# Connecting
# Policy to Practice
## in the Human Services

# Connecting
# Policy to Practice

## in the Human Services

Brad McKenzie and Brian Wharf

OXFORD
UNIVERSITY PRESS

# OXFORD
UNIVERSITY PRESS

8 Sampson Mews, Suite 204, Don Mills, Ontario, M3C 0H5

www.oupcanada.com

Oxford University Press is a department of the University of Oxford.
It furthers the University's objective of excellence in research, scholarship,
and education by publishing worldwide in

Oxford   New York

Auckland   Cape Town   Dar es Salaam   Hong Kong   Karachi   Kuala Lumpur   Madrid   Melbourne
Mexico City   Nairobi   New Delhi   Shanghai   Taipei   Toronto

With offices in

Argentina   Austria   Brazil   Chile   Czech Republic   France   Greece   Guatemala   Hungary   Italy   Japan
Poland   Portugal   Singapore   South Korea   Switzerland   Thailand   Turkey   Ukraine   Vietnam

Oxford is a trade mark of Oxford University Press in the UK and in certain other countries

Published in Canada by Oxford University Press

Library and Archives Canada Cataloguing in Publication

McKenzie, B. D. (Bradley Douglas)
Connecting policy to practice in the human services / Brad McKenzie and Brian Wharf. — 3rd ed.

Includes bibliographical references and index.
ISBN 978-0-19-543009-7

1. Canada—Social policy. 2. Social planning—Canada. 3. Human services—Canada. I. Wharf, Brian II. Title.

HN107.M33 2010      361.6'10971      C2009-904327-0

Cover image: Fancy Photography/Veer

Printed and bound in Canada
3 4 5 6 — 13 12 11 10

Oxford University Press is committed to our environment.
The pages of this book have been printed on paper which has been certified by the Forest Stewardship Council

# Contents

# Introduction

There are three primary objectives of the third edition of *Connecting Policy to Practice*. Two of these remain the same as in earlier editions: to identify gaps between policy and practice and to argue the case for improving the connections between these two somewhat discrete domains from a social justice standpoint. The third objective is to provide an overview of what social policy, in its many manifestations, is all about. New information on policy relevant to this objective not only serves as a platform for discussions on connecting policy to practice but also provides basic information about the place of social policy in both Canadian society and the global context.

The underlying rationale for these objectives is that more inclusive approaches to policy-making will both empower front-line practitioners by creating a work environment conducive to effective practice and lead to improved program and service outcomes for service users. At the same time we recognize that inclusive approaches advancing the rights and benefits of service users will not always succeed, particularly in heavily bureaucratized work environments that emphasize organizational accountability and compliance with these norms over the needs of service users. Strategies that take up these causes in other ways—both inside and outside the system—will be required. We explore some opportunities for policy change efforts, including resistance to regressive policy measures that move beyond the margins of methods and procedures likely to be sanctioned by senior policy officials, later in the book. In developing the general themes in this book we draw on relevant research and literature; in addition we incorporate experiential evidence from practice in the form of illustrative examples and case studies. However, this book is more than just an argument for different approaches to policy-making. If we are to develop progressive policy changes we must have a good understanding of the policy-making environment, the structures and processes pertaining to policy-making, and an ability to use methods of policy-making, including policy analysis, implementation planning, and policy evaluation within a more inclusive, value-critical framework. Information and tools consistent with this broad purpose in the second edition have been retained but new material has been introduced on theories of public policy, the role of the federal government in making social policies, neo-liberalism, and globalization; as well, more examples of strategies which may influence policy outcomes have been added. We are grateful to reviewers who recommended some of these changes.

It will be apparent from the opening paragraphs that this book is not a neutral and dispassionate appraisal of social policy formation and outcomes. In our view it would be difficult to be value free about social policy since it is, by its very nature, concerned with making choices about contentious issues. In addition, the policy process is riddled with disputes about the merits of different approaches to policy-making and policy change. Given this context, we support a value-critical approach to policy-making in the human services. As described in Chapter One, this approach requires that one identify and defend the values that will shape the analytical process and its outcomes.

We draw attention to two terms that appear throughout the book. We adopt the term *service users* instead of *clients* in most cases, and this is intended to reflect the fact that these are individuals who receive services or with whom professionals work. We also frequently refer to practitioners as *front-line* in order to distinguish these service providers from senior program managers in agencies or organizations. However, at least some of the issues confronting *front-line practitioners* may also be applicable to those who are their immediate supervisors. Thus the experiences attributed to front-line practitioners may be applied to those in immediate supervisory roles in a number of situations. Because the primary readers of this book are likely to be students we have included selected readings and critical thinking questions at the end of each chapter. In addition, we identify a number of websites in the Appendix in an effort to facilitate further research on social policy issues. Most identified websites are Canadian, given the special focus on Canadian social policy in this text.

## Social Policy: Toward a Definition

Social policy is not an easy term with which to come to grips. Some appreciation of the slipperiness of the term can be found from the listing of no less than eight different perspectives on social policy (Graham, Swift, and Delaney, 2003). Definitions include the very broad and all encompassing, such as those formulated by MacBeath (1957: 3), who describes social policy as 'the right ordering of relationships between men and women who live together in society', and Gil (1990: 523) who views social policies as 'guiding principles for ways of life, motivated by basic and perceived human needs'. According to these views social policy is virtually synonymous with public policy and encompasses all of the actions of governments in their continuing but not always successful attempts to ensure the safety and well being of citizens.

A somewhat more restricted definition is that proposed by Westhues (2006: 8): 'Social policy is a course of action or inaction chosen by public authorities to address problems that deal with human health, safety or well being.' She then goes on to define public authorities to include those who work directly with service users, bureaucrats working in international organizations and government, and elected officials. We appreciate the clarity of this basic definition, and the additional elaboration that social policies may be 'chosen' by those who work directly with service users as well as senior policy-makers. However, there are important characteristics of social policy that merit additional consideration.

One is the distinction between *grand* and *ordinary* issues (Lindblom, 1979). The grand issues include the distribution of income and wealth, of political power and corporate prerogatives. The grand issues are dealt with at the national and, increasingly, the international levels. They represent the major economic and fiscal challenges faced by the state. While the rhetoric of government often holds that the challenges are dealt with in ways that benefit all citizens, our view is that the grand issues are often, if not usually, resolved in favour of wealthy and powerful individuals.

The ordinary issues of social policy are concerned with more personal matters such as the provision of health and social services, income support, housing, and planning for the development of cities and neighbourhoods. Ordinary issues affect the lives of Canadians in very direct and significant ways. Given that one of the primary objectives of this book is connecting policy to practice in the human services we focus more directly on ordinary issues.

A second and somewhat related consideration is the issue of choice. As noted above, policy is all about choosing and the values that inform these choices. Indeed there is considerable scope for policy-makers at provincial and local levels to determine how health and social services will be provided. Consider the following examples of different choices. Some provinces fund private schools and others do not. Most provinces provide child welfare services through provincial departments or ministries but Ontario, and to a large extent Manitoba and Nova Scotia, have created private, non-profit organizations to deliver services. And whether these agencies are provincial departments or voluntary organizations they can, within the limits prescribed by provincial legislation and funding, decide whether to favour a preventive, community-based approach or whether to focus primarily on crisis-oriented investigation and surveillance services after referrals of abuse or neglect.

Given the special emphasis on 'choices' in social policy we have selected an old, but still useful, definition to establish the tone for our discussion throughout the book:

Social policy is all about social purpose and the choices between them. These choices and the conflicts between them have continuously to be made at the governmental level, the community level, and the individual level. At each level by acting or not acting, by voting or not voting, by opting in or contracting out we can influence the direction in which choices are made. (Titmuss, 1974: 131)

We draw attention to the relevant parts of this definition: purpose, choice, and level. Policy is all about choosing directions in situations where evidence is, at times, incomplete and contradictory and where values inform the fundamental question of who pays and who benefits. The purpose of the policy and the choices related to this purpose are made at a variety of levels: the federal level, the provincial level, the organizational level, the program level, and the service provider level.

We acknowledge that the service provider or practitioner level is often omitted as rather unimportant in policy-making. This is reflected in the view that policy is what needs to be done 'in general' whereas practice is what needs to be done in 'a specific situation', implying that the two domains are, by their very nature, quite disconnected. Although this distinction has a ring of truth, we argue that practitioners consistently face difficult 'policy choices' in their day to day work. For example, physicians, nurses, and others in health care are often faced with the choice of trying to maintain the elderly in their own homes or to place them in a nursing home. Similarly, when confronted with situations of child neglect or abuse, social workers must decide whether to recommend to the family court that a child should be apprehended and placed in the care of the state or remain at home. Such choices are just as complex as those that baffle policy-makers. In addition, practitioners often have to act quickly while being fully aware that their choices will have significant consequences on people's lives.

## The Principle of Affected Interests

While the issue of participation is addressed in later chapters it is necessary to clarify our position at the outset, namely that those who are affected by a policy have a right to participate in its formation and in determining its eventual outcome. Dahl (1970: 64) calls this *the principle of affected interests* and while he acknowledges that it is a broad and ambitious principle that cannot always be acted on, it nevertheless deserves attention whenever possible. For us this is an important principle. We argue throughout the book that, as currently organized, policy-making in the human services largely excludes those who are most affected by the outcomes. Simply put, most policies are planned and funded by those who will not be affected by the outcomes. We are aware of the argument that those most directly affected by social policies are incapable of making a contribution. This argument holds that service users are so buffeted and tired by coping with the pressures that affect their lives on a daily basis that they have no energy left to participate in policy formation. In addition, the view, whether stated or not, is that because service users cannot manage their own lives without assistance from the state or other organizations they do not have the skills or knowledge to contribute in any meaningful way to policy development. These arguments are quite pervasive within policy-making contexts, but we counter these views with the following story from practice.

The story involves an incident that occurred in a project designed to change the practice of child welfare workers in a number of offices of the Ministry of Children and Family Development in British Columbia. Essentially the project, *Protecting Children by Empowering Women* (Callahan, Hooper, and Wharf, 1998; Callahan and Lumb, 1995) sought to introduce group and community work approaches into practice. During a group meeting with single parent women and child welfare workers, one of the workers commented that she and many of her colleagues were stressed out because of high caseloads, the introduction of a new computer system, and the seemingly endless number of training sessions required because of new legislation. Indeed she noted that no less than five workers were on leave because of stress. When she had finished one of the mothers exploded: 'You think you are stressed out—what a bunch of crap! You have a well paying and secure job, you live in a nice house in a good neighbourhood, and have a car and a husband and kids. Look at me, no job, living on social assistance in a crappy apartment, deserted by my husband and you lot took my kids.'

When she had finished the group members remained in silence for awhile. Then the coordinator of the project spoke up and asked if she would like the group members to get involved in thinking about and sorting out her problems. The young mother acquiesced and slowly the group members volunteered information about how they had handled similar matters.

The fact that members of the group had experienced many of the same problems as the young mother who spoke up made their questions legitimate and their responses helpful. But the contribution of the group leader, a professional child welfare worker, should not be ignored. Without a professional who recognized that benefits can be obtained from group discussion, who organized the meetings, and who chaired the discussion in a way that facilitated the open sharing of experiences, these insights from service users would not have been voiced. This example raises a key question. If this approach of problem solving by a group of service users can work, if these service users can contribute to the resolution of problems facing them, why would their contributions not be equally useful and valid in the creation of new policies?

We earlier noted two objections to the involvement of service users in the policy-making process, and it is recognized that there are also important practical issues to consider. First, policy-making that is initiated from the bottom-up may often be a long-term process with indeterminate outcomes, and it is often a question of whether an investment in these processes is worth the bother. In the case of service users, they may have other priorities and may choose not to participate. These choices need to be respected. However, the participation of service users is likely to be more sustainable on policy issues that matter more directly to them, where their voice will be seriously considered, and where the time horizon for policy change is more predictable. Second, service users may feel unwanted or face challenges around such things as meeting times, transportation, and child care. Special invitations, alternative approaches to enabling input such as special forums for service users, and compensation for time spent or related expenses may help to overcome some of these issues. Third, a more participatory policy-making process involves more time, and in some circumstances there may be an imposed time restriction on the phases of the policy-making process. In general, a more inclusive policy-making process may require extending the timelines for decision-making. Although this may not always be possible it is a small price to pay for policy outcomes that may reflect a better fit with the needs of service users.

As earlier noted, service users are not the only ones excluded from policy-making; indeed, practitioners often have little opportunity to contribute to the policies they are expected to implement. The role of policy-makers has traditionally been reserved for staff with long-standing service records, and until recently these individuals have been primarily privileged men (i.e., white and middle-class or well-off). The consequences are readily apparent: policy-making roles have been a male preserve while the roles of practitioners are filled more often by women and, more recently, Aboriginal people and immigrants of colour. This raises questions of differences based on gender, race, ethnicity, and other forms of diversity. For example, because the values of men and women often differ on gender-related matters, such as care-giving, this gender imbalance has exacerbated the gap between policy and practice. It is also recognized that while many practitioners recognize that their 'clients' are harassed individuals doing their best to manage in circumstances that would drive many middle class professionals to distraction, still others have become so inured and accustomed to the poverty ridden lives of their 'clients' that they have normalized these conditions.

An additional policy-practice gap is created by the location of policy-makers in head offices, which are too often far removed from the realities of day to day practice. Rein (1983: 65) refers to the knowledge of policy-makers in these contexts as 'cold and remote'. By contrast the knowledge of practitioners is 'hot'— it is directly and intimately connected with particular circumstances of service users. To continue the Rein analogy, mixing these two kinds of knowledge in this disconnected fashion all too frequently results in 'tepid knowledge': too little and too late to significantly improve the lot of either practitioners or service users. What is needed is a way to inject the 'hot' knowledge from practice experience directly into the policy process. In our view this can be accomplished by having practitioners and service users as active partners in the development of policies.

Finally, we note that disconnections between policy and practice are exacerbated by the way that we have organized the delivery of many of our human services. Most services are provided through departments or ministries of government or large organizations that are best described as 'quasi-government' agencies because, although located outside of government, they receive their mandate and almost all of their funding from government. As a result they are largely responsive to the policy-making decisions that occur at a governmental level. Most of these organizations are structured in a hierarchical fashion where the chain of command flows from the minister, through additional steps to the chief executive officer and through several additional steps to front-line staff responsible for service provision. This structure, which reflects a corporate style of management, involves what Kouzes and Mico (1979) describe as three organizational domains: policy, management, and practice. The policy domain is legitimized as the primary responsibility of politicians and senior bureaucrats, often preoccupied with policies and programs that must enhance the image of the party in power even while (hopefully) responding to the needs of communities and service users. On the other hand, practitioners are largely confined to their own domain which involves service delivery in compliance with new policies and standards. Management is caught in the middle, trying to assure policy-makers that the programs they conceived are being run as efficiently and effectively as possible (so policy-makers can assure the public on such issues), and at the same time trying to respond to the demands of practitioners for additional resources or other changes. Although this description oversimplifies policy-making and implementation structures, the differences in these domains can become so large that one of two scenarios is created. One is that the interactions between these domains become so discordant that a disproportionate amount of time is spent on asserting conflicting perceptions of policy or practice 'realities'. A second is that resignation and withdrawal from engagement occurs, reinforcing the isolation of the policy and practice domains from each other. In either case opportunities for collaboration and joint problem-solving are squandered.

## Ideologies and Their Impact on Policy

'It is not what we know, but what we believe in that matters' (Lemann, 2002: 99). This quotation points out that ideologies or belief systems play a profoundly important part in developing social policies and in determining their outcomes. For example, the 1980 *Family and Child Service Act* in British Columbia was passed by a very conservative government and as a result it contained no provision for support and preventive services. Although some of these programs were developed later, they were contracted out to voluntary agencies. Ministry staff was left with two roles: investigators of complaints of child neglect and abuse, and case managers of the services provided by voluntary agencies. Missing were the long-standing social work roles of counselor and advocate.

Belief systems are discussed at length in the literature on social policy but one framework that has stood the test of time identifies three distinctively different views of the responsibility of the state for the well-being of its citizens: residual, institutional, and social development. The residual view severely limits the role of the state to intervening or assisting only when other resources of family, church, and neighbourhood have been exhausted. By contrast the institutional view of social policy suggests that providing health, education, and social services is a normal and expected responsibility of the state—these are provisions required so that all citizens can enjoy a healthy and productive life. The social development view extends the institutional approach by arguing that citizens have a right to participate in the affairs of the state—that active citizenship is just as important as the benefits and services provided by the state. In addition this approach insists that social policy is equal to economic policy and should be given equal attention in public policy.

Belief systems are also expressed in the form of political philosophies. Although these employ different labels from those noted above, they express similar views.

## The Relationship between Ideologies and Social Policies

| Criteria | Selected Proponents | Relationship to Social Policy |
|---|---|---|
| Neo-liberal | Stephen Harper<br>George W. Bush<br>Margaret Thatcher*<br>Mike Harris* | A residual approach based on the 'Charity Model' is advocated, reflecting the belief that social programs destroy individual initiative: public spending restraints and the provision of social programs only as a last resort are advocated. |
| Liberal | Pierre Trudeau*<br>René Levesque*<br>W.L. Mackenzie King* | Public social programs are important in addressing general risks to well-being, but these are subservient to economic issues. An institutional view of social welfare is advocated. |
| Democratic Socialist or Social Democrat | J.S. Woodsworth*<br>Tommy Douglas* | Universal programs and a social development model are more commonly advocated. Social policy is seen as equal to economic policy in importance and social provision should be based on need. |

*Margaret Thatcher was the Conservative Prime Minister of Britain between 1979 and 1990; Mike Harris was the Conservative Premier of Ontario from 1995 to 2002; Pierre Trudeau was the Liberal Prime Minister of Canada from 1968 to 1979 and 1980 to 1984; René Levesque was the founder of the Parti Québécois and Premier of Quebec between 1976 and 1985; W.L. Mackenzie King was the Liberal Prime Minister of Canada for 22 of the 27 years between 1921 and 1948; J.S. Woodsworth was a Member of Parliament between 1921 and 1942, was a tireless advocate for socialism in Canada, and became the first leader of the federal Co-operative Commonwealth Federation (CCF), the predecessor of the New Democratic Party (NDP) in 1932; Tommy Douglas was the CCF Premier of Saskatchewan from 1944 to 1961 and medicare was introduced under his leadership; he was then elected leader of the federal NDP, serving for 10 years in this capacity.

The political philosophies in vogue at the present time in Canada are neo-liberalism associated with the residual view, and liberalism, with its middle position between more radical and conservative approaches to social policy, is consistent with the institutional approach. Social democracy favours a social development orientation. These are depicted in very general terms in the following table.

## Summary and Conclusion

This chapter has outlined the purpose and objectives of the book, including our general perspective on current approaches to policy-making. We have identified our general commitment to policy-making models which engage both service users and service providers as active participants in shaping the policies that affect their interests. However, we also recognize that these strategies will not always be welcomed. In circumstances where regressive service or benefit changes are being imposed or where procedures are being introduced that limit the ability of front-line practitioners to provide quality services, other activities from both inside and outside the system, designed to resist these strategies or changes, need to be considered. In this chapter, we introduced a definition of social policy and drew a distinction between grand and ordinary policy issues. We also identified some of the reasons for the gaps that exist between policy and practice. Ideology and its expression through different political philosophies contribute to the disconnection between policy and practice. Although we argued in favour of participatory approaches to policy-making a note of caution is in order. The promotion of public participation is not always associated with progressive policies as is illustrated by efforts to mobilize public support for harsher penalties for young offenders and for reopening the debate on choice with respect to an abortion.

Before concluding this chapter, we wish to acknowledge a critique noted by a reviewer of the last edition to this book. In her review Smith (2005) noted that while inclusive approaches might have worked in an era characterized by a more vibrant, liberal democracy, these strategies are unlikely to be effective in the current neo-liberal policy environment. Indeed, Smith argued that inclusive strategies may obscure 'power imbalances', co-opt those who engage in such strategies, become 'vehicles for creating changes that are illusory', and shore up the 'very inequalities' such strategies are designed to address (2005: 139). We agree that many social policies are the creatures of neo-liberal governments dedicated to reducing the size and scope of the human services and to managing them in a highly regulated and controlled fashion. These governments have no genuine commitment to bringing progressive reform to the human services that will address fundamental social problems on a long-term basis. We also agree that many practitioners are overwhelmed in their day to day work by heavy caseloads and never ending paperwork requirements. Given these oppressed working conditions many are unable to contribute to the development of progressive social policies within institutions, and in many circumstances such efforts may simply co-opt participants to serve the overarching goals of neo-liberalism. Although the pervasive domination of neo-liberalism and its influence over social welfare today presents a more challenging policy environment that requires efforts to resist and subvert policies, these are not enough. Despite the many obstacles to more inclusive policy-making, we demonstrate in *Connecting Policy to Practice in the Human Service* that opportunities still exist for active engagement of progressive policy-makers, practitioners, and service users to influence policy processes in ways that make a difference to policy outcomes.

Chapter One reviews three themes of public policy-making, discusses the role of elites in the policy process, and outlines five models of policy-making relevant to the human services.

# Acknowledgments

We thank members of the Oxford 'team' who helped to make the third edition of *Connecting Policy to Practice in the Human Services* possible. Nancy Reilly, acquisitions editor, not only initiated the process for a third edition but commissioned four reviews of the second edition. These reviews pointed to a number of gaps in content, such as the need for additional information on the role of the federal government in social policy. With the benefit of this information, Nancy engaged with us in a collaborative fashion in developing the final outline for the new edition. We are also grateful to these anonymous reviewers and trust that our effort to address many of their suggestions has resulted in a more useful text for students and practitioners in the human services. Development editor Dina Theleritis guided us through the writing process and provided a helpful, independent perspective on essential content. Her understanding of our circumstances regarding deadlines and our perspectives on content was particularly appreciated. And Jessie Coffey was both prompt and meticulous in her role as copy editor.

We owe a great deal to the individuals who contributed chapters to this edition: Marilyn Callahan, Bruce Wallace, and Tim Richards. The contents of these two chapters, one on feminism and social policy and the other on resisting welfare cut-backs, add a great deal to the main theme of the book.

As in the previous editions, Claudette Cormier was an invaluable source of assistance in word processing and formatting.

Most of all we thank our wives for putting up with us in yet another writing endeavour. Both Madeline McKenzie and Marilyn Callahan also came to our rescue when early drafts of new content were in need of repair.

Finally, we acknowledge the interest of readers who share a commitment to policy-making from a social justice standpoint which includes the perspectives of practitioners and service users, and who also recognize that the theory and knowledge of planning for progressive social change must be translated into action in order to make a real difference in the lives of the most vulnerable in our society.

# Chapter One

# Policy-Making and Policy-Makers

In the first part of this chapter we introduce theories of public policy and advance the argument that elites exercise a disproportionate amount of control over public policy-making, particularly around decisions made with respect to the grand issues at the federal government level. The second focus of this chapter is on policy-making models and their connections to practice. Five policy-making models are described and assessed to identify their potential for connecting policy to practice. These include the comprehensive rational model, incrementalism, mixed scanning, the value criteria model, and the garbage can model.

## Theories of Public Policy

Ideologies, which were briefly outlined in the Introduction, have a significant influence on social policy in two interrelated ways. First, the ideology of the government in power, including its world view, its view of the role of the state, and the focus of its analyses, influences the nature and scope of social policies that will be introduced. For example, the Ontario government under the leadership of Mike Harris was more extreme than a number of other provincial governments in its approach to cutting welfare benefits in the 1990s. Second, ideologies influence theories of public policy. Theories are important to the politics of policy-making because they offer explanations of why things happen the way they do (Miljan, 2008). As Miljan explains, theory is characterized by abstract reasoning on the basis of empirical observation. Although theory is frequently described in symbolic terms, its value is enabling one to predict future events with some degree of accuracy. Miljan goes on to distinguish between *normative* and *positive* theories, describing positive theories in the field of public policy as efforts to explain politics as it is, 'without any explicit political interest, ideology or agency to promote' (2008: 24). Theories such as Marxism, pluralism, and public choice are described as *positive* theories insofar as they attempt to describe political behaviour rather than justify some course of action based on moral imperatives. We have reservations about labelling such theories as positive because in our view they are not merely descriptive. For example, the normative implications (i.e., value preferences) of these theories are evident in the variables selected for analysis (and those excluded), the interpretations that are offered, and the implications that are drawn from these theories—even if these are not explicitly stated. Selecting a theory of public policy, then, is not unlike the selection of a preferred social policy, in that it involves both empirical and normative considerations.

The specification of theories of public policy to be included in this book is made more difficult by the variety of perspectives presented in the literature and the variations among key authors of Canadian public policy in their selection of relevant theories. For example, Howlett and Ramesh (2003: 22) identify six theories within a classification described as 'general approaches to the study of political phenomena'. These include public choice, Marxism, and transaction cost analysis, which are classified as deductive theories, and welfare economics, pluralism, and statism, which are classified as inductive theories. Miljan (2008) outlines two general groups of theories to explain the political process of public policy-making but these are labelled as structuralist and dynamic. In the structuralist camp she places Marxism, environmental determinism (including globalism, feminism, and culturalism), institutionalism, incrementalism, and systems theory. In the dynamic camp are pluralism, game theory, and public choice. On the other hand, Brooks (1998) limits his list of perspectives to three: Marxism, pluralism, and public choice. We adopt the more parsimonious approach advanced by Brooks, but note that these theories are also common to the other authors cited above. Although some precision may be lost by focusing on only three theories, we argue that these represent the most common prototypes used to explain the relationship between political processes and policy-making in the Canadian context. However, we do make one adaptation in describing Marxism under the more general label of *structural theories*.

## Structural Theories

The Marxist theory of policy formation is the most influential structural theory. It has four main elements: (1) there is a division of society into classes determined by one's relationship to the means of production; (2) there are major divisions between the dominant class ('capital' or those who own the means of production) and the subordinate class ('labour' or those who largely work for the dominant class); (3) class conflict between the dominant and subordinate class is based on political and economic inequalities; and (4) the state is biased in favour of the dominant class because the state is disproportionately controlled either directly or indirectly by the dominant class or bourgeoisie. There are a number of variations of Marxism but the inherent conflict between the interests of the dominant and subordinate classes is central to understanding this view of public policy-making.

Over time Marxist theory has modified its understanding of class conflict and the role of the state. For example, the effects of class conflict are muted by two factors. First, society's dominant ideology, which is reinforced by institutions in society, including the media, leads many within the subordinate class to develop a *false consciousness* about their own best interests and to connect these interests to prevailing liberal-capitalist ideology that sees the market economy as the ticket to upward socio-economic mobility. Second, the state has a moderate degree of autonomy. Although it operates primarily in the interests of capital, it does respond to pressures from the working class and its advocates in enacting policies favourable to this class. However, government also risks a loss of business confidence and related impacts on economic growth if it imposes too many restrictions on business during times of economic downturn, when there may be increased pressure to respond to the needs of the subordinate class rather than the needs of capital.

As Miljan (2008) notes, policy development in a liberal-capitalist democracy is seen by Marxists to evolve from contradictions between two policy pressures at the state level. One is the pressure to introduce *legitimation* policies to reduce inter-class conflicts. These consist of the provision of benefits to the subordinate class that also serve to reduce their dissatisfaction with the inequalities associated with the market. These policies, which include health care and economic benefits such as Employment Insurance (EI), promote social harmony (as well as false consciousness) by legitimizing the capitalist system in the eyes of those who benefit least from its operation. A second pressure is to introduce *accumulation* policies, which largely support businesses through grants, tax subsidies, state expenditures on public works required by business (e.g., roads and other infrastructure), and bailout loans or guarantees to corporations. It is important to emphasize that not every state action supports the interests of the dominant class in that some policies, often bowing to public pressure from the subordinate class and related interest groups, provide important and necessary benefits to those in need. At the same time, the primary burden for payment of these benefits comes not from the dominant class (including corporations and their owners) but the taxes paid by those within the subordinate class, particularly those who are defined as 'middle class'.

Other structural theories, including feminism, environmental determinism, and colonialism are based on somewhat similar descriptions of the politics of policy-making. For example, a central premise in feminism is the structural imperative flowing from patriarchy; this acts as the dominant force in the adoption of policies affecting women. Similarly colonialism, which has characterized Canadian public policies towards First Nations and other indigenous people, is based on a structural model that defines differences in terms of a fundamental conflict between the dominant mainstream society (i.e., the colonizer) and the subordinate group (i.e., the colonized). In each case, it is the structure of society that creates an unequal distribution of power between dominant and subordinate groups. That is, dominant control in society rests with individuals and groups that are not representative of women or Aboriginal people, and the dominant group ensures that policies evolve in a manner that largely preserves the status quo of the dominant group. Because of the similarity in these theories about the central cause of economic and social inequalities (i.e., the structure of society into more and less privileged groups) we adopt the more general label of *structural theories* for this perspective even though we have focused on Marxism as the exemplar of these theories.

There are, of course, criticisms of structural theories. For example, it is argued, particularly in the case of Marxism, that intra-class difference in interests and preferences are minimized by a dichotomous division into dominant and subordinate classes. A somewhat related criticism is that policy changes to provide increased benefits to those in need cannot be fully explained by class conflict or the influence of the subordinate class on decision makers; indeed it is argued that many such changes have a more complex causal chain.

## Pluralism

Pluralism reflects the observation that interest groups influence the outcomes of governmental decisions. Although society is a collection of individuals, these individuals recognize the value of organizing as groups to advance their collective interests. Policies are shaped primarily by the outcomes of competition between groups. Although some pluralists suggest that there are relatively equal competitions among interest groups with the state as an independent arbiter of these conflicts, many pluralists have come to recognize a wide number of divisions in society, based on economic, gender, ethnicity, culture, and ideological considerations. These factors influence the capacity of groups to compete on equal footing within society but, according to pluralists, this is not indicative of divisions into dominant and subordinate classes as defined by structural theorists. Miljan (2008) notes how pluralists recognize and reconcile policy-making in a democratic society as a competition between elites. First, it is argued that competition for political office is a contest among political elites (e.g., political parties); however, voters do get to choose between the policies of different political parties, thus preserving the democratic nature of the way these elites are selected. Second, once in power, governments have to be somewhat responsive to popular demands because of the risk they may be replaced at the next election, and because shifting coalitions among interest groups can place political pressure on governments to take certain actions.

As noted, some pluralists have recognized the fact that some groups possess greater resources than others. In addition to being able to sustain lobbying efforts over a long period of time, these groups (i.e., business) tend to receive a more sympathetic hearing from government than others. In addition, large corporations carry a 'big stick' in that they can exercise significant influence by deferring new investment or perhaps relocating their businesses to other countries or regions. These adaptations of pluralism can lead to the provision of additional resources or preferences for disadvantaged groups so they are more able to represent their own interests, even if the 'playing field' remains heavily biased in favour of more privileged groups. Although pluralism may recognize a preference for a level playing field efforts to redress this problem under pluralism have largely failed to make much of a difference. In part, critics argue that this reflects the pluralists' failure to recognize or address the disproportionate power exercised by elites in the policy-making process.

## Public Choice Theory

The application of public choice theory to policy-making in the Canadian context, particularly in relation to the budgetary process at the federal government level, was developed by Trebilcock, Hartle, Pritchard, and Dewees (1982); however, earlier work by authors such as Buchanan and Tullock (1965) provided the framework for this model. We draw on Brooks (1998), Miljan (2008), and Trebilcock et al. (1982) in describing the main features of this theory.

The public choice perspective is based on the classical theory of microeconomics where the only political actor that really matters is the individual. Although it is similar to pluralism in some respects, analysis focuses on individuals rather than groups. These individuals are assumed to make rational choices based on their own self-interest in political behaviour as they would in purchasing goods or services in a free market context. Thus they will seek to maximize their self-interest or personal gain and minimize losses in any transaction.

Within government, politicians, bureaucrats, and interest group advocates are defined as political entrepreneurs. Although policy-makers are guided by utility-maximizing behaviour, they are somewhat constrained by the preferences expressed by voters at the ballot box. The activities between these political actors are played out in what is described as a series of 'games' characterized by bargaining and negotiation. Exchange theory is used to explain the nature of behaviours that occur between actors involved in these games, and policy outcomes are the result of transactions that occur. Four distinct games are hypothesized: the political game, the bureaucratic game, the interest group game, and the media group game. Each game has its own set of rules and complex relationships among players and teams can involve coalitions and conflicts. However, the rules place some limits on the nature of conflicts and how each game is played. The general relationship between these four groups is shown in Figure 1.1. The electorate confers power on politicians, but it is the perceived capacity of the media to influence the views held by voters on issues or political parties that gives them significant influence. The influence of special interest groups is affected by their ability to mobilize supporters and allies for collective action which may either offer credible support or a significant threat to politicians. For their part, bureaucrats exercise control over the flow of vital information and the delivery of programs. The capacity of politicians within governments to manage the public agenda and to confer benefits on voters or special interest groups whose support is up for grabs, or alternatively to soften the adverse effects of policies on their supporters, will determine the nature of policies that are developed and their ability to maintain power.

**Figure. 1.1    The Policy Process According to the Public Choice Perspective: Four Interrelated Games**

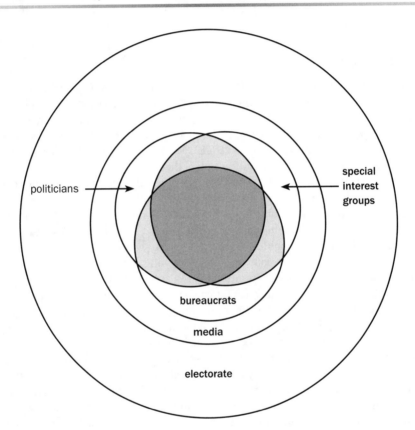

Notes
1.    The darkest area in the centre is the heart of the decision-making process and the lighter shaded areas show the interplay between each pair of policy participants.
2.    The media interact with each set of policy participants and are the channel through which the electorate perceives participants.
3.    The voters are treated as non-participants in decision-making but choose the players in the political game.

In the political game certain kinds of benefits and costs are accepted. For example, politicians gain personal prestige and knowledge of the system once elected, which is enhanced by the effective use of power and influence. They also acquire the right to favours from participants in the system in exchange for favours provided to them. However, costs can include the investment of one's own time and money, loss of privacy, loss of time with family, and the possible risk for career advancement in a position one held prior to running for political office. In order to maximize benefits relative to costs it is in the interests of the politician to be elected, to be a part of the governing party, and to be a minister in an important portfolio. There are generally accepted rules in the political game, including trading favours (e.g., supporting another's position in return for a future favour from that individual) and putting the party's interests ahead of personal interests after extracting the best possible price (i.e., a future benefit or position of some kind).

In the bureaucratic game, senior bureaucrats often sacrifice some monetary income for pride and prestige, and normally receive greater tenure and job security than is afforded the politician. Most senior bureaucrats are friendly adversaries with other bureaucrats, competing for budget, ministerial time, and appointments to other offices of greater prestige. They also attempt to enlarge the span of control and budget of their own departments as a means to achieve greater recognition both for themselves and their minister.

There is some similarity between the media and interest group games. Both interest group leaders and media professionals need access to decision-makers yet the nature of their roles often place them in positions where they become a public critic of government policy or expose issues which can be embarrassing to government or a particular individual. For example, the special interest group leader often needs to develop strong, and often critical, positions of current policies and actions to mobilize interest group membership. Yet at the same time the leader's influence is often dependent on access to ministers or senior bureaucrats, and one's perceived ability either to deliver something of value to them (e.g., support or votes) or to impose negative sanctions that might impede policy adoption. On the other hand, the successful media professional is one who uncovers 'hot information' that can make the major headlines, and access to key decision makers is essential in securing such information. Although some of this information may lead to positive coverage and enhance the image of the political party or government with the public, too much negative publicity can lead government officials to impose restrictions on access to information or limit the access of particular individuals to key sources of information. Whether justified or not, the Harper Conservative government has regarded many in the media as adversaries. Because of this, it has imposed several restrictions on media coverage including limiting the access of media professionals to public events and controlling the nature of interaction that occurs between the media and government representatives.

It has been argued by some public choice theorists that the nature of these games within the government leads to inefficiencies within government in both policy formation and expenditure allocation. For example, the short time horizons of government often lead senior bureaucrats to favour short-term solutions to long-term problems. On the expenditure management side, departments generally strive for increased expenditures and budgetary control whether these are justified or not. Departments are discouraged from running surpluses as these are generally clawed back by the central financial authority at the end of the year; as well, surpluses may lead to a reduction in allocations in the following year because future budget allocations are often based, in large part, on expenditure patterns from the previous year rather than evidence-based decision-making.

At a macro-policy level, many public choice theorists identify a growing trend among voters to seek more and better programs from government, subject to certain limits in taxes they are prepared to pay, because it is in their interests to do so. According to public choice theorists, this leads to an increase in the level of state intervention which interferes with the natural operation of the market, as conceptualized by theorists such as Milton Friedman. In short, welfare state programs are seen as encouraging 'free riders' who do not require such programs. Thus public policy, it is argued, should focus on supplementing the free market only when necessary, providing social programs as a last resort, and reinforcing individual responsibility as much as possible in policies and programs that are enacted.

The underlying orientation of public choice, which is based on the ideology of a free market and a residual orientation to social policy, has many critics both at home and in an international development context (see Klein, 2007). But, it is the description of public policy-making, as earlier described, which is of primary interest to us here. Public choice explanations of governmental policy-making share certain characteristics with those associated of the pluralist model. For example, they share the same competitive world view, and the role of the state is largely seen as responsible for mediating conflicts over scarce resources. In public choice theory there is some evidence to support the nature of relationships among the various political actors described in the political and bureaucratic arenas, but there are also significant limitations. Similar to pluralism, public choice theory ignores the fact that the deck is stacked so that too often it is a small minority that wins approval for what they want over the preferences of the majority. This is largely a result of the ability of those with more power to influence the nature of choices that are made either inside government or by the public in elections. In the latter case, considerable influence is exercised over public opinion through advertising or the media, and major control over these institutions remains in the hands of those with the most power. Another criticism of the public choice explanation for policy-making is its assumption that all actions are based on rational economic choices motivated by self-interest. If this were the case, individuals would recognize that participation in many interest groups, particularly in the social policy sphere, involve more costs than benefits, and therefore decline to become involved. In politics as well, many choose to advance policy goals and positions that may not get them elected, or if elected, fail to be in a position that would allow them to be a part of government. Although Olson (1965) in his critique of public choice concluded that politically active people are not motivated by self-interest but by altruistic or idealistic goals, we draw a more cautious conclusion; that is, policy actors in political and bureaucratic arenas include both those driven more by self-interest and those espousing more altruistic goals. However, clearly motives other than self-interest play a role in policy-making, and even Trebilcock (2005) acknowledged that the influence of ideas and ideals, which are not based on self-interest, had been underestimated in his earlier writings on the application of public choice theory to governmental policy-making.

## Making Sense of Theories of Public Policy

Each of the theoretical perspectives summarized vary in their interpretations of the focus of analysis, the constraints on the policy process, and their views on the role of the state. First, Marxist analysis (and other structural theories as well) focuses on classes or major divisions in society, pluralism focuses more on organized groups, and public choice identifies the individual as the unit of analysis. Second, structural theorists define the dominant ideology of capitalism or the prevailing power of other forms of domination as major constraints to policy reform, and this is largely absent from other perspectives. Third, each perspective contains very different views of the state. For the pluralist, the state is essentially democratic but can pursue some of its own interests in addition to mediating between different societal interests. For the public choice theorist, the state is both active in pursuing its own interests and reactive in needing to respond to non-state actors such as voters, special interest groups, and the media, who are perceived as having the capacity to influence its goals. Thus, public choice adherents see the state as democratic but also heavily bureaucratic. Structural theorists tend to see the state as having a margin of independence from the narrow interests of capitalists or the dominant class and able to respond to the demands of a much weaker subordinate class; however, it generally identifies with and acts on behalf of the dominant class.

What is the evidence for these different perspectives? It is unlikely that there will be agreement among policy advocates for each perspective on the evidence because at least some data will be interpreted through an underlying value or ideological screen. For example, class differences for the pluralist may be interpreted as evidence of multiple divisions between groups and interests in society. These divisions, Marxists will argue, are a contradictory outcome of legitimization policies which when coupled with other strategies, including advertising and control of the mainstream media, convey the message that the current system acts in the public interest. This message, it is argued, is accepted by many; the result is that subordinate class efforts to organize and take more unified action against the interests of the dominant class are diffused. On the other hand, growing inequality between the wealthy and all other strata may be interpreted by those sympathetic to a Marxist perspective as an indication of the growing polarization between the dominant and subordinate classes.

Although differences exist between the theories there is also evidence of behaviours and trends within each of these theories that may resonate with our experiences. But are these the defining elements that shape the nature and scope of policies or are there other important factors to be considered? A final question relates to whether one's position on these theories matter. The answer is 'yes' because this will have some influence how one approaches policy change, not only in relation to grand policy issues but also in relation to the ordinary issues. More specifically, the extent to which both individual and structural conditions are considered reflects different political stances regarding the role of the state and how individual and social responsibilities and obligations are allocated. Although we identify more strongly with the critique offered by the structural perspective, and the extent to which structural factors contribute to policy-making by elites, it is important for readers to develop their own perspectives on these theories. It is also important to consider how the three theories we have just summarized are related to the models of policy-making outlined later in this chapter (i.e., the rational model, incrementalism, mixed scanning, the value criteria model, and the garbage can model). These models illustrate different approaches to planning but, with the possible exception of the garbage can model, do not refer to the political processes that influence policy-making. Theories of public policy, on the other hand, provide us with models for understanding the relationship between the political process and public policy.

It follows, then, that those adopting a particular theoretical approach to understanding the political side of making public policies may use any one or more of the policy-making models described later in developing new social policies.

## Who Makes Social Policy?

In our view the grand issues of social policy are controlled primarily by a relatively small number of individuals holding key positions in business and in the federal government. In some cases they may exchange positions, serving for a time as a senior bureaucrat or politician and then assuming responsibilities in the business world. Our conclusion about the dominance of elites in the decisions that are made about the macro level policies is based on two considerations. We first examine the theories of public policy that have just been summarized to identify their explanations about who influences the major policy decisions at a senior governmental level. We then consider the literary evidence from the Canadian context on this question.

Each of the theoretical perspectives that have been described draw different conclusions about the policy-making process and the level of importance that is attached to the influence of elites. Nevertheless, each theory is remarkably similar in highlighting the disproportionate influence of those with privilege. Structural theorists are the clearest about the role of elites. For Marxists, the elite includes representatives of the capitalist class who exercise primary control over the economy, and by extension the state; for feminists the elite is composed of a dominant class of primarily males in positions of power who are opposed to gender equality; for Aboriginal Canadians it is those dominant representatives of mainstream cultural values and perspectives in power who fail to recognize the different aspirations of Aboriginal people. Although pluralists initially viewed the state as a somewhat independent arbiter of shifting coalitions of interest groups, many have recognized the dominant position of business in the political marketplace (Lindblom, 1982; Lowi, 1979), and their ability to maintain privileged access to decision-makers. This view has been extended to the role of policy communities. For example, Coleman and Skogstad (1990) found that groups enjoying political advantages were able to exclude other groups from the policy-making process, and it was policy communities within the business and financial sectors that enjoyed the most success in advancing their interests with government. In the pluralist view elites are more dispersed, although there is significant attention to their presence. Public choice explanations of government policy-making focus on the roles of two key groups of individuals—politicians and bureaucrats—and how their self-interested actions affect policy outcomes. Based on this analysis and the preferred solution of public choice theorists to devolve more authority to a private market dominated by corporations it is clear that policy directions in the public choice traditions will be dominated by elites, even if this is not a major foundation of the theory. And although many pluralists and public choice advocates might hold that elections at least provide the public with a choice over which elite is to govern, the declining percentage of eligible voters who actually vote in elections raises additional questions about the effectiveness of representative democracy as it is currently being practiced in Canada.

The literary and empirical evidence of who makes the major policy decisions in Canada is based on a number of studies dating back to the groundbreaking research of Porter (1965), and then the continuing work of Clement (1983, 1975), Panitch (1977), and Newman (1981, 1975, 1998). These studies found that a relatively few individuals, mostly male of Euro-Canadian descent, prospered greatly under existing policies and structures, enjoyed a disproportionate amount of influence, and exercised this power to ensure that these conditions remained in place.

Compelling accounts of who rules in Canada and the influence of elites are also provided in a series of books by Linda McQuaig. The series began with an examination of the tax system (*Behind Closed Doors*, 1987), followed by an inquiry into free trade and the GST (*The Quick and the Dead*, 1991), then by an investigation into the reductions in funding for social and health programs (*The Wealthy Bankers Wife*, 1993), and finally by an examination of the reasons for the national debt (*Shooting the Hippo*, 1995). All of these books reveal consistent themes: the growing influence of elites, including the growth of multi-national corporations and their independence from control by the state, the unequal distribution of wealth and income, the lack of progressivity in the tax system, and the declining support for the health and social service sector. A more recent study by Brownlee (2005) demonstrates how the corporate elite in Canada, aided by conservative think tanks such as the Fraser Institute, were able to promote the neo-liberal agenda in Canada.

One of the outcomes of the disproportionate control by elites is inequality, and this theme is explored in more depth in Chapter Two. As documented by the Canadian Centre for Policy Alternatives, inequality in Canada is on the increase:

Canada's gap between the rich and poor is growing and this is during the best of economic conditions. In 2004 the average earning of the richest 10% of Canada's families raising children was 83 times higher that earned by the poorest 10% of Canadian families. That is nearly triple of the ratio of 1976 which was around 30 times higher. (Yalnizyan, 2007: 1)

The report concludes with the sobering observation that 'the rich are getting richer, the poor aren't going anywhere and there are fewer people in the middle to mediate the two extremes. We ignore these trends at our peril' (2007: 6).

The theoretical arguments and research summarized above pertain to who rules on the grand issues of policy. At first glance it might appear that a more balanced picture of participation would occur with respect to ordinary policy issues. These include the decisions made by municipal governments, health facilities, school boards, social service organizations, and special commissions. Such decisions affect people very directly in their day to day lives and the opportunities for public participation, including services users and providers, would seem to be quite easy to facilitate.

Indeed, some recent experiences in Canada with respect to participation in ordinary issues tend to confirm that opportunities are available and that people do take advantage of these opportunities. For example 'tens of thousands of Canadians' provided input to the Romanow Commission established to chart the future of health care in Canada (Romanow, 2002). In British Columbia, the Citizens Assembly on Electoral Reform held 50 public meetings across the province, attended by 3,000 people, before issuing its report in 2004. And in Ontario, the Citizens' Assembly on Electoral Reform incorporated a wide range of participatory processes, including a website that led more than 50,000 different visitors to download at least 10,000 key documents pertaining to electoral reform in that province (Institute on Governance, 2007).

Yet closer examination of participation in the ordinary affairs of policy-making is required to determine whether those who are engaged are truly representative of service users. For example, in a study of citizen participation in health reform in British Columbia, Wharf-Higgins (1997: 280) found that the participants were generally 'well off, well educated and well spoken'. They came from the middle and professional classes to the relative exclusion of low-income individuals and users of health and social services.

In general, those who are most often affected by decisions around health care, welfare reform, or housing availability are the least able and least likely to participate. If these individuals are to participate in decision-making, then the sites, times, and formality of the meetings must be adapted to respond to their needs and schedules.

# Policy-Making Models and Their Connection to Practice

The policy-making process outlined in this chapter introduces five different models. Three commonly identified approaches are the *rational* or *synoptic approach, incrementalism*, and *mixed scanning*. These models are frequently referred to in the literature; in effect, they have stood the test of time, although each has its limitations. A fourth, the *value criteria model*, incorporates values as an explicit component of the policy-making process. This model is an adaptation of the rational model and was developed by the Institute for the Study of Child and Family Policy at North Carolina (Dobelstein, 1990; Moroney, 1991). Rein (1970) and Titmuss (1968) were early advocates of the need to explicitly examine values in the policy-making process.

The final model summarized in this chapter is the *garbage can model*, originally developed by Cohen, March, and Olsen (1972) for universities and related organizations, and later adapted by Kingdon (1995) to explain how policies are developed at the governmental level. This model identifies the importance of both problems and solutions as major ingredients in the policy-making process; however, it also explicitly recognizes the central role of politics, a somewhat neglected attribute of other models. We have selected these models for inclusion because they can be applied to planning and policy-making at both the organizational and governmental levels. The characteristics of each of these models are identified below.

We draw attention first to some of the variables that confound the task of describing these models as they unfold in practice. The policy environment at a provincial, national, and, more recently, global level affects the development of policy in some significant ways. This environment is shaped by ideological, technical, and socioeconomic factors, and these largely determine the resources governments are prepared to commit to new policy initiatives, particularly in the health and social service sectors. These issues are discussed in detail in the following two chapters. As well, the arena or level within which policy-making occurs can influence the process. For example, an organization trying to develop policies to deal with adolescent offenders in its catchment area may be more likely to use a different model of planning that that adopted by a federal government concerned with social security reform. Because of its intimate knowledge of the problem and its limited resources, a local organization may adopt an incremental approach whereas the federal government may use a comprehensive rational approach in reforming social security. Finally, policy-making remains difficult to classify because each situation is unique and the process is adapted, to some extent at least, to that particular situation. One important consideration is whether the government wishes to act quickly without bothering with studies or analyses of any kind. A government with a cause may be impatient with any kind of process, and the absence of process is particularly evident when governments decide to reduce funding or eliminate programs.

In discussing these models we include a number of case examples. Although most of our examples are drawn from the field of child and family services, there are similar examples from other policy fields. If you have experience in another field of practice, try to identify examples from that field that might correspond to some of the models identified below.

## The Rational Model

The rational or synoptic approach is based almost entirely on the analysis of objective data in an orderly sequence. This approach to policy-making is anchored in systems theory and the analysis of factual or observable data using the scientific method. While the irrationality of the policy process may be acknowledged, proponents of this model are more likely to attribute this irrationality to the unwarranted interference of politics, politicians, and political agendas. The preferred role for the planner is that of the expert technician who coordinates the complex tasks associated with policy-making.

The development of the rational model is often associated with the appointment of Robert MacNamara as the Secretary of Defense in John F. Kennedy's administration in the early 1960s. Fresh from his success as the chief executive officer of the Ford Motor Company, MacNamara was determined to transfer business techniques to the public policy field. Analytical tools such as benefit–cost analysis and program policy budgeting systems (PPBS) were adopted. Both reflected a goal-oriented approach to policy development in which goals and measurable objectives are clearly identified, and options are evaluated in terms of benefits and costs. The rational model features five general steps (Carley, 1980):

1.  Define the problem in objective (behavioural) terms.
2.  Develop a list of all feasible alternatives that would resolve the problem under prescribed circumstances.
3.  Project the general consequences that are likely to flow from each strategy and the probability of those consequences occurring.
4.  Collect and examine data appropriate to each alternative strategy; then assess the relationship between predicted outcomes and policy objectives and the relative benefit–cost ratio of each alternative strategy.
5.  Select the strategy that best approximates identified goals and objectives and achieves the best benefit–cost ratio.

Several problems have been identified with the rational model. One is the difficulty of identifying and analyzing all feasible alternatives in determining the single best solution. In social policy development, this can be characterized as an information- or knowledge-related problem in that most policy decisions involve situations or circumstances that are somewhat unique, the consequences cannot be adequately predicted, and only a limited number of variables can be considered (Moroney, 1991). A second issue is that of values. Although a rational model may incorporate value considerations, the assumption is that once values are clarified, they can be ranked and dealt with in the same way as other types of information. In effect, the policy-maker is assumed to play a neutral or value-free role. Thus, policy-making within the rational model stresses technical rationality where the focus is on examining the most efficient means to achieve a predetermined end. However, the focus on means often results in inadequate attention to outcomes and we are then left with policies that may work on technical grounds but that are nonetheless 'bad policies'. Finally, the rational model often assumes that implementation follows logically from policy initiation and formulation and thus pays inadequate attention to the implementation phase.

Although the comprehensive version of the rational model calls for an analysis of all possible alternatives, a later modification of the model ended the consideration of alternatives once a satisfactory one was located. The result was policy development within a framework of 'limited rationality'. While this modification addressed questions of feasibility, it sacrificed the appeal of finding the most desirable policy choice following a comprehensive search for alternatives. A major problem with either the limited or comprehensive rational approach is the lack of attention to values or whether the 'ends' of policies can be justified. In some cases the ends may be predetermined at a more senior level; in other cases the analysis of alternatives may be infused with the values of the analyst, without identifying and defending these value assumptions. In either case, the lack of transparency restricts debate about the validity of goals and the 'goodness of fit' between these goals and alternatives on value criteria.

In social policy sectors such as child welfare, policy development often begins with a data collection phase. The complexity of problems facing policy-makers is such that they often feel overwhelmed. Sometimes task forces, Royal Commissions, or special inquiries will be mandated to outline a policy direction after gathering information, hearing from stakeholders, and initiating special studies. These strategies reflect a rational approach to policy development, and such groups can perform a useful role in policy-making in some circumstances (see Box 1.1 for an example of a rational approach to legislative change). However, the appointment of such bodies by governments or other decision-makers can also be used as a method to avoid taking action on controversial, complex, or costly issues while appearing to give these matters serious attention.

The rational model—or some of its major aspects—is widely used by human service practitioners. The medical model that begins with diagnosis, then the identification of optional treatment approaches, and finally selection of the most appropriate intervention is a common approach to practice, particularly in health and mental health settings. Similarly, the planned change model found in many frameworks for social work practice stresses an orderly, systematic approach to change. The terms applied to the various steps may differ from the medical model but the process is essentially the same. Professionals are cast in the roles of the expert or change agent working on, rather than with, a patient or client, who is considered to be a largely passive recipient of services.

## Box 1.1  New Child Welfare Legislation in BC:
        A Rational Approach to Policy-Making

By late 1991 a number of factors converged to produce the required impetus for major change to British Columbia's child welfare legislation. These included increased criticism of the reliance on statutory authority within the 1980 *Family and Child Service Act*, the election of a new NDP government that espoused a commitment to more family support services and a willingness to consult with the public, and the death of an adolescent in a government-funded youth facility that led to a highly criticized report from the provincial ombudsman. The government appointed a community panel composed of a mix of government and community members, and Aboriginal members formed a separate Aboriginal panel that held hearings in Aboriginal communities. These panels consulted widely; they held public meetings, received written briefs, conducted research, organized several day-long round-table discussions on special topics, and met with professional groups and organizations. This comprehensive rational approach to policy-making included a strong commitment to public participation. For example, the main panel heard 550 presentations in more than 23 communities and received over 600 briefs from individuals and groups. A broad approach to examining the needs of children and families was taken and issues such as poverty, service integration, and the adversarial relationship between child welfare agencies and families were addressed. After several months, two major panel reports were published, each outlining broad recommendations for new legislation and a new, more preventive approach to dealing with communities, families, and children. Many of the more radical recommendations of the panel reports—such as the inclusion of a provision stating that no child would be apprehended due to a lack of family resources—were rejected. Nevertheless, the reports were accepted by the ministry as a framework for drafting new legislation. A Legislative Review Group was appointed to draft legislation, and in the spring of 1993 an implementation Steering Committee was formed to begin preparing the various regions for change. The Legislative Review Group consulted with a variety of groups, including regional staff, and in 1993 a White Paper, *Making Changes: Next Steps*, was released. Work continued on developing a policy paper to outline proposed legislation and this paper was approved by Cabinet in December, 1993. Under the guidance of a new minister, drafting of the new Act was completed in the spring of 1994. In June 1994 the legislature passed the new *Child, Family and Community Service Act*, and its companion legislation, the *Child, Youth and Family Advocacy Act*.

(Adapted from Durie and Armitage, 1996)

## Incrementalism

If the rational model of policy-making is seen as too isolated from the real world of politics and policy-making, a second model—incrementalism—has been criticized for being too closely associated with the status quo. Incrementalism is commonly associated with Charles Lindblom (1959, 1968, 1979), who referred to the process as 'the science of muddling through'. Lindblom argued that change is most likely to occur when one calculates the marginal benefits of small adaptations from current approaches.

Advocates of incrementalism suggest several benefits. First, small-scale changes avoid major disruptions and the possibility of avoiding unanticipated negative outcomes that often result from large-scale changes. If a small change results in positive effects, it can be accelerated; if it leads to adverse effects, it can be halted and reversed without causing major problems. Second, incremental changes can usually be incorporated within existing organizational arrangements. Third, the approach accounts for political and normative realities by incorporating these considerations into discussions of alternatives during the change process. Furthermore, such discussions can include the views of those who make policy, those who implement it, and those who are affected by it.

Incrementalism generally accepts that existing structures, service mandates, and power structures within service organizations are legitimate and appropriate. Thus, it adopts an essentially conservative approach to change (see Box 1.2 for an example of an incremental approach to legislative change). Boulding (1964: 931) captures the limitations of incrementalism aptly in the following phrase: 'We stagger through history like a drunk, putting one disjointed incremental foot after another.'

It should be noted that a counter argument to the charge that incrementalism is always a conservative strategy or somehow limits innovation and change comes from the remarkable success of the Toyota Motor Company. Toyota has 'defined innovation as an incremental process in which the goal is not to make huge sudden leaps but rather to make things better on a daily basis. Most of the ideas are small—making parts on a shelf easier to reach—and not all of them work. But cumulatively every day Toyota knows a little more and does things a little better than it did the day before' (Surowiecki, 2008: 48). Given our interest in participation we should note here that most of these small ideas come from workers on the assembly line: 'Toyota implements a million new ideas a year and most of these come from ordinary workers. Japanese companies get a hundred times as many suggestions from their workers as U.S. companies do' (Surowiecki, 2008: 48).

## Mixed Scanning

Mixed scanning was advanced by Etzioni (1967, 1976) in an attempt to integrate the best aspects of the rational and incremental models. Mixed scanning suggests that situational factors will determine when each approach should be emphasized. It advocates an approach to policy development that begins with a comprehensive scan of the existing policy, including problem analysis and alternatives, and then adopts an incremental approach to the implementation of new policies.

## Box 1.2 Legislative Reform in Manitoba: Incrementalism in Action

In the summer of 1996 the Manitoba government launched a process to update its 1985 *Child and Family Services Act*. However, a very limited approach to reform was undertaken. The public consultation process was limited to a mere few weeks' duration, with only a few presentation dates in approximately six centres throughout the province. Furthermore, presenters were directed to confine their recommendations to a series of specific and quite limited policy questions published in a 'consultation workbook'. These included questions such as whether grandparents should have a right to apply for access to children who are apprehended, whether birth parents under 18 should be able to consent to private adoption, whether private practitioners arranging for adoptions should be licensed, whether teenaged dads should be required to pay child support, and whether child welfare workers should be required to have a minimum level of training. No comments on larger issues related to the general orientation of existing legislation or problems in the current service delivery system were invited. While presenters at public hearings did not necessarily confine themselves to this narrow set of questions, their views on broader policy issues were not stressed in the final report published by the panel. The report of the panel then made recommendations to government on the limited issues identified at the outset, and some of these recommendations were incorporated as amendments to the Act in the spring of 1997. However, these relatively minor changes did not alter the general thrust or philosophy of the existing Act.

Mixed scanning is a cumbersome term for a model that captures what happens on many occasions. Policy implementation often takes place in an incremental fashion, yet the use of comprehensive approaches, including task forces and commissions, to scan the broad policy environment, attests to the influence of the rational model.

There are a number of similarities between mixed scanning at a macro level and strategic planning, which has been widely adopted within human service organizations at the agency and operational level of planning over the past two decades. Although strategic planning has been a popular approach to policy-making at the organizational level, it requires continued organizational investment to realize potential benefits. It is also plagued by two of the difficulties associated with many forms of policy-making: it is difficult to predict consequences, particularly in a policy environment where so much lies outside the effective control of organizations; and most importantly, service users and front-line staff are frequently excluded from or underrepresented in the planning process. We return to a discussion of strategic planning in Chapter Three.

## The Value Criteria Model

There are different versions of the value criteria model, sometimes referred to as the value-analytic model (Gallagher and Haskins, 1984), but they are similar in their overall approach to policy-making. First, the problem is defined and available alternatives for dealing with it are identified. Although responses to a problem may represent only a limited range of alternatives, the problem analysis stage can direct attention to key normative elements of the problem, including causality. For example, the conventional child welfare system has all too often separated First Nations children from their families, communities, and culture. Identifying and analyzing the negative consequences of this approach can spur a consideration of alternatives such as First Nations control over child and family services, the development of more community-based foster care resources, and the development of more culturally appropriate services.

A second step is the development of value criteria for evaluating alternatives. These value criteria should include both universal and selective criteria. Universal criteria may represent general value considerations such as effectiveness, efficiency, and feasibility, whereas selective criteria represent those values that are more specific to the problem or issue being considered. In the example above concerning First Nations child and family services, selective criteria may include self-determination, community responsibility, and cultural appropriateness. The third step involves the gathering of data required to assess each alternative, and the analysis of each alternative according to value criteria. In the final step, the alternative that maximizes the greatest number of values, including efficiency, is recommended or a range of alternatives with identified strengths and weaknesses are discussed.

Although this model has considerable appeal to policy development in the human services because of its explicit consideration of values, it is apparent that conflicts can arise over the criteria that ought to guide final policy selection. For example, if a particular policy choice maximizes more of the selected values but also requires higher costs, how is this conflict to be resolved? And who sets the key values to be used in policy selection—the decision-maker, the policy researcher, the service user, or others?

The selection of value criteria, particularly those that are specific to the problem or issue, is the most controversial stage of this policy model but it should be recognized that other policy-making models incorporate values even if this is done implicitly. In the value criteria model, values are explicitly identified and, at the very least, they become more visible and open to debate. While the selection of value criteria depends on the nature of the policy being considered, this step is the point at which an ethical framework for policy-making can be proposed. Therefore, it is important to identify guidelines, especially for the development of selective value criteria. Saleebey (1990) has identified some broad philosophical cornerstones relevant to policy-making in the human services. These are:

a)   begin with an ethic of indignation about the denial of human dignity and opportunities;

b)   incorporate humane inquiry and understanding based on dialogue;

c)   focus on compassion and caring; and

d)   incorporate a quest for social justice.

These four cornerstones foster empowerment and social change to promote equity.

In a discussion of criteria for theory evaluation in social work research, Witkin and Gottschalk (1988) arrive at similar conclusions. As adapted to our purposes, the steps in developing value criteria for policy-making are:

1.   the approach should be explicitly critical in considering historical, cultural, political, and economic factors;

2.   people must be recognized as active agents in shaping as well as reacting to their environment;

3.   the life experiences of service users must be considered; and

4.   solutions should promote social justice.

The term 'social justice' is frequently evoked, yet it is open to various interpretations. We adopt the position advanced by Rawls (1971), who argued persuasively that social and economic inequalities created in society should be adjusted to provide the greatest benefit to the least advantaged. Social justice, then, is about redressing problems of inequality. Box 1.3 provides an example of how value criteria have been used to shape policy development in a First Nations child and family services agency.

## The Garbage Can Model

As earlier noted, the garbage can model was first developed by Cohen et al. (1972) in an effort to explain how organizations make decisions under conditions of uncertainty. Although universities were the original focus of analysis, application was generalized to other similar organizations. These organizations were described as 'organized anarchies', characterized by problematic preferences, unclear technology, and fluid participation. Four streams or processes were originally conceptualized: problems, solutions, participation, and choice opportunities, although Kingdon (1995), who revised the model for widespread use, reduced the number of streams to three. The 'choice opportunity' in the original model was likened to a 'garbage can' into which various kinds of problems and solutions were dumped by participants as they were generated, and outcomes were a function of the mix in the can and how it was processed.

The modified garbage can model of policy-making developed by Kingdon (1995: 86–8) builds on the earlier work and is an attempt to describe policy-making as it unfolds in the day-to-day life of governments and organizations.

## Box 1.3  An Example of the Value Criteria Model
##              of Policy-Making

The development of West Region Child and Family Services in Manitoba illustrates how the value criteria model can be used to develop policies that shape an agency's overall orientation to practice and program development. Growing awareness of the child welfare system's colonizing effects in First Nations communities in the late 1970s and early 1980s led to the signing of a Master Agreement by Manitoba First Nations, the government of Manitoba, and the government of Canada in 1982. This Agreement paved the way for the transfer of administrative control of child welfare services to tribal council authorities in the province, and in 1985 West Region Child and Family Services, serving nine First Nations reserves, became a fully mandated child and family service agency. This agency paid special attention to assessing the impact of the conventional child welfare system on family and community life, an impact represented by the loss of hundreds of children from their families and communities, and by the presence of powerlessness within many of these families and communities. This led to the new agency's adoption of four key philosophical principles used as guidelines for policy development. These principles, which may be expressed as value criteria, are Aboriginal control, cultural relevancy, community-based services, and a comprehensive team-oriented approach to service delivery. Thus, a service model has been adopted that relies on community-based staff working with local child and family service committees that have considerable authority. Specialized service teams have also been developed to provide support and back-up services to community-based staff. In addition, the agency adopts a broad approach to child and family services by undertaking initiatives in training, recreation, and community development.

Cultural relevancy shapes policy development through such things as an emphasis on hiring Aboriginal staff, providing culturally relevant staff training, and incorporating the wisdom of elders. Furthermore, the agency has played a leadership role in developing culturally appropriate foster homes, including the widespread use of extended family care. The agency is managed by a Board of Chiefs, but there are also extensive efforts to incorporate a broader level of community participation in policy development. For example, an Operational Planning Workshop is held every two years in which representatives from each community engage with agency staff in identifying new service needs and priorities. Today, few children require care outside their community or their culture, and external evaluations have demonstrated that the agency provides both high quality services and a supportive, sustaining work environment for its staff.

(Adapted from McKenzie, 1999; McKenzie and Shangreaux, 2006)

Three 'families' of processes are observed to exist in setting organizational or governmental agendas: problems, policies, and politics. These are likened to separate streams that often operate quite independently of each other. First, there is a 'stream of problems' that captures the attention of policy-makers in a government or an organization. Second, there is a policy community of specialists, which may include people inside or outside the organization that concentrates on generating policy proposals. These individuals or groups advance a 'stream of solutions'. Some of these ideas and solutions are taken seriously, while others are not. The third ingredient, the 'political stream', is composed of elements such as public opinion, election results, administration changes, ideological shifts, and interest group campaigns. Participants in the policy-making process may be active in all three process streams at the same time or they may be active in only one or two of these streams.

Each of the actors and processes associated with these streams can function as either an impetus or a constraint to change. Although there may be some overlap and some connection between the streams (e.g., groups may propose both their understanding of a problem and their preferred solution), they are largely separate from each other, governed by different considerations and styles. For example, key problems with feasible solutions may not emerge on the policy agenda because of an absence of political support. The lack of political interest in a feasible solution may be due to the fact that the solution has emanated from a think tank with a different ideology from that of government. In addition, feasible solutions may not gain acceptance if governments anticipate strong public resistance.

Although these streams usually operate independently, they do connect at times. This opens a 'policy window' (see Figure 1.2) that can lead to problem recognition, agenda setting, and the creation of new policies or programs. However, if these opportunities are missed (e.g., if no action is taken or if the political mood shifts), then the policy window will close and the opportunity will be lost, at least for the time being.

A key stage in the process is problem recognition and possible definition. Recognition, according to Kingdon, generally occurs through three mechanisms. The first is a change in indicators such as unemployment rates, economic growth, interest rates, or the rate of children in care. A second mechanism is a focusing event that directs attention and sometimes action in response to an issue. The third mechanism is normal feedback from the operations of programs, including the role of evaluation in influencing policy development.

Pal (1992: 135) elaborates on Kingdon's list of mechanisms leading to problem recognition by identifying criteria that can be used to determine when a problem becomes a public problem. In order to define something as a public problem, he suggests that it must affect a substantial proportion of the public, offend or affront widely held public views or mores, or be the direct result of previous public policies. The example of changes to the Canada Pension Plan is briefly noted here. Actuarial information in the mid-1990s indicated that without substantial changes, the plan would not be able to meet future benefit payments for retiring

**Figure 1.2    Policy Window in the Garbage Can Model**

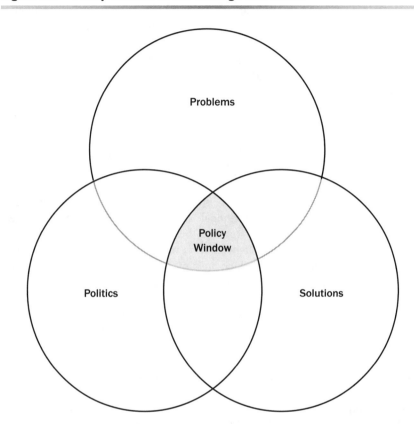

Canadians. In addition, the crisis was intensified by previous government policies that resulted in benefit payouts to beneficiaries that were in excess of the value of their contributions. In this case, the problem affected a wide number of Canadians, and resulted, in part, from the failure of previous policies. After a great deal of debate around the relative merits of public versus private pension plans, the federal government decided in favour of the former and raised the premiums paid by contributors to the plan.

It is often difficult to predict which issue will be defined as a public problem in that recognition depends on a combination of objective data and subjective perceptions that change is required. Indeed, in some cases, subjective perceptions become more important than objective data. Youth violence in Winnipeg provides one example. In recent years there has been growing concern about high levels of juvenile crime, particularly within the inner city. However, although gang violence has increased, the actual rate of youth crime has declined over the past several years. This has not prevented a growing perception among the public that youth crime is increasing, a perception fuelled by increasingly intense media attention on the operation of organized street gangs. In turn, this perception has led to heightened demands for a more punitive approach to the problem of youth crime.

Issues can remain on the policy agenda for some time, although the weighting of certain issues may vary at different times depending on how the three streams interact. Furthermore, items can fall off the policy agenda because they cannot be sustained or because the problem may appear to be solved.

The garbage can model provides useful insights into the policy-making process, and it directs attention to the political environment that plays such a significant role both in determining how the process unfolds, and ultimately, in the outcomes that emerge.

A summary of the policy-making steps in each of the models is provided in Table 1.1, although we stress that these steps rarely follow each other in a linear fashion. We have also presented the models as discrete approaches, but in the real world of policy-making, this oversimplifies the policy development process. First, policy-making often combines elements from more than one approach, and it is this combination of approaches, which often provides a more accurate description of the policy-making process in a given context (see Box 1.4). Second, policy-making is a process of trying to decide what to do in situations in which values and opinions are often in conflict and where the final choice is heavily shaped by differing ideologies.

**Table 1.1    Models of Policy-Making: A Summary**

**A. The Rational Model[1]**
1.  Define the problem in objective terms and classify goals.
2.  Develop a comprehensive list of alternatives to address the problem.
3.  Project possible consequences and the probability of occurrence for each set of alternatives.
4.  Examine data for each strategy in relation to goals and benefit–cost calculations.
5.  Select a strategy to maximize goals and to achieve the best benefit–cost ratio.

**B. Incrementalism[2]**
1.  Calculate the marginal benefits of current choices for addressing the problem.
2.  Initiate small choices toward a solution that would achieve marginal benefits.
3.  Increase the emphasis on choices that produce positive results; reduce the emphasis on choices leading to negative results.
4.  Policy emerges from a combination of choices that work.

**C. Mixed Scanning**[3]
1. Define the problem and classify goals.
2. Conduct a comprehensive scan of alternatives.
3. Select alternatives for detailed analysis based on potential for goal achievement and feasibility.
4. Collect data and select the alternative best able to maximize goals and feasibility considerations.
5. Project incremental incorporation of policy choices.

**D. The Value Criteria Model**[4]
1. Define the problem and identify policy alternatives available to deal with the problem.
2. Establish universal and selective criteria (values) for evaluating alternatives.
3. Gather data related to each alternative, and assess each alternative relative to value criteria.
4. Recommend the alternative that maximizes the value criteria, or offer a range of alternatives that maximize different criteria in different ways.

**E. The Garbage Can Model**[5]
1. Three types of processes exist in agenda setting for policy-making. These are characterized as streams of problems, solutions, and politics.
2. These streams exist somewhat independently of each other, and each of actors and processes can act as an impetus or constraint to change. The streams are conceptualized as floating around in a garbage can where on occasion, the streams may come together and a window of opportunity opens. A key stage is public recognition of a problem and three mechanisms can contribute to this stage. These are a change in economic or social indicators, an unpredictable event, or feedback from program operations.
3. Once a policy window opens, the combination of problems, solutions, and political opportunity can lead to a new policy with the outcome dependent on characteristics associated with the problems, alternatives, and participants included in this mix.
4. If the opportunity is missed or if no action is taken, the policy window closes, and one must wait for the next opportunity. Issues can also sit on the policy agenda although they may be weighted differently at different times. In addition, items can fall off the policy agenda because interest cannot be sustained or because the problem appears to be resolved.

[1] (Adapted from Carley, 1980: 11); [2] (Adapted from Lindblom, 1959); [3] (Adapted from Etzioni, 1976); [4] (Adapted from Dobelstein, 1990: 71); [5] (Adapted from Kingdon, 1995: 86–8)

## Box 1.4 Policy-Making Often Involves a Combination of Planning Models

In response to the Aboriginal Justice Inquiry–Child Welfare Initiative launched in Manitoba in 1999, four separate authorities for the delivery of child welfare services in the province were developed. Three of these were Aboriginal (First Nations North, First Nations South, and Métis), and one is known as the General Authority. The three Aboriginal Authorities assume primary responsibility for services to children and families based on membership affiliation and the General Authority has primary responsibility for providing services to non-Aboriginal service users in the province. Legislation mandating these changes was passed in 2002 and implementation occurred between 2003 and early 2005. Ongoing implementation of this form of devolution has not been without controversy, and several highly publicized deaths of children who had received services from the child welfare system led to a series of reviews beginning in 2006. These reviews identified a wide range of recommendations to improve the system. Government's willingness to fund a broad range of these recommendations resulted in a coordinated implementation planning initiative called *Changes for Children* to implement these changes.

In describing the policy-making models used by government, the former Coordinator of the *Changes for Children* initiative notes that none of the policy models provides a complete explanation for how policies emerged from the *Changes for Children* initiative, but when several models are combined the development process is more accurately depicted. At an early stage, *framing* of the problems occurred, and as options were generated there was often a reframing of the issues to be addressed. Of importance was a political commitment to maintain the newly created authority structure but also to invest in options to improve the system.

The government's action to appoint committees to conduct comprehensive reviews (one of the service delivery system, one of children in institutions, and another of child deaths) and bring forward recommendations reflects steps associated with the *rational model*. At the same time, shifting the understanding of problems from a recognition of the high number of children in care to the inadequate front-end response to this reality, which when combined with several possible solutions (e.g., more training, more front-line staff, a different model of service) and the political commitment to the Authority model of service delivery, reflects a number of the processes outlined in the *garbage can model*.

In its response to the reviews, the government committed $130 million to system improvements over a three-year period, embraced a differential-response model of services (i.e., better front-end assessment and two streams of service: child protection and earlier intervention and support) and set up a special committee to coordinate planning and implementation. This committee first identified principles (i.e., value criteria) to guide its work against which any new measures to be implemented would be assessed. This step draws on the *value-criteria model* of planning. Finally, planning proceeded by outlining strategic directions based on recommendations from the reviews but quickly proceeded to a series of tasks, such as defining better assessment instruments and identifying pilot projects to test the new differential response system. This approach is consistent with a *mixed scanning model* of policy-making.

(With acknowledgement to Jay Rodgers, CEO, General Child and Family Services Authority, Winnipeg, Manitoba.)

Finally, it is important to emphasize that regardless of the approach, social policy is also permeated by politics. In the last analysis, the major decisions are made by politicians and governments whose pre-eminent concern is to meet enough of the people's needs to be re-elected. Thus, all-important policies will be assessed through the political lens of votes. But governments, and organizations for that matter, do not *always* follow the most politically expedient route. They are sometimes driven by causes that reflect a deeply held conviction or ideological commitment, and policy directions under these circumstances are not easily compromised. For example, the Saskatchewan NDP government led by Tommy Douglas withstood significant public pressure in 1961 when it adopted Canada's first medicare program. On the other side of the political spectrum, the Mike Harris Conservative government in Ontario, with its ideological commitment to a residual model of welfare, cut monthly welfare payments by 22 per cent and cancelled the Jobs Ontario program, an employment support program, after coming to power in 1995.

## Summary and Conclusion

In our summary we consider how the policy-making models connect to the work of practitioners in the human services, and to the lived experience of service users. At the outset we acknowledge the difference in purpose between policy and practice, a difference that often creates a gap between the two that is difficult to bridge. Policies represent an overall course of action to deal with a need or problem that affects a large number of individuals, whereas practice is concerned about what should be done for one or more service users in a particular context. Too often policies, when rigidly adopted, fail to consider the specific circumstances or needs of individuals or communities, which are, in fact, the primary concerns of both service users and practitioners. One way of closing the gap between policy and practice is to include service users and practitioners in the development of policy. Moreover, if policies in the human services retain some elements of flexibility, practitioners will be able to adapt these to the particular needs of individuals, families, and communities. We give special attention to inclusive models of policy development in Chapter Six.

Do any of the policy-making models ensure that the wisdom of practitioners and service users will be combined with that of policy-makers? The rational approach is primarily a top-down process that clearly assigns a primary role to policy analysts who are responsible for drafting new policies or legislation. As the name suggests, incrementalism is a more informal process that may well facilitate partnerships between policy-makers and practitioners. Although a series of small steps can eventually lead to substantial changes, it is more likely that these steps will continue in a well-established direction, and will not significantly challenge accepted ways of doing things, whether in policy or practice. Thus, incrementalism is unlikely to lead to major reforms; instead incrementalism is more likely to promote an environment in which policy becomes routinized and practitioners become its caretakers. Although incrementalism allows for some limited contributions from practitioners, opportunities are not usually extended to service users. Like the rational approach, it is not seen here as the approach of choice. Although there are some advantages to mixed scanning because it represents a combination of both the rational and the incremental approaches, this combination means it cannot escape some of the limitations associated with these approaches. The value criteria model is an adaptation of the rational model; however, it incorporates the explicit treatment of values. This is its most important strength, but its ability to serve as a useful tool in connecting policy and practice is highly dependent on what values are selected for consideration and on how the process of value analysis is conducted. The garbage can model of policy-making incorporates political processes as a consideration in policy adoption. This model also recognizes a role for policy communities that contribute to the stream of solutions by recommending particular policies. Although practitioners and service users may be involved in these policy communities, their involvement is often quite limited. One of the reasons is that policy communities must usually sustain their efforts over a relatively long period of time to obtain relatively modest gains. Such long-term commitments are often difficult for practitioners and service users.

Each of these approaches may be adapted to be more inclusive in ways that increase the potential of connecting policy and practice; however, none insist on inclusiveness. The value criteria model comes closest to realizing this potential in that it allows for the specification of value criteria that can include consultation and/or decision-making input from practitioners and service users. Clearly, this policy-making model must adopt the central principle of inclusiveness if it is to succeed in connecting policy and practice concerns. But in order to achieve this principle, policy-making must be transformed from a process in which decisions are made in secret at the highest level of the organization, and then packaged within this arena for marketing to an apparently resistant and largely uninformed group of practitioners and service users.

Chapter Two describes the policy-making environment and its impact on policy-making processes.

# Recommended Reading

R. Titmuss, *Social Policy* (London, UK: George Allen and Unwin, 1974). This book is a classic on social policy, and provides insight into the origins of the value-criteria model of policy-making.

M. Howlett and M. Ramesh, *Studying Public Policy: Policy Cycles and Policy Subsystems*, 2nd edn (Don Mills, ON: Oxford University Press, 2003). This book provides an in-depth study of the policy-making process.

L. Miljan, *Public Policy in Canada: An Introduction*, 5th edn (Don Mills, ON: Oxford University Press, 2008). This book focuses both on the public policy-making process and policy developments in six fields of practice in Canada, including the social services.

# Critical Thinking Questions

1. Three theories were outlined to explain political behaviour and policy-making. What are these theories and which one do you think best describes policy-making at the federal level? Provide a rationale for your choice.

2. Low voter turnout in local, provincial, and federal elections is often taken as a sign of alienation and a feeling that one's voice does not matter in the political process. This may be one indication of a decline in civil society. In your opinion what are some of the reasons why people don't vote or don't engage in the political process? What might help to change this?

3. Select a recently developed policy or program with which you are familiar. What model(s) of policy-making best explain the process of developing this policy? What is your critique of the process that was used?

4. What are the differences between the value-criteria model of policy-making and the rational model? What is your critique of each model?

5. The public recognition stage of a problem is defined as a key stage in the garbage can model of policy-making. What are the three mechanisms that can contribute to this stage? Can you illustrate two of these stages with examples?

# Chapter Two

# The Social Policy Environment

There are a number of general factors to be considered in understanding the art and science of making social policy in Canada. These include certain aspects of our political culture, the influence of ideology, the centralization of power, globalization, social and economic characteristics such as poverty and inequality, and policy-making structures.

Political culture refers to dominant and relatively durable beliefs and values in a society. However, these are difficult to define in the Canadian context because of the recognition of the unique status of Quebec, First Nations and other indigenous groups, and the general Canadian commitment to multiculturalism. The delivery of health and social services was ceded to the provinces in the *British North America Act*, but the unique status of Quebec has encouraged the devolution of other national social policies to Quebec, and sometimes to other provinces as well. The Indian Act sets out the special responsibilities of the federal government to First Nations communities and the Inuit, and their aspirations for greater self-determination are shared by other indigenous groups.

Canadian social and economic policies are also heavily influenced by Canada's proximity to the United States (US). Canadians generally regard their differences from the US, particularly in relation to social policies such as public health care, as assets. However, the dominance of American media and cultural communication, as well as the extensive economic linkages between the two countries make true autonomy difficult to achieve when one lives in the 'shadow of the elephant'.

Policy-making structures include the federal and provincial governments, the *Charter of Rights and Freedoms*, and the Supreme Court. Our model of parliamentary government was inherited from the United Kingdom (UK) and is enshrined in the *Constitution Act, 1982* (formerly known as the *British North America Act, 1867*);

however, when compared with the UK, our version of federalism is much more decentralized in the area of social policy, in that provincial governments play a major role. The role of these structures in making social policy is described in more detail in Chapter Three.

Ideology and its relationship to social policy, poverty, and inequality, and the influence of globalization receive primary attention in this chapter. A consistent theme across the first three chapters of the book is the centralization of power among a social and economic elite and the extent to which this restricts the adoption of a more inclusive and democratic approach to policy-making. Although much of the contents of this chapter identify some daunting challenges for making progressive social policies, we conclude by reviewing some of the developments that suggest that there are also opportunities for making policy changes that can make a difference in the lives of those who are deeply affected by the problems of poverty and social exclusion in our society.

The general relationship of ideology to social policy was summarized in our Introduction. That is, neo-liberalism was associated with a residual approach, liberalism with an institutional model, and democratic socialism with a social development model. The social democratic label is often applied to contemporary advocates of democratic socialism and others who support a more comprehensive social welfare state as well as a stronger role for government in economic matters.

We now turn to a discussion of the ideology of neo-liberalism, which has dominated the political landscape in Canada and a number of other western countries for most of the last three decades.

## Neo-liberalism and Globalization

Neo-liberalism can be defined as an approach to economics and public policy that strengthens the power of private businesses and competitive markets in society and focuses state activity on areas of policy that reinforce the private market, including the generation of higher profits for private corporations. Stanford (2008) traces the roots of neo-liberalism to the appointment of Paul Volcker as head of the US Federal Reserve in 1979. Prior to this, more attention had been paid to the issue of unemployment and the need for government to stimulate the economy in 'hard times' through government spending and the adjustment of taxes and interest rates. Direct public investment to stimulate employment was a prominent aspect of public policy but when 'good times' returned government could often become less interventionist in job creation and emphasize more of a regulatory role. This Keynesian approach to economics, popularized in the 1930s, stressed a more activist role for government; in the 1980s under Volcker, this gave way to strict monetary policy.[1] Based on the ideas of Milton Friedman, the monetarist approach paid little attention to the goal of full employment. Instead high interest rates were introduced in an almost single-minded focus on controlling inflation, which would, it was argued, make it attractive for the private market to invest in new economic ventures. In turn, 'trickle-down economics' would benefit the masses because of expanding jobs and increased consumer participation in the private market. The political architects of this approach were Margaret Thatcher, who became the UK Prime Minister in 1979, and Ronald Reagan, who was elected as the US President a year later.

According to Stanford (2008), this era of capitalism has been described by different labels, including neo-conservatism and the corporate agenda; the term neo-liberalism is commonly used today. It is a confusing term because liberalism in the reformist sense normally refers to a political ideology often associated with the centre of the political spectrum. However, Stanford notes that in economics, liberalism means 'an absence of government interference' (2008: 48). Neo-liberal goals are to control or reduce inflation, to restore insecurity as a way of disciplining labour markets so workers will work for lower wages or reduced benefits, to roll back government programs and activities to meet business needs, and to cut taxes. The tools of neo-liberalism include the adjustment of interest rates to regulate inflation, privatization (including private–public partnerships which most often result in higher costs for the public sector and higher benefits to the private sector) and deregulation, a reduction in social security benefits, and the use of free trade agreements to expand markets and contain the power of government.

There are two additional points to emphasize about neo-liberalism. First, the pursuit of neo-liberal policies is not restricted to political parties or actors on the right (i.e., neo-conservative), although it will be apparent that neo-liberalism is most often fully embraced by representatives of this political philosophy. Nevertheless, governments of all stripes, including the Liberal Party and the New Democratic Party (NDP), can adopt a neo-liberal policy agenda. For example, the actions of the Liberal government of Canada in the 1990s, which painted social spending as a major cause of the deficit, and the related adoption of policies which reduced social spending, reflect a neo-liberal agenda. Second, it is a mistake to classify all governments, either in Canada or in the developed world, as equal proponents of a neo-liberal form of capitalism. For example, there are significant differences between the United States and Canada and between these two countries in general and the Nordic countries in their perceptions of the role of government and their approach to managing social welfare.

The neo-liberal agenda of cutbacks, privatization, and deregulations can have disastrous effects on both the economy and well-being of families as illustrated in the sub-prime mortgage crisis that surfaced in the United States in 2008 (see Box 2.1). The effects of this crisis triggered a world-wide credit crisis and a global recession. It is important to note that the effects of such a recession are not limited to the developed world; indeed Saunders (2008) describes how the economic meltdown resulted in major job losses in the villages of the developing world as well. The economic crisis has raised questions about the lack of regulatory oversight and the inflated salaries of CEOs. At a more fundamental level it highlights the failure of neo-liberal policies which extol the benefits of an unregulated market, as well as the readiness of neo-liberal champions to turn to government for corporate handouts following the failure of laissez-faire economics. Requests for economic bailouts

## Box 2.1 Neo-liberalism and the 2008 Economic Crisis

The 2008 credit crisis in US financial markets surfaced with the unraveling of sub-prime mortgages in 2007, but its origin dates back to 2001 when former Federal Reserve chairman Alan Greenspan, a monetarist in the Milton Friedman mould, cut interest rates to extremely low levels. If this was not enough to stimulate a tidal wave of home-buying, mortgages were offered to individuals with limited collateral at even lower rates, under an escalating interest arrangement which required increased payments after an initial period of time. The cost of homes escalated, driven by market demand, and major US investment banks tripled their profits between 2002 and 2006. In the absence of adequate regulatory oversight, investment banks, which had borrowed money several times their own worth to buy mortgages of questionable quality, repackaged these debts and sold them as securities to other national and international institutions. By the summer of 2007, many people could not meet their mortgage payments. Defaults on mortgages grew and home prices began to tumble. Investment banks were left with mortgage assets no one wanted to buy and these financial institutions could no longer borrow enough money to meet growing liabilities.

Like a 'house of cards' the system began to collapse in the summer and fall of 2008. Trillions of dollars were lost, investment banks went bankrupt, investors' portfolios plummeted in value, and other companies, in need of loans to cover costs, had difficulty borrowing money. In an attempt to prop up the system the US government approved a bailout which initially cost taxpayers between $700 billion and $1 trillion, but costs are already much higher than this. Meanwhile, one of the now-bankrupt investment banks—Lehman Brothers—paid its CEO about $350 million in the years leading up to the bank's collapse (2000–07). The credit crisis then spread to Europe where government intervention was required to prop up banks which had lost money on securities bought from US investment banks. The spillover effects of the crisis on the global markets, including Canada's, has been significant. Although a global recession has been triggered, the long-term effects are not yet clear. What is clear is that one trillion dollars was equal to Canada's economic output for approximately one year in 2008, and would have funded AIDS prevention around the world for 100 years.

(With information from Carmichael, 2008; Hershfeld-Davis, 2008; McKenna, 2008).

and loan guarantees have been widespread, and in the United States the CEOs of the big three automakers (General Motors, Ford, and Chrysler) were ridiculed by some members of Congress in late 2008 when they flew to Washington, each in his own private jet, to make their pitch for public funds to Congress. It will also be apparent that these expenditures have both direct and indirect effects on the well-being of citizens and related social programs. Direct effects include job losses and pressure to limit wages and benefits; indirect effects may include longer term cutbacks in social spending as an outcome of increased government debt arising from expenditures to prop up a faltering economic system.

Neo-liberalism has become more closely integrated with economic globalization over the past two decades. Economic globalization, with its emphasis on free trade and the mobility of capital, is advocated by neo-liberals because it reflects 'good business', which is defined simply as higher profits for the large corporate structures able to compete in the global marketplace. But how does globalization affect social policy and the well-being of citizens living in specific nation states?

Globalization is not really new in the sense that it can refer to the strengthening of international economic linkages for the purposes of trade through the development of free trade agreements, improved communications, and better transportation systems. There are obvious benefits to globalization through increased opportunities for trade, and it is neither desirable nor feasible to eliminate these exchanges. However, it is the combination of neo-liberal policies, often supported by governments, and globalization that often produces adverse effects on one or more of the participating partners.

There are three key international bodies that have played major roles in imposing a neo-liberal agenda of free-market, pro-business structures on the world economy in the past two decades: the International Monetary Fund (IMF), the World Bank, and the World Trade Organization (WTO).[2] The IMF and World Bank were established after the Second World War. The former was to focus on stabilizing and freeing the international flow of money, and the latter was to assist poor countries with economic development.

Free trade agreements are one of the primary features of economic globalization. Although such agreements must be assessed from the perspectives of all parties, and through a social justice lens, as well as an economic lens, we focus here on Canadian experiences with the North American Free Trade Agreement (NAFTA) and the earlier Canada–US Free Trade Agreement (FTA). Viewpoints on free trade agreements are often deeply divided. For example, Miljan (2008: 141–5) provides a largely positive assessment of NAFTA whereas others identify job losses and the threat to Canada's network of publicly provided health and social services as major disadvantages (see Box 2.2). There is some evidence of overall job loss among major Canadian companies; however, there have been other factors, in addition to free trade, that contributed to these losses. Of additional concern to many are the ongoing efforts of the corporate elite, supported in large part by the Canadian government, to deepen the nature and scope of economic integration with the United States and Mexico. The current vehicle used for this purpose is known as the Security and Prosperity Partnership of North America (SPP), which was formed in 2002 at the urging of the Canadian Council of Chief Executives (CCCE),[3] the most powerful corporate body in the country (Dobbin, 2007). Representatives of the business and government elite of the three participating countries have been meeting in secret over the past few years to plan for increased linkages between the

Box 2.2 The Problem with the North American
Free Trade Agreement

---

Canada is regarded as an energy 'superpower' but NAFTA guarantees that Americans, not Canadians, will be the primary beneficiaries of Canada's ouput. As of 2008, Canada exported 63 per cent of its oil and 56 per cent of its natural gas to the US. Moreover, a requirement of NAFTA, known as the 'proportionality clause', requires Canada to continue exporting the same proportion of our oil and gas forever— even if there is a domestic shortage—unless it reduces its own usage by the same proportion. If processing of this oil occurred in Canada, rather than the US, 18,000 new jobs would be created annually over several years.

One of the most insidious provisions in NAFTA is the one that allows foreign investors to sue the Canadian government directly if any public policy or government action denies them investment or profit opportunities. As of August 2008, Canada had been hit with 15 such lawsuits costing more than $18.5 million, with another $533 million in claims pending. One example of a pending claim occurred in July 2008 when a group of 200 private American investors filed legal papers to force the government to permit a private American-operated surgical centre in British Columbia. In addition, these investors are claiming damages of $154 million based on delays in obtaining approval of their for-profit medical facility.

(With information from Dobbin, 2008; Russell, 2008a, 2008b).

economies of Canada, the United States, and Mexico. Because US economic and corporate interests dominate the North American economy, it is not hard to predict whose interests are likely to be first served in any agreements that might arise out of these talks. More important is the absence of transparency and any evidence that input from those other than key elite power brokers will even be permitted.

The new era of globalization is led by transnational corporations (TNCs), and these parent companies and their affiliates produce 25 per cent of the world's economic output (Silver, 2002: 30). TNCs differ from the older version of nationally-based companies in that they are motivated only by profit with minimal regard for the interests of host countries. Thus, they move their operations on a whim to countries where labour is cheapest and environmental laws are the most lax. As Rice and Prince (2000) note, the state is increasingly unable to regulate the activities and tax the surplus of globalized capital because of the fear that these corporations will relocate to other countries, and this contributes to a reduction in the powers of national governments. As well, neo-liberal governments frequently collude with these corporations in actions to further the aims of globalized capital.

In developing societies, working people are at risk of losing employment through plant closings or the transfer of production to non-union, low-wage sites. Technological advances also reduce the need for human labour and workers are transferred from permanent jobs to short-term employment in order to reduce wage and benefit packages. Meanwhile, one-fifth of the world's population (some 1.2 billion people) were living on less than $1 per day in 2000, and 100 million children were estimated to be living or working on the streets (United Nations 2000 Human Development Report, quoted in Canadian Centre for Policy Alternatives, 2000: 3).

The IMF and the World Bank have contributed to the impoverishment of many countries by lending money that could not be repaid. Structural adjustments programs (SAPS), designed by the IMF and supported by the World Bank, are imposed on nations that apply to the IMF for refinancing because they have fallen behind in their payments. SAPS require debtor nations requesting financing to foster trade by eliminating restrictions on imports and exports, privatizing national resources and public utilities, cutting back in public services such as health and education, devaluing currency, and making loan payments a priority (Prigoff, 2000). While these 'adjustments' are supposed to make these countries competitive in a global market, the social costs of adjustment have been extensive, especially for women and children. Only recently has the World Bank acknowledged some of the adverse effects of their adjustment policies and responded by allocating some resources for social investment.

These developments also affect Canadian social policy. First, because they give priority to countries characterized by low wages and few benefits, TNCs impede the development of progressive social policies. This strategy can also be observed within Canada: large corporations may play off one provincial government against another. These tactics limit the power of governments to establish fair labour practices or rates of taxation, and they also restrict the power of unions at the bargaining table in trying to establish a fair wage rate or related social benefits like pensions. Second, in determining where they will establish their enterprises, TNCs and other corporations place pressure on governments to provide tax holidays or incentives that restrict government revenues that could be used for social programs. In addition, they often exert influence on government to reduce the level of benefits in income support programs like welfare and Employment Insurance (EI) to ensure a ready supply of cheap labour and to relax protective legislation such as minimum wage laws or environmental protection legislation. While companies may place direct pressure on governments regarding such changes, the influence is also exerted through comparisons with other jurisdictions that are being considered as a place to locate. This results in enormous pressure to design policies to serve the interests of the market economy rather than the needs of the public at large.

Perhaps one of the most important effects of globalization is its influence on civil society. Civil society is a concept that is frequently associated with community capacity-building and the development of local democracy. In our view, one of the essential attributes of a civil society is the ability to hold others, including institutions, accountable for their actions. This may occur through informal actions, formal complaints, the influence of public opinion, redress through the legal system, and elections to replace those in power. Although accountability mechanisms are often imperfect, they do exist, even in the case of elected officials. When some of the powers normally vested in government and local institutions are transferred to TNCs that are accountable not to the citizens of the country where they are located, but to international shareholders primarily concerned with profits, the equation is altered. While globalization is not the only reason that people feel unable to influence the policies that affect their lives, it contributes to the weakening of civil society, particularly in relation to social policy, by placing the authority for these decisions out of reach by local citizens.

Economic globalization may be an inescapable reality, but stringent national and international controls are required if the public interest in both Canada and other countries is to be protected. Two possible scenarios related to diminished state power in the globalization era have been identified by Marchak (1991). First, decreasing state power may lead to the mobilization of actions to promote policy reform on a more global scale. One example was the mobilization of support to defeat the Multilateral Agreement on Investment, a proposal by the 29 richest companies in the world to ease the movement of capital across international boundaries in 1998. The growing international resistance to the concentration of power among TNCs is also reflected in protests that occur at all major meetings of groups such as the WTO. The international scope of such actions is significant, and Hawken (2007) estimates there are over a million—maybe more—organizations around the world working toward ecological sustainability and social justice. In Canada, for example, groups like the Council of Canadians are active in coordinating Canadian opposition to the social costs of globalization. It can also be argued that the goals of these social movements will become more achievable with growing awareness of the failures of current neo-liberal policies. However, a second possibility is that social policy will adapt to an environment characterized by a diminished state role, particularly with respect to the state's capacity to regulate the national economy. As earlier noted, there is also evidence that supports the growing influence of neo-liberalism on social spending and the operations of health and social service organizations. If the 'diminished state role' scenario prevails, we will become increasingly unable to rely on government to protect the health and social programs we have come to value in Canada.

# Poverty and Inequality in Canada

Poverty in Canada is our most persistent social problem; it is also widely recognized that Canada has the capacity to eradicate poverty. The relatively weak public policy response to poverty is recognized by many within Canada, and the social and economic costs are immense. Those who grow up poor are less likely to be able to locate well-paying employment, more likely to require health care, and more likely to be involved in crime. When research findings from US studies (Holzer, 2007) are adjusted for the Canadian context, the social costs of child poverty in Canada are estimated at approximately $40 billion annually (Finn, 2008).

Most governments in Canada were preoccupied with their annual operating deficit (identified as a first step in addressing a growing public debt) as a single-minded agenda in the 1990s.[4] Public spending cuts, particularly to social programs, coupled with increased tax revenues and low interest rates led to balanced federal budgets beginning in 1997–98. The erosion of funding for social programs associated with this trend has also shaped the struggles of the past decade. For example, medicare remains on the critical list despite recent infusions of new funding. And despite the federal government's action to restore some of the cuts to social transfers to the provinces in the late 1990s, funding levels for education and social programs remain well below the levels required to meet the growing needs in these program sectors. Although unemployment rates over the past decade in Canada have declined, these have increased sharply as result of the recession triggered in 2008. It is also important to note that poverty rates have remained almost unchanged over the past two decades. Using the Statistics Canada Low Income Cut-Off (LICO)[5] as a poverty line, the national child poverty rate in 2006, after tax adjustments, was 11.3 per cent (the before-tax rate is much higher at 15.8 per cent), almost identical to the 1989 rate (11.7 per cent) when the House of Commons unanimously resolved to eliminate child poverty in Canada by the year 2000 (Campaign 2000, 2008b: 1). As noted, there is a significant difference between before-tax LICOs, which include income after government transfers but before payment of income taxes, and after-tax LICOs, which reflect disposable income after taxes. While it is probably more common to use after-tax LICOs, one must also ensure that any comparisons also use the after-tax income available to individuals or families. Campaign 2000, a coalition of anti-poverty groups in Canada, goes on to note that about one in nine children in Canada (760,000) were living in poverty in 2006 when income is measured after taxes and social transfers.

The rates of child poverty vary considerably across the country. In 2006 the rate was highest in British Columbia, Saskatchewan, and Manitoba (16.1 per cent, 14.4 per cent, and 12.4 per cent respectively) and lowest in Prince Edward Island, Alberta, and Nova Scotia (4.0 per cent, 6.9 per cent, and 8.7 per cent respectively). Child poverty rates are quite similar to poverty rates for all Canadians. For example, the Canadian Council on Social Development (2008: 1) notes that more than 11 per cent of Canadians (or 3.5 million people) were living in poverty in 2004. Lone parents, particularly women, carry a disproportionately high burden. In 2006, one in three mother-led lone-parent families lived in poverty. Children in visible minority, new Canadian, and Aboriginal families (both on and off First Nations reserves) were disproportionately affected by poverty. Children with disabilities are also at increased risk of poverty (Campaign 2000, 2008b: 2).

Poverty in First Nations and other Aboriginal communities is all too common. Almost one in four First Nations children live in poverty and the rate of disabilities is almost double the rate for all Canadian children. Additionally, overcrowding in First Nations homes is almost double the Canadian rate. In 2006, Canada ranked eighth when applying the United Nations Human Development Index whereas

First Nations communities in Canada would rank 68th among 174 nations (Assembly of First Nations website, 2008).

A snapshot of the number of children or families living in poverty is a serious indictment in a country that has enjoyed unprecedented economic growth over the past two decades, but poverty is more than statistics (see Box 2.3). The examples included in Box 2.3 raise other factors about poverty that must be considered. One is the 'poverty gap'. The poverty gap represents the income required by an average family living in poverty to bring that family up to the poverty line. The average low-income family in Canada was living on an annual income that was $9,000–$11,000 below the LICO poverty line in 2005 (Campaign 2000, 2008a).

## Box 2.3  Living in Poverty

Stories of living in poverty can vary a great deal and living in poverty is not only about hardship and despair; there are stories of resilience, strength, and success. But, too often, there are struggles against steep odds that make it hard to get ahead—struggles that wear on the body, mind, and soul. The four excerpts below reflect the struggles of some of those without enough to eat.

- You feel hungry all the time, depressed and tired like a car that ran out of gas. . . . I don't feel good enough because I can't build energy. Your self-esteem is so low and my self-confidence, because I can't provide food for my kids.
- My son was embarrassed that we used the food bank. He doesn't always understand there is little or no money. It affects my mood and ability to sleep.
- I have worked all my life, 35 years, and yet right now I'm injured and I can't work. . . . I am so disappointed at how life is here. I have lost my dignity having to get stuff from others.
- Once bills and rent were paid I had $30 for the month for groceries.

Poverty is also about struggling to get ahead. For example, if one is a lone parent with a two-year-old child and with a reasonably good education, it can be hard to escape poverty. If you find a part-time job so you can still spend time with your child, much or even all of your income could be clawed back. You will not get ahead and may even be worse off after employment expenses like clothing and transportation. If you can land a full-time job that could allow you to get off welfare, you will sacrifice time and energy for your child. Depending on your salary, you might even risk losing subsidized housing, adding to your costs and the family stress of yet another move.

(The four excerpts about struggling to find food were selected from Fayant and Kerr, 2007.)

A second important factor to consider is the extent to which poverty, with its experience of material and social deprivation, leads to social exclusion, that is, the opportunities to participate in activities commonly available to citizens in an industrialized country like Canada. This understanding of poverty supports a relative approach to the definition and measurement of poverty, rather than a minimalist or absolute approach. A relative approach to poverty directs attention both to income inequality and measures to promote social inclusion. In this context, Canada's poverty problem is also about inequality and there is convincing evidence that the 'inequality gap' is growing (Lightman, 2003; Osberg, 2008).

Osberg's (2008) analysis of income distribution trends summarizes the share of aggregate income for Canadians based on quintiles. Between 1981 and 2005, the share of income received by the poorest 20 per cent of Canadians declined from 4.6 per cent to 4.1 per cent whereas the share of the richest 20 per cent increased from 41.6 per cent to 46.9 per cent. Middle-income earners were also net losers as their share declined from 17.7 per cent to 15.6 per cent. However, collapsing figures in this way masks some of the disparity. For example, in 2004 the bottom 5 per cent of income earners had 0.2 per cent of the taxable income whereas the top 5 per cent had 24.1 per cent of the taxable income in the country. The growth in income for those in the very high-income bracket reflects the unequal dollar value of compensation packages paid to the economic elite. Even though not all of those in the very high income category are CEOs of major companies it is of interest to note that between 1992 and 2004 Canada's top 100 CEOs saw their 'earnings' jump from 107 to 218 times as much as the average worker (Canadian Labour Congress, 2008: 1). In 2007, the average of the 100 highest-paid Canadian CEOs working for a publicly traded company earned more than $10 million in pay, an increase of 22 per cent over the previous year. To put this in context, it took the average CEO just 12 hours in 2007 to earn the average annual wage of a full-time Canadian worker (i.e., $40,237).

The growing gap is even more apparent when the distribution of wealth is considered. In part, wealth inequality is exacerbated by the fact that our taxation system has become less and less progressive over time. Simply put, wealthy individuals and companies are much more able to employ tax lawyers and financial planners to identify tax avoidance strategies that are either unavailable or unknown to hourly-paid employees. The growing inequality in Canada has not escaped international attention. In a 2008 report by the Organization for Economic Cooperation and Development (OECD), the significant growth in income poverty (poverty rates based on income before tax adjustments) and inequality over the 10 years prior to 2005 was identified as a growing problem. The OECD report also noted that income inequality in Canada exceeded the OECD average and that Canada ranked a dismal 18th place in OECD countries ranked from best to worst on income inequality. The report noted that Canada spends less on cash benefits such as unemployment benefits and family benefits than most OECD countries, and because of this, taxes and transfers do not reduce inequality by as much as in these other countries. Furthermore, the effects of these benefits on inequality have been declining over time.

Other indicators of the growing problem of poverty include the number of homeless persons and the increased use of food banks. For example, 720,000 Canadians made use of food banks in March 2007 and between 150,000 and 300,000 people remained homeless in 2007 (Rainer, 2008: 8). These numbers can only be expected to get worse as the effects of the recession triggered in 2008 become more apparent. Two reasons for the persistence of poverty in Canada are the relatively low minimum wage and the inadequacy of welfare rates for those dependent on welfare. For example, EI, which in 1989 covered 77 per cent of men and 70 per cent of women who were unemployed, covered only 40 per cent of men and 32 per cent of women out of work in 2006 (Townson and Hayes, 2007). Meanwhile, the accumulated surplus in the EI fund in 2007 was over $50 billion (Canadian Labour Congress, 2007).

Welfare incomes vary across the country for different types of recipients so inter-provincial comparisons are difficult to make. However, the inadequacy of welfare rates and the failure of these rates to keep pace with the cost of living is one of the reasons for a large poverty gap among those who are dependent on welfare. Using 2007 data, the National Council on Welfare (2008) constructed 53 different welfare case scenarios, and welfare incomes were less than two-thirds of the after-tax LICOS for 24 of 53 scenarios. Quebec and Newfoundland and Labrador were demonstrably better than other provinces in integrating welfare incomes with Child Tax Benefits and these are provinces with well-integrated strategies for preventing and reducing poverty. For example, lone parents in Newfoundland and Labrador received income at 101 per cent of the after-tax poverty line in 2007 (National Council of Welfare, 2008: 1).

Although some provinces are making somewhat better progress, the examples summarized above demonstrate the failure of the federal and provincial governments to respond to social justice objectives, including closing the inequality gap and alleviating poverty. But this is not simply our observation. Indeed, these issues have been highlighted by the United Nations Committee on Economic, Social, and Cultural Rights that chastised Canada for its failure to do more to address problems of poverty and inequality in 1998 (when it made 21 recommendations), and again in 2006 (Osberg, 2008).

This failure is not just a question about the availability of resources, because cutbacks in social programs are currently justified on moral as well as economic grounds. It has become popular to advance the view, bolstered by groups like the Fraser Institute and newspapers like *The National Post*, that what the poor need most is more hardship and more stigmatization—not improved opportunities or resources—to rise out of poverty. These differences reflect fundamentally different discourses on poverty, which are summarized by Raphael (2007) as MUD, RED, and SID. The Moral Underclass Discourse (MUD), which is the dominant view, sees poverty as the responsibility of the individual who is poor because of a lack of motivation and moral fibre. Government benefits, it is argued, must be made unpleasant in order to motivate individuals to join the workforce. The Redistribution Discourse (RED) sees poverty as a result of the social exclusion of individuals from the economic and social resources required for meaningful participation in society. In this discourse, problems of poverty are not caused by individual failings but the failure of society to meet the needs of citizens. To the extent that dependency does occur it is a result of excluding people from social and economic opportunities. In this discourse proposed solutions include increased benefits, the reduction of inequality, and more opportunities for the excluded to be active participants in defining and realizing their rights. The Social Integrationist Discourse (SID) recognizes the exclusion of individuals by virtue of living in poverty, but focuses solutions on integrating the non-working poor into the labour force. Although this strategy has some merit (e.g., provision of employment training opportunities) its policy manifestations in Canada have included programs, such as workfare, where punitive provisions for non-participation have more in common with a MUD discourse on poverty.

## Challenges and Opportunities

Neo-liberalism stands both in opposition to the welfare state and in favour of completely free markets unimpeded by state intervention. Although some (see for example, Marchak, 1991) have argued that the rise of this political ideology parallels the failure of the state to provide social services free of debt, others (see Cameron and Finn, 1996) have noted that government spending on social services since the 1970s was responsible for only about six per cent of the federal debt. It is also important to qualify general statements on welfare state expenditures. For example, despite the cutbacks in benefits in a number of programs, welfare state expenditures, including health care, have increased over time and account for approximately 40 per cent of federal spending (Miljan, 2008: 150). But social spending varies significantly by type. When expressed as a percentage of Gross Domestic Product (GDP), Canada spends a relatively high amount on health care (7th highest of 29 developed countries) but low amounts on disability-related benefits and income supports to working families (Raphael, 2007: 347). As earlier noted, however, overall social spending in Canada is below the average for OECD countries, and in spite of this reality, the neo-liberal agenda continues to emphasize lower social spending and increased privatization of the social services.

Neo-liberal arguments do resonate with the concerns of many people. But it must be recognized that ideology does not exist independently from people's lives; rather, daily life reflects and shapes one's ideological commitments. Citizens are faced with rising taxes, declining incomes, poorer services, the past failures of social programs, and concern about the debt. In addition, the media in Canada, which is dominated by a neo-liberal orientation, is always ready to highlight these concerns. These experiences influence the views of the public on social spending. The fact that federal and provincial governments were able to reduce social spending in the 1990s, including major cuts to welfare rates, without major protests demonstrates a hardening of public attitudes towards social programs in the late twentieth and early twenty-first century.

Policy-making in the health and social service sector today cannot ignore broader questions about the Canadian political economy. But it is not a matter of learning to accept less. Despite significant challenges, there are several arguments that highlight opportunities and support a more activist stance. One pertains to the influence of neo-liberalism and globalization. As noted, there have been modest successes in the struggle against undemocratic forms of economic globalization and across the world there are social movements which are actively campaigning for a more ecological, social-justice-oriented agenda. Governments today are under enormous pressures from the corporate sector and their autonomy from these forces is diminished. However, some governments are more likely than others to support this model of globalization; moreover, even in those cases where the state chooses to support a more neo-liberal model of globalization, it can be held accountable for its actions through interest group pressure and the ballot box. The growth in the ecology movement and the incorporation of environmental issues within the policy agenda of the Green Party, the NDP, and the Liberal Party in the 2008 federal election may be a reflection of a new agenda which can challenge the current neo-liberal model of globalization.

Neo-liberal approaches to domestic social policies can also be successfully challenged, and one example of this is described in Chapter Nine. At a more general level, governments can and do make different choices—influenced by the citizens of that country—about their social policies. It is well known, for example, that many countries in Europe spend significantly more than Canada on social welfare, and these expenditures reflect both different policy objectives and different results. The Swedish welfare state, for example, embraces a stronger commitment to full employment, social equality, and the abolition of poverty than Canada. Sweden's poverty rate is among the lowest in the world and its child poverty rate is one-third that of Canada (4 per cent versus 12 per cent) (Olsen, 2008). Anti-poverty strategies have been adopted in other countries including the UK and New Zealand. In the UK about 800,000 children have been lifted out of poverty since 1999, and in 2003 New Zealand adopted a new social development approach where greater attention is paid to social investment for disadvantaged populations (Regehr, 2008).

Social policy responses from other countries are often dismissed because contexts, including demographic characteristics, differ. Although this argument has some validity, the nature and scope of different policy choices cannot be fully explained by contextual factors. And even if one is not persuaded by these international comparisons, it is important to consider the opportunities that exist within Canada. One of the most important of these is the efforts of Campaign 2000 and coalition partners across the country to promote poverty reduction strategies at both the federal and provincial government levels. Regehr (2008), who is the Director of the National Council of Welfare, suggests there are four cornerstones of a workable national strategy for poverty reduction in Canada. These include a national anti-poverty strategy with a long term vision and measurable targets and timelines; a plan of action and a budget to coordinate initiatives within and across governments and with other partners; a government accountability structure for ensuring results and consulting with Canadians on the design, implementation, and evaluation of actions that will affect them; and a set of agreed poverty indicators that will be used to plan, monitor, and assess programs. And some progress is already being made. Provincial governments in Quebec and Newfoundland and Labrador are implementing poverty reduction strategies and the early evidence on impacts is encouraging (National Council of Welfare, 2008). The government of Nova Scotia is in the process of establishing poverty reduction strategies, and Ontario released its poverty reduction strategy called *Breaking the Cycle* in December 2008 (Taylor, 2008). The Ontario strategy sets clear targets, including a promise to reduce child poverty by 25 per cent within five years, although significant federal increases to the Working Income Tax Benefit and the National Child Benefit Supplement will also be required to reach this goal.

In Quebec a law against poverty and social exclusion was adopted in 2002 as a response to the actions of grassroots organizations and coalitions that were mobilized around this issue. Over time an action plan was designed and it is in the process of being implemented. While it is difficult to assess outcomes in any definitive way yet, public opinion surveys indicate strong support for those strategies (Lauzière, 2008). Although most other provinces have yet to develop poverty reduction strategies, there is growing public pressure on governments to do so.

We have noted the centralization of power among the elites in Canada, and this is also discussed again in Chapter Three. However, power is not only exercised in a top-down manner; it can be acted upon by individual and collective action through structures which mediate the rights and claims of citizens and the state. Thus, governments, and policy-makers within government, can play an important role in facilitating new and potentially beneficial policies even in times characterized by political and fiscal conservatism. In concert with government actions or when there is resistance at the state level, third sector and grassroots community groups play important roles in building civil society by providing the means for citizens to participate in influencing social policies. Two examples serve to illustrate how small scale policy initiatives can make a difference both to the people served by these policies and as program models or options that can contribute to larger and more comprehensive changes. Shelters for abused women were initially developed by concerned citizen groups on a very small scale, but these have expanded with public funding until a network of these resources now spans the country. A second example involves a small disadvantaged neighbourhood in the north end of Winnipeg well known over the past several years for high rates of poverty and crime, including prostitution and drug use (see Box 2.4). Progressive policy-making is all about influencing and shaping more of these kinds of policies at the local, provincial, and federal levels.

Box 2.4  Rebuilding the Neighbourhood

In June 2007, the children of a local school made national headlines when they appealed to Governor General Michaëlle Jean for help. This appeal became a catalyst for local action that began with the local Women's Centre and an energetic local leader who helped to mobilize community involvement. An initial focus was public safety and the residents' committee set up an email account that allowed residents to send tips about criminal activity, which were then referred to police. New relationships were established with police; 30 crack houses were shut down over an eight-month period; the crime rate declined by 70 per cent over a one-year period; and community meetings and events, which once had trouble attracting a dozen members from the community, now involve more than 100 at each event. More children can be seen playing outside in the neighbourhood and residents now feel free to walk the streets any time, day or night. Renovated and restored homes outnumber abandoned ones and a major plan for redeveloping the neighbourhood is to be established with city and provincial assistance.

(With information from Lett, 2008).

# Summary and Conclusion

In this chapter, several key factors that affect the making of social policy in Canada were reviewed. A number of characteristics were identified, including geography, political culture, and proximity to the United States. But two interrelated themes were given special attention. These were neo-liberalism and globalization, and poverty and inequality. These are especially important to consider in advancing social policy reforms in Canada.

Neo-liberalism has reinforced the prominence of the free market ideology over the past two to three decades, although in truth the ideal market advanced by this ideology is anything but free. Whereas government was seen in a welfare state economy as playing an important mediating role in reducing the adverse effects of capitalism, neo-liberalism advances the goal of centralized corporate control within a global economy with little regard for those who are marginalized by the corporate brand of capitalism that flourishes under this ideology. When neo-liberalism is combined with economic globalization it reduces the power of individual nation states to exercise control over their own economic and social policies because these companies can transfer their operations at will to other locations. The decision-making processes of these international corporations, which have profound effects on economic and social policies, are beyond the reach of ordinary Canadians. As a result we experience a loss of civil society because we lose more and more ability to hold institutions in our society accountable for the decisions that are made.

Social policy reforms in Canada will remain modest unless there is serious attention to the problem of poverty and inequality. In this regard several provinces have adopted poverty reduction strategies, and coalitions that are broadly representative of community interests may be able to influence more widespread adoption of measures to address the many faces of poverty in Canada. However, the longer term impact of the 2008–09 recession is uncertain. On one hand, it provides an opportunity to advocate for a more interventionist style of government that responds not only to the concerns of corporations but also to the needs of citizens. In order for this to occur, governments must embrace a commitment to planning and new social investment similar to that which occurred after the Second World War. On the other hand, the effects of increased budget deficits and lowered economic growth could also relegate policies, such as poverty reduction, to the 'back burner' of government priorities. If new investment is limited to short term measures, and there is some indication by the federal government that this is all that is intended, we will return to a neo-liberal formula that includes reduced social investment to those in need and miss an important opportunity to repair our frayed social safety net.

Chapter Three examines policy-making structures and processes at the federal, provincial, and organizational levels.

# Recommended Reading

D. Raphael, *Poverty and Policy in Canada: Implications for Health and Quality of Life* (Toronto: Canadian Scholars' Press, 2007). This book provides an excellent review of poverty and social exclusion in Canada with coverage of the international context as well.

J. Stanford, *Economics for Everyone: A Short Guide to the Economics of Capitalism* (Halifax, NS: Fernwood and the Canadian Centre for Policy Alternatives, 2008). This is a primer on the Canadian economic system in an era of globalization that is both pragmatic and idealistic.

National Council on *Welfare, Welfare Incomes, 2006 and 2007* (Ottawa: National Council on Welfare, 2008). This publication provides a detailed examination of welfare incomes, including LICOs, recent trends, and information on child benefits. These data are generally updated on an annual basis.

Campaign 2000 website. Available at http://www.campaign2000.ca. This source provides reports and ongoing updates on poverty in Canada.

Canadian Centre for Policy Alternatives website. Available at http://www. policyalternatives.ca. The Canadian Centre for Policy alternatives website includes useful reports and information on poverty, inequality and other social policy issues from a progressive standpoint.

# Critical Thinking Questions

1.   Locate a recent opinion article or editorial on poverty or welfare in the local newspaper. What are the author's arguments? Is the author's perspective an example of the MUD, RED, or SID approaches to poverty reduction? What is your critique of the author's arguments?

2.   Try to locate the latest child poverty information for your city, province, or territory. Identify any advocacy groups that are working on this issue in your area. What is the focus of their work?

3.   What do you think are the benefits and costs of globalization for Canada? Can you identify any strategies that might help reduce the adverse effects from the neo-liberal model of globalization?

4.   Who is likely to be most affected by a recession and why? How should the most vulnerable be protected?

5.   Locate current information on welfare rates for your city, province, or territory. You may wish to select a certain category of recipients, such as a lone parent with two children, a single employable person, or a person with a disability. How adequate are these rates?

# Notes

1. 'Monetarist policies' refer to actions taken by the central bank, acting on behalf of the national government, to control the money supply. Monetarism is generally associated with neo-liberalism or neo-conservatism because it is designed to ensure the full play of market forces. The major goal is to control inflation, primarily through adjustments in interest rates. It is argued that if inflation is low, prices will be determined competitively through supply and demand, and in this environment capitalism will flourish. These policies, which have been popular since the mid-1980s in many countries, can be contrasted with Keynesian policies that support government or state intervention, particularly in recessions, to stimulate the economy by injecting demand (e.g., new employment programs or new money) into the system. While Keynesian policies create or sustain employment, they increase the amount of money relative to available goods and services and can increase inflation. Keynesian policies are associated with the development of the welfare state because they support state intervention to modify the free play of market forces in order to redistribute income and opportunities. Monetarist policies generally oppose state intervention or investment, and are less concerned with problems such as high unemployment. Because they are associated with a reduced role for government in managing the economy, these policies also support the expansion of a global economy based on free market principles. According to monetarists, the problem of high unemployment will be addressed as the benefits of new investment, encouraged by low inflation and a free market, increase economic growth and new jobs 'trickle down' to those currently out of work.

2. The World Trade Organization was established in 1995 as a successor of the General Agreement on Trade and Tariffs (GATT). The GATT was one of the earlier treaties regulating international trade and the imposition of protective tariffs on imported goods.

3. The Canadian Council of Chief Executives (CCCE), which changed its name in 2001, was formerly known as the Business Council on National Interests. It was initially formed in 1976 to represent the interests of the financial and business community in Canada. It is composed of the CEOs of Canada's largest companies.
4. One needs to distinguish between the operating deficit of a government in its annual budgeting cycle and the 'public debt' that represents the accumulated debt resulting from annual deficits over a period of time. Government borrows money from both Canadian and international sources to finance a deficit in any given year and pays interest on these amounts. These are often referred to as the cost of 'servicing the debt'. It is normal for government to carry a certain amount of debt that is related to infrastructure investment for future use; however, there is an ongoing debate about whether or not the amount of debt in Canada is a major policy concern. When budget surpluses occur, governments are faced with determining how much emphasis should be placed on three public policy choices: paying down the debt, investing in new public programs, and reducing taxes.
5. The Statistics Canada Low Income Cut-off (LICO) is an income threshold below which a family is likely to devote a larger share of its income to the necessities of food, shelter, and clothing than the average family. Different LICOs are established by Statistics Canada for families living in rural areas and urban centres of different sizes. These also vary by the number of people living in a family. For example, the before-tax LICO for a single person in a city of more than 500,000 was $21,666 in 2007 whereas the LICO for a family of four in a centre of this size was $40,259. Comparative figures for the after-tax LICO were $17,954 and $33,946 (National Council of Welfare, 2008: 137). There is a debate about whether one should use before-tax LICOs or after-tax LICOs. One argument against after-tax LICOs is that although Statistics Canada takes into account the redistributive effects of federal and provincial taxes, they do not include the effects of other taxes, such as sales taxes, which have a disproportionate effect on low-income Canadians. The before-tax LICOs are higher than the after-tax LICOs because of differences in average incomes before and after tax and differences in the rate of expenditures on food, shelter, and clothing in these two scenarios. Thus, any family spending more than 54.7 per cent of its pre-tax income on food, shelter, and clothing fell below the pre-tax LICO in 2005, and any person spending more than 63.6 per cent of its after-tax income fell below the after-tax LICO. Raising the bar in this way reduces the poverty in Canada by about 4–5 per cent.

Although the LICO is the most widely used 'poverty line' in Canada, it is not an official poverty line. Other poverty measures include the Market Basket Measure (MBM), the Low Income Measure (LIM), and the Fraser Institute poverty line. The Statistics Canada MBM is based on constructing a market basket of necessities for two adults and two children. The Statistics Canada LIM is a relative measure of poverty that defines poverty as any family attaining less than one-half of the median gross income for Canadian families. The Fraser Institute poverty lines are based on a market basket of basic necessities but the identified necessities are much more limited than the Statistics Canada MBM. For example, expenditures on social amenities like school supplies and recreation are excluded. Sarlo (2008), who writes for the Fraser Institute, has estimated a 2005 poverty rate of between four and five per cent in Canada based the Fraser Institute poverty line. Estimates of poverty based on this approach are widely criticized as underestimating the incidence of poverty in Canada.

# Chapter Three

# Making Social Policy in Canada: Structures and Processes

This chapter focuses primarily on policy-making structures and processes at the federal and provincial levels of government. Although these two levels of government are particularly important to the development of social policies, we should not dismiss the role of third level governance structures such as cities, towns, municipalities, and First Nations Band Councils. Third level structures can often develop or influence policies related to recreation, housing and urban renewal, responses to policing and crime, and by-laws related to such issues as smoking. As well, in Nova Scotia and Ontario local governments have some jurisdiction in social services, and in Ontario this includes a role in funding social assistance, child care subsidies, social housing, and community health. As we move down the policy-making ladder we encounter the organizational level and the ways policies and programs are designed and implemented at this level has a significant impact on service users. We can operationally define the organizational level to include private and non-profit organizations in the non-government sector, faith communities, and government organizations at the service delivery level. Although the latter group of organizations is a part of government, they are some distance from the central policy-making apparatus of government and maintain some degree of control over elements of the policy-making agenda. Within non-government organizations (NGOs), non-profit organizations that provide services mandated by legislation and funded primarily by government, including child and family service agencies and regional health authorities in some provinces, often have no more real control over the policy-making than service delivery units within the government sector. In this chapter we include a discussion of small scale policy-making which is more applicable to the policy-making processes that occur at the organizational level. We do not specifically address policy-making at the city or municipal level; however, some aspects of our discussion on small scale policy-making may be applicable to this third level of government, particularly within First Nations communities where local or regional governance structures may have significant influence over the development and management of human service programs.

# Social Policy and the Federal Government
## Constitutional Issues and the Division of Powers

The federal government's role in social policy is somewhat overshadowed by the role of provincial governments. This is a function of arrangements established in the *British North America Act (BNA), 1867*, as incorporated now in *The Constitution Act, 1982*, which ceded much of the responsibility for local affairs, including the delivery of health and social services, to the provinces. The Canadian Constitution is comprised of a number of documents and Acts but the primary sections dealing with the division of powers are Sections 91 and 92. Section 91 sets out the major responsibilities of the federal government, including laws related to peace, order and good government, trade and commerce, banking, defense, Indians and Indian lands, and primary responsibility for taxation. Section 92 outlines areas of provincial jurisdiction, including local works and undertakings, property and civil rights, the administration of justice, hospitals and health care, municipal affairs, and direct taxation within provinces. Section 93 gives jurisdiction over education to the provinces. Concurrent powers for agriculture and immigration were recognized in Section 95. Although 29 enumerated federal powers are listed in *The Constitution Act*, residual powers were also left to federal government. Coupled with primary control over taxation and laws that permitted the federal government to overrule the provinces on matters deemed to be of national interest, a strong central government was assured at the time of Confederation. Although the delivery of health and social services remained a provincial area of responsibility, state involvement in social welfare was relatively minor at the nation-building stage. Thus these powers were regarded as relatively inconsequential in 1867.

Over time the involvement of both levels of government in social policy has increased. First, the nature and scope of services provided for health, education, and social welfare has grown and the costs of these services have increased accordingly. Regional differences and the federal government's central role in revenue generation have required the federal government to play a significant role in funding these services. There are two major fiscal transfer programs. One is the federal transfer of funds to provinces for health care, post-secondary education, and social assistance, and the second is equalization payments which can be used for a broader range of public services. These transfers are a significant source of revenue for many provinces and in 2000–01 transfers paid to Nova Scotia, Newfoundland, and Prince Edward Island accounted for more than 40 per cent of their total revenues (Asselin, 2001: 6). The principle of cost-shared services for health, social services, and post-secondary education, as well as a broader range of public services, has been a central feature of Canada's federated structure for a long time. However, the role of the federal government in the human services increased as a result of the provinces' inability to respond adequately to the needs of its citizens during the Great Depression, and recognition that federal government involvement was required in order to implement the welfare state reforms that emerged after the Second World War.

The federal role in social policy has been established through several methods. In some situations, as in the case of EI, this responsibility has been added to the list of federal powers; in other circumstances (e.g., Old Age Pensions), the concurrent power of both levels of government has been recognized. Shared cost programs, where the federal government provides some funding but leaves service delivery to the provinces, were established for post-secondary education in 1952, hospital insurance in 1957, and medical insurance in 1968. Within the social services the most significant shared cost program was the 1966 *Canada Assistance Plan* (CAP), which provided federal funding for certain social services, such as child welfare and income assistance (welfare) on a 50–50 cost shared basis. As well, the federal government uses the tax system to provide a number of benefits to both low income Canadians (e.g., Canada Child Tax Benefit) and those with higher levels of income (e.g., Registered Retirement Savings and investment tax credit programs).

Despite the growth in the federal government's role in social policy there have been countervailing forces that have promoted greater provincial autonomy. Jurisdictional challenges have been raised by many provinces, but Quebec has been the most vocal in asserting provincial rights. The assertion of provincial jurisdiction led to the *Established Programs Act* in 1965, which allowed provinces to opt out of conditional grant programs and continue to receive federal funding as long as they offered equivalent programs (Dyck, 2004). In addition, the ideological orientations of some federal governments, particularly in the neo-liberal era since the 1980s, have often favoured the transfer of responsibility to the provinces.

Cost sharing arrangements have been a constant source of conflict between the provinces and the federal government. For example, when health insurance payments were transferred from a conditional grant to a block grant under the *Established Programs Financing Act* in 1977, the federal government's contribution levels were no longer guaranteed at 50 per cent. Further federal cuts occurred during the deficit cutting era of the 1990s as social spending became a convenient, but unwarranted, target for cost-cutting. In 1996–97, with Paul Martin as Finance Minister, CAP was phased out and all funding for post-secondary education, health, and the social services was combined under one grant, known as the Canada Health and Social Transfer (CHST). The 1995 budget also included reductions in transfers to the provinces of $7 billion over three years for these programs (Finkel, 2006: 292). The provision of a block grant provided the provinces with greater flexibility in how the money could be used but health care often takes priority over other issues when funding is being reduced. Concerns about the allocation of federal funding eventually led to the division of the CHST into the Canada Health Transfer and the Canada Social Transfer in 2004.

Although some of the federal cuts to transfers for the human services were restored after 1996–97, the replacement of CAP with a block grant arrangement enabled the federal government to gain more control over its own spending on the social services. Thus it had more flexibility to target resources to new initiatives and to benefit from the political capital resulting from such expenditures.

Reductions in funding and the unilateral actions of the federal government in cost-sharing arrangements were particularly contentious with the provinces after 1995. This led to a series of discussions among first ministers about inter-governmental relationships and the signing of the Social Union Framework Agreement (SUFA) in 1999. This agreement includes a number of joint commitments to consultation on intended federal social policy reforms.

While we have briefly summarized the somewhat complex role of the federal government in making Canadian social policy, and the related federal–provincial tensions that have accompanied this role, it is also important to note that this level of government has primary responsibility for policy development and funding for services to First Nations people, particularly those living on reserves, the Inuit, and others who qualify for services under the *Indian Act*.

## The Federal Policy-Making Apparatus

All organizations create formal mechanisms—referred to here as 'structures'—for developing policies and this section examines the general structures at the federal government level. Although many of these structures, including the role of the parliament, remain somewhat impervious to change, the governing party may alter the approach to governing, including the number and role of committee structures inside government in ways that can have significant effects on how policy-making processes are carried out. In addition, the role of the Prime Minister and cabinet is influenced by the personalities of those occupying these positions. For example, the degree of centralized control exercised by the Prime Minister over policy-making increased during the Chrétien years and this control, even over the role of ministers in dealing with the media was extended even further when Prime Minister Harper and the Conservatives came to power in 2006.

Canada's governmental model can be described as a constitutional monarchy with operating principles based on the Westminster model. The Westminster model, based on British parliamentary traditions, locates considerable power in the hands of the Prime Minister and cabinet. This is often referred to as the Executive branch of government. There are also two other branches of government known as the Legislative branch (i.e., the House of Commons and the Senate) and the Judiciary (federal and provincial courts). Locating the Executive branch inside the Legislative branch (i.e., the House of Commons) is unlike the model in the United States (US) where the President is elected through popular vote and the Cabinet serves the president without direct accountability either to Congress or the US Senate. In the Canadian model, the Prime Minister and cabinet are given considerable freedom to govern but they must account for their actions to the

House of Commons. In turn the House of Commons has a responsibility to ensure cabinet answers for its use of executive authority. If the Prime Minister or the governing party loses the confidence of the majority of members of the House of Commons, it can be defeated. This is unlikely to occur if the government holds a majority of the seats because party discipline normally ensures that all members vote with the government, particularly on matters of confidence. When there is a minority government, this outcome is less certain and the defeat of the government on matters of confidence such as the Throne Speech, the budget, legislative changes, or motions of non-confidence will bring down the government (see Box 3.1).

Legislative accountability in the House of Commons occurs in ways other than confidence motions. For example, the opposition has an opportunity to debate government sponsored legislation, particularly at the second reading stage; as well, there are special debates including those related to the Throne Speech and the budget. There are also 25 'opposition days' set aside in each parliamentary session during which motions proposed by the opposition parties form the basis for debates. Finally, question period offers an opportunity to raise questions about the performance of the government. Although there is value to question period it is also widely criticized for its staged performance where the opposition seeks to embarrass the government and the government seeks to avoid direct answers by deflecting attention to past actions of the opposition or general assurances that the matter is being adequately addressed.

There are independent officers of the House of Commons, including the Speaker, who is elected by all members in an independent vote and the Clerk who is a non-elected official. Other independent officers include the Auditor General, the Chief Electoral Officer, the Commissioner of Official languages, the Privacy Commissioner, the Freedom of Information Commissioner, and the Integrity Commissioner. The Auditor General plays a particularly important role in reviewing public spending and management.

Although the Senate is an aspect of the Legislative branch because it must approve new legislation, it plays a relatively minor role in government. Originally designed to reflect regional interests by a make-up that included 24 seats each for Ontario, Quebec, and the three Maritime provinces of Nova Scotia, Prince Edward Island, and New Brunswick (24 seats were later added for the four western provinces, then six seats for Newfoundland, and one for each territory), it has become largely a location for patronage appointments by the Prime Minister of the governing party. Occasionally the Senate has exercised its power to obstruct or delay the government's legislation, and it has sponsored inquiries into a variety of policy issues, including studies of poverty, public health care provision, and children affected by separation and divorce.

The Queen's representative in Canada is the Governor General, and this role is exercised by Lieutenant Governors at the provincial level. Even though these individuals represent the Queen, appointments are made by the federal government. These individuals formally assent to laws passed by the Legislative

## Box 3.1 Canada's Parliamentary System in Action

Canada's parliamentary system is based on the notion of electing a representative assembly (i.e., parliament) to govern the country. In a parliamentary system three types of government are possible: a majority government where the governing party holds a majority of the seats, a minority government where the governing party holds less than the majority of seats but receives support from other parties or individuals on motions of confidence so that it is not defeated, and a coalition government where the government is composed of more than one political party. Coalition governments are uncommon in Canada but they are the norm in most parliamentary systems worldwide; some even argue they are more democratic because coalitions reflect the opinions of a broader spectrum of citizens than government by one party alone.

Usually, the party with the most seats will be given an opportunity to govern even if that party does not hold a majority of seats in the House of Commons. The leader of the governing party becomes the Prime Minister but the Prime Minister and his or her government remains in power only as long as they maintain the confidence of the House of Commons. If the governing party is defeated on a motion of confidence, most likely in circumstances where it does not hold a majority of the seats, it must resign. The Prime Minister must then formally request that the Governor General dissolve parliament.

Normally this triggers a new election but the Governor General also has the option of asking the opposition to form a government, and this has occurred on rare occasions in Canadian history. In October 2008, Stephen Harper and the Conservatives were returned to power without a majority. Faced with an economic crisis and the need for government intervention to stimulate the economy, the government proposed spending cuts, a balanced budget, and restrictions on collective bargaining. The Opposition parties were incensed and an agreement to form a NDP–Liberal coalition government with support from the Bloc Québécois on confidence motions was signed. The Conservatives launched a nation-wide attack on the proposed coalition government, demonizing the coalition as dominated by 'socialists' and 'separatists'. In order to forestall certain defeat, Prime Minister Harper asked the Governor General to prorogue parliament for approximately seven weeks, after which a new budget was presented. The Governor General could have refused to accede to the Prime Minister's request, and if the government was defeated, she could then have asked coalition partners to govern. Instead she made a precedent setting choice to prorogue parliament to give Prime Minister Harper an opportunity to develop an economic plan that was presented to the House of Commons in January 2009. In January, the plan received enough support from the opposition to avoid defeat of the government.

branch, and perform tasks such as reading the Throne speech. However, as noted in Box 3.1, they can play a central role in decisions regarding the dissolution of parliament or provincial legislatures.

The Judicial branch, which includes both provincial and federal courts, is the third branch of government. At the federal level, the courts making up this branch include the Federal Court of Canada, which hears matters related to such things as citizenship appeals and appeals related to privacy, and the Tax Court of Canada, which deals with tax disputes involving the federal government. However the most important body is the Supreme Court of Canada. Essentially, the courts deal with two types of disputes. First, there may be disputes related to constitutional law and these may include matters related to the division of powers or appeals by citizens under the *Charter of Rights and Freedoms*. These matters are dealt with by the Supreme Court at the federal level, and decisions at the provincial level may be appealed to the Supreme Court. Second, the Judicial branch is also concerned with administrative law, that is, whether rules and regulations of policy are followed and whether these have been applied in a fair and consistent manner.

Individuals or groups may file complaints of discrimination under the *Human Rights Act*; however, the *Charter*, which was added to the *Constitution Act* of 1982, is of particular importance because of the nature and scope of rights that it outlines. These include political freedoms, democratic rights, mobility rights, language rights, and equality rights. The equality rights section, and related decisions based on these provisions, has recognized rights pertaining to sexual orientation, the decriminalization of abortion, and certain economic rights for women. At the same time, a number of other *Charter* challenges, including action to prohibit the corporal punishment of children, have failed.

The Prime Minister's (PM) influence over government is significant because of the powers attached to this office. For example the PM makes all appointments to cabinet, the Senate, and other senior level posts in government, including the Bank of Canada. There are between 20 and 30 ministers in a typical cabinet, and about 10 junior ministers or secretaries of state whose responsibilities lie within the portfolio of another minister.

The committee structure within the Executive branch is of particular importance to the exercise of power. Government committee structures can vary but several core committees play key roles. A central committee, identified in the Harper government as the Priorities and Planning Committee and chaired by the Prime Minister, provides strategic direction on government priorities. The Treasury Board has a great deal of influence over expenditures and is supported by a highly specialized bureaucracy known as the Treasury Board Secretariat. Executive support to Cabinet is provided by the Privy Council Office (PCO). The Prime Minister's Office (PMO) is also an important centre of power. Unlike the PCO, which is composed of career civil servants, the PMO is made up of appointees selected because of their loyalty to the Prime Minister. They provide ongoing advice to the PM, and manage communications and media relations. Central agencies like the PCO, the PMO, the Treasury Board, and the Department of Finance overshadow the role of Cabinet in policy-making and exert significant influence over the general direction of government policy at the federal level. Although cabinet used to have a central role in setting policy directions, strategic decision-making more often occurs now within committees of cabinet or through direct control by the Prime Minister.

There are two other important elements that affect policy-making. First, a great deal of policy-making occurs at the departmental level or across departments. The interplay among ministers and between ministers and senior department staff shapes the nature and scope of these policies as well as how they are implemented. As a result, the bureaucracy is a very important aspect of the policy-making apparatus. Bureaucracy is much maligned for its inefficiency by both politicians and the public. These claims are sometimes exaggerated but they have encouraged a number of reform efforts aimed at increasing the efficiency and effectiveness of public sector bureaucracies. Unfortunately, many of these reforms have been driven primarily by ideology. Although some changes have been positive, others have tended to reduce the degree of democratic accountability of the system through the development of somewhat independent units of government and the separation of policy-making functions from service delivery.

The other important element in policy-making is the influence of interest groups, social movements, and think tanks. An interest group may be defined as any group seeking to influence government without contesting an election; generally such groups focus on single issues or a relatively narrow set of issues. Social movements, on the other hand, can be defined as an informal network of organizations and/ or interest groups, who on the basis of a collective identity and shared values engage in political or social action to bring about some change within society or government policy (Dyck, 2004). The notion of a policy community or a policy network is somewhat related to a social movement although this concept is usually reserved for a particular group of government agencies, interest groups, and other organizations with a particular interest in a policy issue. Participants attempt to establish the legitimacy of a particular policy problem and undertake coordinated efforts to advocate for solutions. Examples of recent policy communities include the environmental lobby and the groups and organizations supporting Campaign 2000 in its efforts to address poverty.

Think tanks include policy research and advocacy organizations, such as the Canadian Council on Social Development (CCSD) and the Caledon Institute, which focus more explicitly on social policy. Others such as C.D. Howe Institute, the Institute for Research on Public Policy, the Fraser Institute, and the Canadian Centre for Policy Alternatives focus on a broader range of public policy issues and adopt a more identifiable ideological stance in their analysis of public policy. We return to the role of interest or advocacy groups, think tanks, and social movements in policy-making in Chapter Seven.

Once a policy problem has been identified government must choose a method for addressing the issue, and these methods can be broadly classified as policy instruments (see Table 3.1). The neo-liberal era in Canadian politics has increased

Table 3.1     Instruments Used by Government to Address
              Policy Problems

| | |
|---|---|
| 1. Privatization of Conflict | Government takes no action and either ignores the problem or refers it to a private sector authority. |
| 2. Symbolic Response | Government states concern and may appoint a task force or royal commission as a substitute for real action. |
| 3. Exhortation | Government urges the public to take action perhaps through advertising and public awareness campaigns. |
| 4. Tax Expenditures | Tax expenditures consist of tax credits and deductions which operate as incentives in using income in certain ways. |
| 5. Public Expenditures | Public expenditures require the actual disbursements of funds acquired and controlled by the state. |
| 6. Regulation | Many aspects of our lives are subject to regulation by government, and although these are often resisted as an infringement on individual liberties, these are generally designed to serve a public purpose such as improved health, safety, order, or protection from corporate exploitation. |
| 7. Taxation | Taxation is often considered to be more intrusive than regulation because it requires individuals and/or corporations to make contributions to government. However, a reduction in taxes has the effect of reducing those contributions, and this approach has become more common in the neo-liberal era. |
| 8. Public Ownership | Public ownership often takes the form of a Crown corporation and is most commonly used in public utilities and some public housing projects. |
| 9. State of Emergency | In situations of national disasters or a major military threat the government may assume special powers, often suspending normal procedures pertaining to civil rights or policy guidelines. |

Source: Adapted from Dyck, 2004: 485–9.

the tendency of government to simply *ignore policy issues* or to undertake more *symbolic responses*, particularly in relation to social policy. *Exhortation* is a common policy response, and examples of this include campaigns against drunk driving and smoking, and efforts to promote the conservation of water and electricity. Tax credits and deductions involve expenditures in that they represent revenue that is foregone. These are quite popular because they are often less controversial ways of providing benefits. Public expenditures for social programs have been constrained in recent years but the economic crisis of 2008 gave rise to some new public investment, primarily in job creation and measures to stimulate the economy.

Government *regulation* is a widely used policy instrument; this is apparent in areas of public health policy, such as sanitation and the licensing of pharmaceutical drugs. But it also applies to a number of other public policy areas. Over the past three decades, the corporate agenda has emphasized deregulation. This is often reflected in agreements to promote free trade or in the lifting of regulatory controls over the operation of financial markets. Increases in *taxation* are never popular, and the trend at all levels of government over the past two decades has been to reduce or maintain current taxation rates, and to increase user fees for various types of services. Although user fees can be justified in some cases, the imposition of fees for essential services like recreation and public education amount to increases in taxation by another name, and these costs fall disproportionately on the shoulders of those with lower incomes. *Public ownership* has been largely out of favour over the past three decades; indeed the trend is in the direction of privatization or private-public partnerships where the focus is on selling public assets to the private sector. *Emergency related measures* apply in very special circumstances. The best known Canadian example is the imposition of the *War Measures Act* in the First and Second World Wars and then again in 1970 to deal with the FLQ crisis.

# Social Policy and the Provincial Government
## Key Policy-Making Structures at the Provincial Level

The dominant role of provincial and territorial governments in the development of social policy requires us to pay particular attention to this level of government. Although structures such as cabinet committees may vary somewhat from province to province, the processes of policy-making within different provincial governments are quite similar. The Manitoba government is selected as an illustrative example in the following discussion, and readers from other provinces or territories are encouraged to locate additional information on the governmental structures that exists in their province or territory.

The premier and cabinet, often referred to as the Executive Council, is the central policy-making authority even though other structures are created to mediate its role. At the federal government level we noted the important role of the PMO, and provincial premiers will also have a staff complement headed by someone who occupies the role of a chief of staff. The premier and his or her chief of staff will exert a great deal of control over policy initiatives that are politically sensitive. Beyond this, the level of control is somewhat dependent on whether a premier operates in a more centralized fashion or relies on cabinet debate and discussion to shape policy.

In Manitoba, the structures of government are relatively simple. There is a Policy Management Secretariat made up of staff that provides support to the premier and cabinet. There are also four standing committees: Treasury Board, Community Economic Development, Healthy Child Manitoba, and Aboriginal Issues. The Aboriginal Issues Committee was created in 2003 in an effort to coordinate policy initiatives affecting Aboriginal people in the province. Although Treasury Board is common to all governments, the nature and role of other standing committees can differ. Standing committees will have their own complement of staff, but in Manitoba staff from the Policy Management Secretariat help to connect the work of these committees to cabinet. Standing committees are comprised of ministers of the government and in Manitoba, Treasury Board is chaired by the Minister of Finance. Whereas staff of standing committees are likely to be career civil servants, staff of the Policy Management Secretariat are appointed by the party in power.

Treasury Board is supported by a secretariat within the Department of Finance, and this committee reviews and makes recommendations on all new initiatives, particularly those involving new expenditures; therefore it exercises considerable control over policy development. Analysts with Treasury Board play a key role in reviewing all submissions, and referring submissions back for revisions, if required. Although Treasury Board makes a recommendation to approve or decline a new initiative, cabinet ultimately reviews and approves these recommendations. Treasury Board can be an obstacle to new initiatives in some governments if it tries to micro-manage the development of new policies; if this posture is assumed, it will often delay new initiatives by repeatedly referring these back to committees for more information.

One other structure that has become increasingly important to governments over the years is the mechanism used to manage information flow and communication with the public. In Manitoba, this responsibility is carried out by the Cabinet Communications Secretariat, led by the Premier's Press Secretary. This group works directly with ministers designed to put a positive spin on government initiatives in a manner that connects with the public. For example, in 2002 the Kyoto Accord on greenhouse gases was being hotly debated across the country and the Manitoba government had come out in support of this treaty. As a means of connecting with the public, a communications strategy was designed to draw attention to the effects of inaction on the ecosystem of polar bears. Why polar bears? First, almost everyone likes the image conveyed by polar bears. And second, it was seen as a way of simplifying and packaging a very complicated issue so that it would garner the support of the general population.

Although we have provided a brief overview of one example of provincial government structures that play a role in policy-making two important points must be emphasized. First, cabinet decision-making and approval plays a somewhat more important role at the provincial level than it does at the federal level. Second, although we have noted the role of cabinet and standing committees, we should not underestimate the policy-related activities associated with each department or ministry. As described below, each department will have research and policy analysts, and this number will vary with the size and importance of the department. These staff may carry a number of roles, including research and policy analysis tasks, but at least some of these staff will also be tasked with providing briefing notes and answers to questions raised or anticipated from the opposition during sittings of the Legislative Assembly.

Governments are often slow in adopting major innovations in social policy, at least of the progressive variety, and new policies are often prompted by initiatives initially developed in the non-governmental social service sector or by the advocacy efforts of policy networks and lobby groups. There are several reasons for this. First, government is risk-aversive; it always has one eye on how the public will react and how this might 'play out' in the next election. Because new social policies generally require new public spending, there is bound to be some level of public resistance. This tends to make governments more conservative, particularly in their approach to social spending. Second, as described above, government operates like a bureaucratic machine with layers of decision-making structures, each with its own set of requirements that serve to slow down the policy-making process. Finally, the financial resources available to government are often more restricted than it might appear. For example, the ongoing operations of government departments might require up to 95 per cent of the revenues available to the government, leaving relatively small amounts for new initiatives. While internal reallocation or expenditure cuts can increase the amount of resources available for new investments somewhat, there is always intense competition among departments for new money.

Despite resource constraints, provincial governments play an important role in policy-making. The state, through its general ability to create legislation and policy affecting the general population and to direct expenditures and other resources, has a major influence over policy development. However, while individual ministers of departments may have significant influence over matters in their own department, their influence over general government policy is much more circumscribed. Instead, general government policy is more likely to be heavily influenced by the premier, senior staff, and a few key ministers. And although other elected members from the government may be appointed to provide some support to cabinet ministers with larger portfolios, similar to the pattern of junior ministers within the federal government, elected members who are not members of cabinet have very limited influence.

## How New Policies Are Developed Inside Government

New policies are developed in response to problems that appear on the agenda of governments. This agenda is shaped by issues that arise from the cycle of government planning or the influence of interest groups. Issues that appear on the government's agenda may be foreshadowed in items such as departmental priorities, throne speeches, or the budget; in these circumstances 'policy windows' or opportunities for new initiatives may exist. Usually governments undertake more new initiatives in the first two years after being elected than they do in the last two years of their mandate. Policy windows can also be triggered by unexpected events such as a crisis, results from an inquest, or the exposure of an issue by the media or pressure groups.

Developing policy in response to policy windows has become increasingly complex as governments engage in efforts to coordinate policies across departments or other levels of government. Policy specialists with knowledge and experience about the policy environment play an important role in determining the success of these endeavours. Some of these specialists are located in policy and planning branches of departments which are instrumental in generating planning options and advising the minister of the department. Three different types of policy-making within government are identified here.[1] One type of policy-making is confined to the bureaucratic structures of the department. Indeed many of the activities carried out at the departmental level will receive only limited attention from the minister. New policy directives, regulations, policy manuals, and protocols for service delivery may be established within departments without any significant discussion at the ministerial level and without ever entering the radar screen of cabinet.

A second type of policy-making involves issues that require political attention. An issue may come to the attention of the department because of external pressure or because it has been referred to the department by another level of government. Departments of government are usually composed of divisions (program areas) that might be headed by assistant deputy ministers. These individuals are accountable to a deputy minister who is the chief staff member to the minister. Detailed policy changes may be developed by staff within program divisions. For example, an income assistance division might draft policies related to a change in eligibility requirements for social assistance. These might then be forwarded to a senior departmental level, such as a policy and planning branch, which undertakes further development and reports directly to the deputy minister and minister.

If a new issue or opportunity emerges and becomes a policy priority for government, a process like that depicted in Figure 3.1 may unfold. At an early stage, there may be efforts to educate others about the need for a policy response or to advocate for a particular solution. In some cases, research may be undertaken or a demonstration project may be launched. If the need for a particular policy response is substantiated, it will be brought forward to the political level of the department (i.e., the minister) by champions and/or legitimizers who try to

**Figure 3.1    Government Policy Process in Response to an Issue
Beginning at the Department Level**

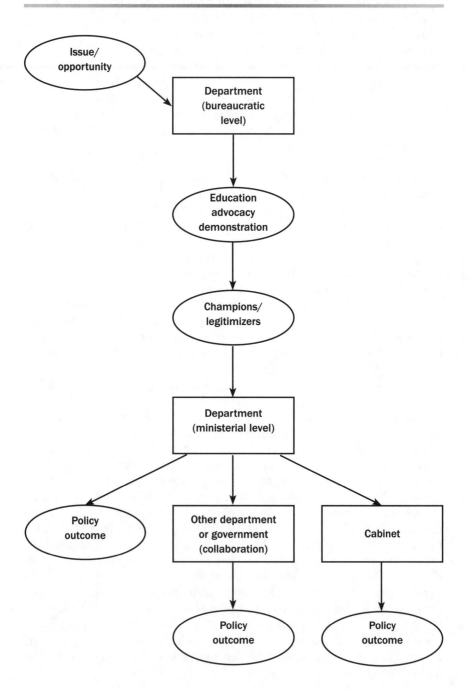

establish the credibility of a recommended policy response. Policy champions and legitimizers may be from inside government, from outside government, or be a combination of insiders and outsiders. If the minister is convinced that a policy response is required, three possible actions may be taken. First, where the minister has the required authority he or she will initiate the policy response leading to an outcome. Second, if the minister decides that sanction for a policy response must come from central government then the matter will be referred to cabinet. Third, in some cases collaboration with other departments or governments may be required. While collaboration with another department may be initiated by the minister directly, cabinet may also demand this. Collaborative efforts with other levels of government are usually sanctioned by cabinet or the premier's office, and will often involve activities by one of the standing committees of cabinet.

The third type of policy-making within government unfolds more directly at the political level (i.e., cabinet). In this case an issue or opportunity is viewed as important enough to require the immediate attention of cabinet, a number of departments, and staff from the central government secretariat. In these matters policy is led by central government (cabinet, the premier's office, and related staff), which assumes the role of the policy-making authority even though matters may be referred back to various departments for action. As indicated in Figure 3.2, policy is coordinated from the centre in these circumstances. One example was the development of the *Aboriginal Justice Inquiry Child Welfare Initiative* in Manitoba. This initiative involved the transfer of responsibility for all child welfare services provided to Aboriginal people in the province to newly created Aboriginal authorities between 2003 and 2005. Because implications transcended several departments and the issue was politically sensitive, the government's general response was developed centrally with more specific actions assigned primarily to the Department of Family Services and Housing.

Policy-making within government occurs at three levels: the department, cabinet, or the legislature. Matters that require the assent of cabinet are referred to as Orders-in-Council whereas the budget and changes in legislation require the approval of the Legislative Assembly. Documents submitted to cabinet are of two types: those requiring final approval by cabinet and those that seek cabinet approval but must also be presented to the legislature (i.e., new legislation or requests for new expenditures). Documents submitted to cabinet are organized in a prescribed format that contains information on the policy/program request, cost, and the service and political implications of the requested change. Matters that require only cabinet-level approval include regulations for new policies or bills that have been approved by the legislature, a wide range of other matters that are considered to be within the government's policy and expenditure plan approved by the legislature, and proposals for new initiatives, such as the creation of a committee to hold hearings on changes to child welfare legislation. Quite often governments try to shift the authority for making decisions from the legislature to cabinet to avoid public and opposition scrutiny of controversial issues. Although this enables government to manage sensitive issues more effectively, it often

**Figure 3.2    Government Policy Process in Response to an Issue Beginning with Central Government**

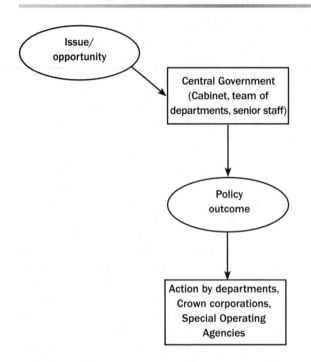

contributes to a policy-making process that contradicts the essential principles of transparency and accountability.

The Canadian parliamentary system has a well-entrenched protocol that must be followed when changes in legislation are required, and these processes are similar at both the federal and provincial levels of government. Although bills may be introduced by any member of the legislature, private member bills require unanimous approval if they are to be further considered. Because this occurs only on rare occasions, most changes to existing legislation or new bills are introduced by government through the respective ministers responsible for the policy issue being considered.

Legislation is normally introduced into the legislature in the form of public bills. These bills result from a process that normally includes policy review and development, the minister's approval, cabinet approval, the drafting of the bill, and detailed approval of the bill for introduction to the legislature by the Cabinet or a committee of government (see Figure 3.3). Once a government bill is introduced to the legislature, government members are expected to support the bill, thus ensuring its passage if the governing party holds a majority of seats. In Manitoba, a new bill requires two days' advance notice, although the Legislature may give unanimous consent to shortening the notice period or waiving it entirely.

## Figure 3.3   How a Government Bill Becomes Law

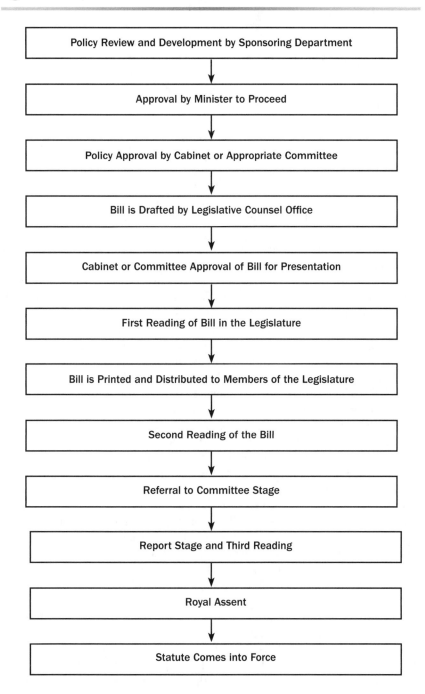

The minister's first introduction of a new bill is known as 'first reading'. Although the minister may give a brief explanation of the purpose of the bill at first reading, no detailed statement is given, and debate is not permitted at this stage. The vote that takes place on first reading simply signifies the approval of the House to consider the bill and to approve printing. The bill is printed after the first reading and distributed to all members of the legislature, although in practice, printing may have occurred prior to first reading. This speeds up the process and allows for the distribution of the bill immediately after first reading.

'Second reading' normally cannot occur until at least two days after the bill has been distributed. Second reading begins with the sponsoring minister making a motion that the bill be given second reading, making a speech to explain the bill, and opening debate. Any member of the Legislative Assembly may speak on the bill. Debate on the second reading is generally confined to the basic principles of the bill rather than specific provisions. After debate ends, a vote is taken. If the motion passes, the bill is considered to have been given second reading.

After second reading, normally the bill is referred to a standing or special committee for review. On rare occasions, such as when emergency legislation is being considered, the bill may be simply referred to the Committee of the Whole (i.e., the legislature). In addition, supply bills and taxation bills are also considered in Committee of the Whole rather than by a standing or special committee. Both government and opposition members sit on standing and special committees. The sponsoring minister of a bill is a member of the Committee and departmental officials may sit with the minster to provide advice. The purpose of the committee stage is to allow members of the committee to receive representation from the public, and representatives may speak for or against the bill or specific provisions in the bill. Following public presentations, the bill is considered 'clause by clause' by the committee. Each clause is voted on, and it is at this stage that amendments can be moved by the minister and by opposition members.

On completion of the committee review, the chairperson of the committee reports to the Legislative Assembly on the committee's deliberations, including any proposed amendments. After these amendments are considered in the legislature, the bill is given 'third reading'. Before it becomes a statute it must receive royal assent by the lieutenant-governor. The bill has the force of law once it is given royal assent unless the bill contains a provision that indicates it comes into force on a specified date or on a date fixed by proclamation. Legislation that is complex or requires the development of new regulations, forms, and procedures is often not proclaimed until some time after royal assent. This gives departmental staff the opportunity to develop new regulations and procedures. If no fixed day of proclamation is specified, an Order-in-Council must be passed by cabinet directing the lieutenant-governor to issue a proclamation that the statute comes into force on the date specified by cabinet.

Almost all government bills contain a provision authorizing government to develop regulations that guide the specific implementation process of a new policy. Regulations set out the details of the policy, yet they do not come under the scrutiny of the legislature or require its approval. In this regard, the legislature is prevented from holding government accountable for the detailed interpretation of policy or the intended steps in implementation.

A final aspect of provincial policy-making concerns the nature of issues that become part of the government's policy agenda. Some of these emerge as a result of information generated by the normal operating phases of a department. For example, persistent overexpenditures by Winnipeg Child and Family Services, a voluntary child welfare agency in Manitoba, resulted in the government's decision to assume direct control of the agency in the fall of 2001. Other issues are established as part of the government's policy agenda because of pre-election commitments, or they are established as initiatives that are identified in the Speech from the Throne when a new legislative session commences. Finally, issues or policy proposals may be proposed by policy advocates from outside government.

As we note elsewhere, issues or policy proposals that are presented to government by advocates from outside government, whether at the federal or provincial level, may be incorporated as part of the government's policy agenda or rejected. If a proposal responds to a particular problem in a way that is consistent with existing government philosophy, adoption is more likely. However, even a good proposal may be rejected if it conflicts with the ideology or publicly stated position of the governing political party. Thus a policy initiative that might call for the expansion of publicly provided services is likely to be viewed unfavourably by a government committed to privatization. Prevailing government philosophy, then, can inhibit the capacity to innovate or respond to advocacy efforts. At the same time, there are often differing perspectives among members of government, even within cabinet, and over time the general policy stance of the government can shift in response to public pressure or other changes. For example, in December 2008, the federal minority government led by Stephen Harper presented an economic update to parliament that promised a balanced budget and failed to include an adequate economic stimulus plan to counter the recessionary trends apparent in the economy. This was roundly condemned by economists, industry, labour, and the opposition parties, and it almost led to the government's defeat. Within two weeks the government had changed its tune, and the Minister of Finance said he would do everything necessary to stimulate the economy and that this would lead to a significant operating deficit in fiscal year 2009–10. As this example indicates, changes in government direction do occur, but ministers who want to be creative may also get around the general policy orientation of government by creating exceptions or framing a new initiative in a way that avoids any direct conflict with the overall philosophy of the government. This approach relies on finding 'wiggle room' between a new initiative and prevailing government policy that might appear to be in conflict with the new policy proposal.

Political will is an important variable in policy-making and its influence is difficult to predict. A government with a cause may pursue a particular policy agenda even if there will be significant political costs to bear. This approach reflects political will, defined here as the willingness of a government to take some risks with public opinion by developing a policy response in conditions of uncertainty or where there is a strong ideological commitment to action. Political will can lead one government to follow a social justice agenda and restore welfare benefits to recipients who are unable to survive on existing allowances. Conversely, a neo-liberal government may impose severe public sector cutbacks despite widespread public disapproval.

# Organizational Policy-Making
## Policy-Making Structures in Organizations

Agencies, particularly those in the voluntary sector, will have their own policy-making structures. These are much simpler than those found in government. For example, the board of directors may approve particular policies but policy development may occur through a subcommittee of the board, a joint staff-board committee, or a senior management committee of staff. When major programs or policy changes are contemplated, an agency may establish a committee composed of a cross-section of direct service staff, senior staff, and board members, and, depending on the relative commitment of the agency to inclusiveness, service representatives to develop or frame the new policy. Such 'vertical slices' represent a greater commitment to a participatory approach in the development of new policies. Forms of strategic planning are also used in government and small-scale community policy-making initiatives, and we include a brief discussion of small-scale policy-making in the next section.

Although it is easier to incorporate an inclusive approach to policy-making within organizations than governments, there is no guarantee that this will be the case. Organizations characterized by an elitist, centralized approach to management can ignore the voices of front-line staff and service users in ways that are characteristic of some government policy-making bodies. This raises the issue of governance models in organizations, whether located in the government or voluntary sectors. Governance is not simply about structures for decision-making; as outlined by Graham, Amos, and Plumptre (2003: 1) it is the 'agreements, procedures, conventions or policies that define who gets power, how decisions are taken and how accountability is rendered'. We note in Chapter Six that relatively large organizations with dispersed local offices can create a governance model that renders a significant degree of autonomy to these offices under certain conditions.

If organizations have boards of directors or advisory committees, it is important to consider how staff and service users play a role in decision-making. Is staff represented on the board? Are there representatives of service users? Are committee structures in place to permit input? Is there a practice of consultation and open discussion prior to decision-making? These questions are related to the organization's culture pertaining to legitimacy and voice, that is, who should be involved in decision-making. It will be apparent that a more inclusive governance model will provide greater opportunities for input from front-line staff, community members, and service users. Although boards or advisory committees are important, organizational policy-making is also heavily influenced by the values and style of the person in the primary leadership position. The approach of this individual will have a major impact on whether planning at the third level becomes more inclusive or whether a more traditional, centralized model will be adopted.

First Nations communities and other Aboriginal organizations are gaining greater policy-making authority in the areas of health, education, and social services, and structures developed to implement these programs are usually community-based if authority is assumed at the community level or regionally-based if authority is vested in a regional structure that serves several communities. The structures that are established in these circumstances may resemble miniature versions of those that exist at a governmental level. For example, in a First Nations community, one of the councillors may have a portfolio that includes health and social services. However, the approaches to policy-making are much less complex than those that exist at a provincial or federal government level, and in this regard the structures and policy-making processes are more like those that exist within organizations. As in organizations, the approach to policy-making in First Nations communities can vary a great deal. Some may adopt a more centralized approach to policy development whereas others will attempt to foster a more inclusive, collaborative approach.

## Small-Scale Policy-Making Processes

Our discussion of policy-making so far has focused on policies and programs that are developed at the governmental or larger organizational level. But ordinary issues in policy-making can also include small-scale innovations launched by a single staff person, a small team within an organization, or a community group. These types of initiatives can have a profound effect on the lives of those who receive services, even if the number of service users is relatively small. For example, the expansion of a program that provides mentoring support to pregnant women with substance abuse problems to include a public education prevention component can make a difference to those who don't have access to important information on the effects of fetal alcohol syndrome disorder (FASD) or available community resources. What model of policy-making is appropriate in these circumstances?

The process of small-scale policy-making draws on a number of steps associated with some of the policy-making models outlined in Chapter One, and the stages of policy-making that are discussed in more detail in the next chapter. An important consideration is the initiation stage of a new small-scale innovation. The individual or group launching the initiative must take the time to develop a consensus about the need for action with those who are responsible for approving the project. A particularly important consideration is whether other programs provide services that might be defined as similar or related to those that are being proposed. The potential for community partnerships may need to be explored, particularly if one is developing a new proposal that will require external funding.

A strategic planning approach is often used to launch a new initiative. If it is pursued as a participatory exercise that engages key stakeholders in developing the innovation, it can help to resolve any value differences and reach a consensus on key components of the new policy or program. Although the steps followed in strategic planning vary somewhat, the following tasks are usually covered in some form:

- *Understand the historical context of the agency or problem.* This involves an examination of general information on trends, critical events, and any ideals that characterize the agency or sponsoring group.
- *Establish a vision or idealized image of the service or program three or more years into the future.* This helps to identify any tensions that may need to be resolved and to highlight general goals that are essential in establishing a mission statement for the new initiative.
- *Complete a situational assessment that involves an analysis of both the internal and external environment affecting the agency or sponsoring group.* The strengths and weaknesses of the internal environment are identified along with the opportunities and threats in the external environment.
- *Identify the issues for which there are yet no obvious solutions.* Strategic issues may emerge from tensions that surfaced during the visioning stage or from the situational assessment.
- *Develop strategic options and select the preferred alternative to address each major unresolved issue.* The activities involved here are similar to those involved in the formulation stage of policy-making. Alternatives are first identified and then assessed for their ability to meet the general goals of the new initiative.
- *Assess feasibility, including general implementation challenges that may need to be considered.* One should consider the views of service users as well as political, financial, and legal implications of proposed changes. Other considerations include an assessment of key stakeholders and the likelihood of obtaining their support for the new initiative. Strategies will need to be designed to deal with those likely to oppose the new initiative if these individuals will be influential in whether the new policy is adopted. One also needs to consider both the material and non-material resources required to implement the new strategy and possible sources of these resources.

Strategic planning can be useful in resolving differences about general strategies to be adopted and in setting the general direction for a new program or initiative; however, results lack the specificity required for implementing a new program initiative. This stage requires attention to 'action planning', or what is sometimes referred to as 'implementation planning'. Action planning requires clarity about goals and objectives. Goal statements are defined here as general statements of program outcomes or what will be accomplished, whereas outcome objectives are more specific, measurable changes that will be experienced by service users.

The criteria for good objectives are identified in Table 3.2. Because goals are more general in nature, each goal may have several outcome objectives. In developing outcome objectives, one may also need to give attention to performance indicators that will help assess whether the new initiative is effective at various stages of the implementation process. While outcome objectives are important in focusing on the anticipated benefits that will emerge from the project, process objectives can be specified to outline things that must be done to build the operating capacity of the project. For example, a new innovation may require the formation of a management structure and a staff-training program.

**Table 3.2  Criteria for Good Program Development Objectives**

| Criteria | Explanation |
| --- | --- |
| 1. Clarity | The meaning of the objectives should be clear to all those who read it. |
| 2. Realistic | An objective should be reasonable given available knowledge, technology, and resources. |
| 3. Time Frame | The time frame for achieving results should be specified. If specific dates cannot be identified, the time frame may be indicated in months and/or years after implementation. |
| 4. Targets of Change | Outcome objectives should specify the population or elements that are expected to be changed, whereas process objectives will identify the structures or methods to be developed in order to achieve outcome objectives. |
| 5. Products and Results | New programs in the human services are designed to lead to service user changes and these expected changes can be identified as results. Products can be defined as the outputs, processes, or steps to be completed in order to achieve target group results. |
| 6. Criteria for Measurement | Criteria for measurement can include quantitative or qualitative indicators in the case of outcome objectives although performance targets may very over time. In the case of process objectives results may be simply documented (e.g., recruit 25 new foster parents). |
| 7. Responsibility | Responsibility for implementation should either be identified or clearly understood. This is important in ensuring adequate accountability. |

Once objectives are clarified, action plans can be specified for each objective if this is required. Action plans are simply sets of activities that may be required to clarify how the changes specified in the program objectives will be accomplished. The essential elements of action plans are quite similar to the criteria identified in Table 3.2 for good objectives, although an action plan may focus more concretely on the tasks to be carried out, by whom, and within what time frame. Each action plan may involve a number of action steps or tasks that must be carried out in the implementation stage.

In a new innovation, action plans may need to be established to identify tasks related to the following:

- the governance and management structure for the new initiative;
- an outreach strategy to recruit and select service users or the target population;
- a staff orientation and training strategy;
- the service model or technology to be used;
- an approach to be used in evaluating success and monitoring implementation; and
- the protocol for accomplishing tasks or service activities.

Action planning in larger programs may require significant detail. In these circumstances, it is important to establish a timeline where activities are sequenced and integrated within a general policy-making framework. In small programs this can be accomplished by specifying beginning and ending dates for various activities; in larger programs computer modelling can be used to help establish a timeline for program implementation. However, even in small initiatives it is advisable to establish an action-monitoring plan. An action-monitoring plan can be combined with the development of an action plan and might include the following:

- a list of the general set of activities or action plans to be carried out along with information on the resources required, those resources that are available, and what must be done to secure needed resource shortfalls;
- a list of the action steps or tasks for each action plan;
- information on who is responsible for each task and requirements for accountability. In small group initiatives, accountability may be to the group; in larger initiatives a coordinator may be identified and written reports may be required; and
- a timeline for tasks that specifies the start and completion dates for different tasks.

In small-scale policy-making the development of detailed action plans may follow formal approval of the new initiative, and such plans will guide the implementation process.

# Summary and Conclusion

At the nation-building stage most responsibility for social policy and the delivery of human services was deemed to fall within the authority of the provinces. State involvement in the delivery of health and social services was quite limited at the time so this was a relatively minor concession to the provinces. But welfare state programs have grown dramatically over time and the role of both the federal and provincial governments has increased. Constitutional provisions have limited the federal government's direct role in service delivery in many areas, including the delivery of services pertaining to health, justice, education, and social services. However, the federal government does provide funding for these services and is directly involved in the delivery of human services to First Nations people living on reserves. In addition, the growth in the nature and scope of health and social policies has led to more direct involvement by the federal government in areas such as pensions, employment insurance, early childhood education, child care, and the provision of benefits through the taxation system to low income families.

Although we recognize the central role of elites in shaping the nature and scope of social policy it is also recognized that policy initiatives do come from a variety of sources. For example, these may be prompted by the normal operating cycle of the bureaucracy, and priorities that emerge from the ongoing monitoring of services or awareness of the adverse consequences of particular measures.

Government structures at both the federal and provincial government levels were described. Two general trends in policy-making were identified at the federal government level. One is the tendency to decentralize (some would say 'off-load') policy and funding responsibilities to the provinces, and the other is the tendency to centralize power and control in the office of the Prime Minister and one or two key committees of cabinet.

This trend is also apparent in many provincial governments. In these circumstances, the premier's office exercises enormous influence over policy development with limited attention to a review of alternatives or how the implementation process can be managed.

The centralizing trend in government policy-making at the federal level and in a number of provincial governments, has led to concerns about the 'democratic deficit'. Although this term was coined primarily to describe the limited participation and influence of elected members in parliament over policy-making, it has much wider repercussions and clearly makes the job of connecting policy to practice in a more inclusive manner that much more difficult. It also contributes to a general cynicism about government and limits the practice of 'active citizenship' as a major influence in policy processes.

Phillips and Orsini (2002) focus on possible reforms to enhance the role of citizens in political and public sector institutions. Although these authors are somewhat pessimistic about being able to reverse the centralizing trend at the top of the policy-making pyramid at the federal government level, a number of changes to promote more citizen involvement in policy-making are recommended.

One involves reform to both the political party system and Parliament that would promote increased policy-oriented discussions between elected political officials and citizens. Second, more attention to the creation of a civic forum for engaging a broader cross-section of the public in policy debates and discussion is recommended. Third, a change in the culture of governments is required to ensure that citizen involvement begins to be seen as an integral part of the policy process. Fourth, greater investment in promoting civil society is required. This includes such things as relaxing the rules on charitable organizations so they can speak out on issues without fear of losing their funding, and promoting the responsibility of public and community institutions to build approaches that involve service users and community members in policy design. We would add an additional reform that might also serve to reverse widespread public apathy in relation to electoral politics. Our political system which rewards individuals and political parties based on who is 'first past the post'—even if the percentage of the popular vote for the winning candidate or party is between 30 and 40 per cent—disenfranchises the majority of the electorate. Some form of proportional representation, common in a number of countries, might encourage more citizen engagement with our political process, and the ability to use this engagement as a means for influencing public policy. It is also likely to result in a governance model that makes more frequent use of coalition governments. Such governments have the potential to better represent the interests of smaller groups, including minority political parties that remain quite marginalized in our present electoral system. It is also important to note the contradiction between the centralizing trend among some governments and the demand for more input and participation that emerges from commitments to diversity and minority rights. Perhaps this contradiction can be exposed in building more active advocacy efforts that promote social justice rather than profits and free market principles.

Additional strategies to promote inclusive policy-making are discussed in more detail later in the book. However, there is much that can be done to promote the development of small-scale reforms to the policy-making process. One level involves the professional work of staff within their employing agencies where there are opportunities to become involved in activities that include connections to the policy-making process. This can happen within the practitioner's service organization or through involvement as an agency representative on task groups or coalitions that are related to professional responsibilities. One can also choose to invest energy in extra-organizational activities related to a professional association, union, political party, or cultural organization that engages in policy advocacy work. Active participation in policy networks allows individuals the opportunity to be more influential in that their voices are multiplied through that organization and the efforts that are made to build coalitions around social issues. Finally, one can act individually in lobbying key political or agency stakeholders on policy issues that are important to the individual.

In Chapter Four the stages of the policy-making process are discussed in depth and a model for policy analysis is outlined.

# Recommended Reading

E.A. Forsey, *How Canadians Govern Themselves*, 6th edn (Ottawa: Her Majesty the Queen in Right of Canada, 2005). This handbook provides a brief summary of federal government structures and is available online at http://www.par. gc.ca/information/library/idb/fosey/PDFs/How_CanadiansGovern _Themselves - 6ed.pdf.

R. Dyck, *Canadian Politics: Critical Approaches*, 4th edn (Scarborough, ON: Nelson, 2004). This book provides a critical perspective on politics and policy-making at the federal level.

A. Finkel, *Social Policy and Practice in Canada: A History,* (Waterloo, ON: Wilfrid Laurier University Press, 2006). This book provides a general history of social policy in Canada and covers several social policy topics in more depth.

B. Schram, *Creating Small Scale Social Programs* (Thousand Oaks, CA: Sage, 1997). This small book provides a guide to small-scale policy-making.

# Critical Thinking Questions

1.   Review the decision made by the Governor General to prorogue parliament in December 2008 summarized in this chapter. Is this the decision you would have made if you were in her shoes? Why or why not?

2.   What are the three branches of government in Canada, and the structures within each branch?

3.   Do you favour a stronger federal role or a stronger provincial role in the field of social policy? What are the advantages and disadvantages of each option?

4.   An argument was advanced in this chapter that policy-making at the governmental level is heavily dependent on elites, and that the policy-making apparatus, particularly at the federal level, has become more centralized over time. Do you agree or disagree? If you agree what could be done to change this? If you disagree explain why?

5.   Select a recent social policy issue that has been addressed either by the provincial government or an organization with which you are familiar. Try to map out the process and the steps or activities that occurred as the policy moved through the decision-making steps. What did you learn about policy-making by trying to map out the process in this way?

# Note

1. These three approaches to government policy-making were identified by Tim Sale, a former minister, Department of Family Services and Housing, Government of Manitoba.

# Chapter Four

# Stages of the Policy-Making Process

In this chapter we identify the stages of the policy-making process and discuss the similarities between these and the stages that occur in practice within social work and other allied fields. Although the stages can be conceptualized as separate and distinct, they should not be viewed as steps in a linear process. On the contrary, in both policy and practice they frequently merge and flow into each other. Nevertheless, clarity and understanding is aided by discussing each stage separately. This chapter also includes a discussion of policy analysis and its connection to the initiation and formulation stages of policy-making. A model of policy analysis is proposed that includes explicit attention to values.

As Figure 4.1 indicates, there are five stages of the policy process: initiation, formulation, execution, implementation, and evaluation. Analysis should occur throughout the policy-making process; however, it is useful to identify the different ways we apply analysis in the policy-making process. Analysis in the initiation phase can be conceptualized as problem analysis and the critical task of policy analysis occurs primarily at the formulation stage. In our preferred model of policy analysis, discussed later in this chapter, problem analysis and policy analysis are combined because one must clearly understand the nature and scope of the problem before identifying policy options and a preferred strategy. This model also includes activities that involve some attention to feasibility, although this is primarily a concern for the implementation stage. Although some authors extend the nature and scope of policy analysis to include the evaluation stage, we prefer to define this stage as 'policy evaluation'. The execution stage requires little analysis and, given the close connection between policy and practice in implementation, discussion of this stage is the subject of the following chapter.

**Figure 4.1    Corresponding Stages of Policy and Practice Process**

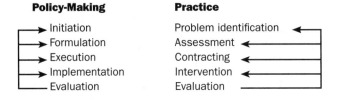

**Policy-Making**

- Initiation
- Formulation
- Execution
- Implementation
- Evaluation

**Practice**

- Problem identification
- Assessment
- Contracting
- Intervention
- Evaluation

# Stages in Developing Policy and Practice
## Initiation and Problem Identification

In both policy-making and practice, action or change begins at a discernible point. In practice, the beginning point might take the form of a request by a service user for assistance, a referral from another agency, or a complaint by a neighbour or another professional. In policy-making, the beginning point might emanate from the pressure created by social movements, the public, or interest groups who have become convinced of the inadequacy of existing policy, or government response to a campaign promise.

In all the possible scenarios, a 'convergence of interest' (Sower, Holland, Tiedke, and Freeman, 1957) or a crisis of some magnitude must occur before action will be initiated. As conceptualized by Sower and his colleagues, a convergence of interest reflects the notion of an idea whose time has come: the perception that something simply has to be done about a particular condition. In the garbage can model of policy development, a convergence of interest is defined as a 'window of opportunity' that occurs when the political stream, the stream of problems, and the stream of policy solutions come together. A convergence of interest is often influenced by the characteristics of the person or organization advocating for change, and these characteristics include authority, legitimacy, and commitment. Thus, an agency director may have the authority to propose a change but may lack the confidence of the agency's staff. A change proposed by such a director may be initiated, but it will encounter resistance during the change process. Conversely, a long-standing staff member who is highly regarded by colleagues may lack authority, but may nevertheless possess a high degree of legitimacy. Both of these people will need to supplement their proposal with energy and commitment; indeed, causes pursued by a dedicated champion may well succeed despite the absence of other factors usually considered essential in bringing about change.

A convergence of interest that leads to initiation is somewhat more complicated in policy-making than it is in practice, and the notion of convergence of interest is expanded here to include a set of factors that need to be considered in assessing the likelihood of policy initiation. These are evidence of need for the change, availability of resources, the complexity of the change being contemplated, organizational readiness, environmental readiness, and the commitment of key actors (see Table

4.1). The answers to the questions posed in Table 4.1 will help to determine whether this is the right time for the policy initiation stage. Thus, a relatively simple change proposed by and backed by the commitment and resources of a minister of social services or a minister of health in a sympathetic environment will in all likelihood be initiated. However, the scenario will shift if the minister's proposal involves a complex issue about which there is widespread disagreement. As we noted earlier, controversial issues will likely be referred to some type of study group. The prospects of a successful launch are more remote if the proposal for change emanates from a backbencher of a party in opposition or from a professional organization lacking close connections with the minister and the party in power.

**Table 4.1     Factors to Consider in Assessing the Likelihood of Policy Initiation**

| Factors | Key Questions |
| --- | --- |
| Need for change | Is the change a political priority or do results from a formal needs assessment support change? |
| Complexity of issue | How complex is the issue and is action required by several sectors? |
| Commitment to key actors | Do key decision-makers support the change? |
| Organizational readiness | Do organizations that must plan and implement the change have the motivation and capacity to do so? |
| Environmental readiness | Do key stakeholders in the policy environment, including the public, support the change? |
| Availability of resources | Are sufficient resources available to implement the change? |

The explanatory power of the concept of convergence of interest takes a different form in the event of a crisis such as the death of a child. Crises can provoke new unanticipated actions, especially if they can be used to reinforce the agendas of those in positions of power and if resources are available. Thus, the 1992 death of Matthew Vaudreuil in British Columbia was interpreted by the minister and senior staff in charge of child welfare as justification to inquire into the internal working conditions of the department and the practices of the front-line staff. In this example, Judge Gove was appointed to conduct a far-reaching investigation of child welfare practices in the province, and his recommendations led to major organizational and service delivery changes in this field.

In practice, the initiation stage begins with a complaint or a referral that is accepted by the agency. Again, the likelihood of acceptance is much greater if the request comes from a respectable and well-known source. When faced with referrals from unknown or poorly regarded sources or requests from service users who have earned a reputation for being difficult, rude, or antagonistic, staff might delay responses or ignore the request. Again, a crisis often spurs a prompt response regardless of the source of the referral or the reputation of the client. Other factors that may influence the acceptance of a referral include the agency's mandate or service priorities. Once accepted, the problem identification phase commences. In cases where a service user wants a particular service, the problem definition phase proceeds through mutual dialogue and exploration. However, this is not the case when the person has not requested a particular service or when he or she has a significantly different view of his or her needs than the service provider.

The most perplexing part of the initiation stage revolves around defining the problem to be addressed. Social problems are notoriously difficult to pin down and yet the definition sets the stage for the rest of the policy-making process. Indeed, the very term 'definition' is problematic because it connotes precision and explicitness. We prefer the term 'framing', which outlines the general parameters of the issue being addressed. Framing provides a sense of direction. It sets out preferences and prescribes limits based on ideologies and experiences, but refrains from the explicitness expected of a definition. Although Rittel and Webber (1973) use 'definition' rather than 'framing', the essence of the latter notion is captured by their description of social problems as 'wicked problems'.

Wicked problems have a number of distinguishing properties, for example:

a)    there is no definitive formulation of a wicked problem;
b)    wicked problems have a no stopping rule: they are resolved over and over again;
c)    solutions to wicked problems are not true or false but are good or bad, depending on one's values and experience;
d)    every solution to a wicked problem is a 'one shot operation'; because there is no opportunity to learn by trial and error every attempt counts significantly;
e)    every wicked problem is essentially unique; and
f)    every wicked problem is a symptom of another problem (Rittel and Webber, 1973: 167–8).

In our view, framing the problem is the most significant aspect of the initiation stage. Thus, if the problem of poverty is framed as the unwillingness of citizens to work, then the solution would be to force people to work or to provide incentives so that more individuals will find and keep employment. Similarly, if the problem is framed simply as the lack of employment opportunities, then attention would focus on job creation programs. However, if poverty is framed as the consequence of a number of faulty and interlocking public policies, including educational preparation, the availability of work, inequality, and the failure to establish a progressive tax system, then the task becomes one of examining the very concept of work, who receives compensation, the adequacy of compensation to lower income individuals and families as well as whether there are sufficient opportunities for employment. Framing the problem in this way implies the need for a more comprehensive and radical examination of options.

Practitioners face similar dilemmas in the problem identification phase of practice. Should a single-parent mother be viewed as a disadvantaged and distressed person with limited resources doing her best to manage under difficult circumstances? If so, then the appropriate response would be to assist her by increasing her resources and reducing her stress. Conversely, the identification of the same person as an inadequate parent requiring training in parenting and budgeting skills will result in referrals to suitable training programs.

An example of framing in practice (see Box 4.1) relates to the project touched on in the Introduction.

This example illustrates the power of framing in setting the course of the policy-making and practice processes. In fact, the framing of wicked problems is heavily influenced by ideologies. We have argued in earlier chapters that many of those who wielded influence in framing and developing social policies in the past two

## Box 4.1 Framing the Problem in the Protecting Children by Empowering Women Project

The *Protecting Children by Empowering Women* project in British Columbia, highlighted in the Introduction, brought together child welfare workers and their clients with the goal of finding ways to meet the needs of these service users and to change child welfare practice. The first step was to identify a number of women interested in the project, to convene a group meeting, and to develop action plans. The coordinator of the project was a former child protection worker. In her previous role her relationship with service users typically began with an investigation of a complaint of neglect or abuse. She acknowledged that her assessments of possible neglect or abuse were, like those of her colleagues, based on pinpointing problems and deficits: Is there evidence of abuse and/or neglect? Are there indications of a poor marital relationship? Are the parents immature? Is the available income adequate? Is the housing satisfactory?

Based on experiences of working more collaboratively with service users in a group work setting, the coordinator of the project now works with service users in a completely different way because her assessments are framed by interactions with a group of motivated women eager to address issues and identify solutions. This frame focuses on strengths: for example, one woman was a carpenter, another was a day-care worker, and a third was an experienced secretary. From the perspective of the people who use services, the opportunity to identify problems, to discuss solutions, and to work with the coordinator as a source of assistance rather than as an investigator also altered the women's framing experience substantially. These women felt validated and motivated to take action in a way that had not occurred to them in the past.

and a half decades reflected a residual view of state-provided services. Thus health care funding was restricted and directed primarily to hospitals and doctors at the expense of health promotion and early intervention, in turn contributing to a crisis in medicare. Similarly, child welfare programs have focused on child protection rather than early intervention and prevention. Paradoxically, this focus has led to higher numbers of children in care and increased costs. These frames have set the context for practice and a deep and continuing fault line has been created by the gap between the needs of service users and the policies ostensibly designed to serve them. As a result, practitioners have been forced to focus their energy on crisis-oriented responses only or on trying to address the gap with too few resources or supports to make a real difference.

While the key actors in the initiation stage of policy-making are more likely to be those possessing some degree of formal power, there are occasions where the initiation of change occurs as a direct result of persistent campaigns by those affected either by the absence of a policy or by an inadequate policy. Examples include the efforts of the feminist movement to establish transition houses for battered women and to change hiring practices in the workforce, and the struggle of First Nations people to settle land claims and to achieve jurisdictional control over their own services.

## Assessing Problems, Needs, and Resources

The problem analysis phase involves careful consideration of both objective and subjective aspects of the problem. Key issues include how many people are affected by the condition as well as how they feel about and react to the issue. Problem analysis in policy analysis differs from the way problems are defined in traditional research. While one is concerned with who, what, and where issues, it is also important to understand the history and causality of the problem, previous attempts to address the problem, and the community's readiness to deal with the problem. There are a number of common questions that can be posed in completing an analysis of the problem and these are included later in this chapter when we introduce a specific model for policy analysis.

Once problems have been framed and defined, they have to be translated into needs. Problems are closely related to needs, but needs reflect the gap between what the situation is and what it should be. If there is insufficient information available on these needs, it will be necessary to conduct a needs assessment. But *need* is a difficult concept to both define and measure. One can distinguish between *needs* and *wants*; whereas *wants* are what people are willing to pay for, *needs* are closer to what people are willing to march for. In this context *needs* take on attributes that are closely related to *rights* or what all people should have available to them. Needs also differ in terms of importance, and these are dependent on circumstances. This is illustrated by Maslow's (1954) approach to the definition of needs for individuals. He argued that needs can be conceptualized in a hierarchical fashion. Therefore, a person is primarily concerned with meeting physiological needs first (i.e., food and shelter), safety and security needs later, and then higher level needs such as love and self-actualization. As a person's needs at a more basic level are met, more attention can be paid to higher level needs. This approach can be illustrated by examining the provision of services to abused women and their children in cases of domestic violence. For example, if the abuse is serious the first response will be to refer the woman and her children to a shelter and only after this basic need is met to consider such things as restraining orders (security and safety), counselling services (to help restore self-esteem), and other options, such as employment and alternative housing (autonomy and self sufficiency).

As the previous discussion emphasizes, need is a relative concept that is affected by both values and context. Standards and attitudes of the public change over time. Thus, the commonly accepted definition of a poverty line in Canada (i.e., the Statistics Canada LICO) is adjusted annually to reflect changing income and costs. Public attitudes and expectations also change. Accessible transportation for the disabled, which is clearly identified as a need in most urban centres in Canada today, would have likely been defined as a want or luxury a generation ago. Because of our interest in relating needs to the development of programs, there must also be some expectation that resources can be identified to respond to these needs, and that the technology is available to solve the problem.

Kettner, Moroney, and Martin (2008) summarize four different perspectives on need: normative, perceived, expressed, and relative (see Table 4.2). Each perspective has both advantages and disadvantages. A normative perspective on need suggests that one can measure the existence of need through the use of a commonly accepted standard. The Statistics Canada LICO, which is used to identify the number of people living in poverty, is one such standard. Other standards have been developed to define the adequacy of housing, nutrition, and the ratio of hospital beds to population in a community or region. Although standards are helpful in defining needs, they are not always available for the problem area in question.

Perceived needs are what people think or feel they need. Perceived needs are measured by asking people what they need through survey methods or interviews. But perceived needs are not always a good reflection of who would actually use services. For example, estimates of those who are sexually abused are commonly provided to demonstrate the prevalence of sexual abuse, yet not all of these victims would use services that might be developed to respond to this need.

Expressed needs can sometimes be confused with perceived needs; however, they are not the same thing. If a need is expressed, there must be some attempt to obtain a service. Wait lists or the number of referrals for service are common methods of measuring expressed needs. Although this approach to needs assessment brings us closer to understanding the demand for a service, it also has its flaws. If people know there are long wait lists for family counselling at a family service agency, they may not bother to register because they are not prepared to wait six months for a service they require immediately. Instead, they may seek out a private practitioner or go without this service. As well, people cannot be expected to express a need by registering for a service that does not yet exist!

**Table 4.2    Perspectives on Need**

**Normative need:** requires comparison to an accepted standard
*Advantage*
• if needs are greater than existing standard, provides support for action
*Disadvantage*
• standards are often not available or accepted

**Perceived need:** reflects what people think and feel
*Advantage:*
• more representative of views of potential target group
*Disadvantages:*
• may not be indicative of actual demand for service or the number of people who would utilize services
• perceptions change over time

**Expressed need:** reflects data on numbers of people who actually try to obtain a service
*Advantage:*
• good predictor of demand for service or the number of people who might utilize a particular service
*Disadvantages:*
• may omit people who have given up trying to obtain a service
• is not a useful measure of need where no service exists for a newly identified problem

**Relative need:** reflects a comparison of data from one area or community with another or with a provincial or national average
*Advantage:*
• allows one to measure gaps where standards do not exist
*Disadvantage:*
• may focus on differences in need rather than the characteristics that reflect the presence of the particular need under consideration

The final perspective is relative need. Relative need does not begin with the assumption that a standard or criterion exists. Instead, the level of need in one area or community is compared with the level in another community to identify differences that may require attention. Comparisons of the unemployment rate in a First Nations community with another community or with the national or provincial average reflect a relative perspective on need. Although a relative approach to needs assessment provides for a wider range of comparisons than might exist if one used a normative perspective, there are potential problems. Comparative studies of child poverty may lead to preoccupation with differences between provinces, and these differences may then divert attention from the substantive issue of child poverty. To summarize, it is most often appropriate to use more than one perspective because this will provide a better picture of the needs pertaining to a social problem.

A number of different methods may also be used to measure needs. The first step is to examine what already exists. This might involve a review of such things as social indicators, including information available through Statistics Canada; local and national research studies; and records on service utilization. New information may be collected through surveys or interviews with service users and providers. Wait lists, trends in the number of referrals, and rates under treatment are examples of information on need that may be able to be obtained from service providers. More interactive techniques, employing primarily qualitative methods, can also be used. These include community forums, focus groups, and nominal group methods. Public hearings, sometimes organized as a component of special commissions, are an expanded version of a community forum in which an individual or group may present a brief on the issue being examined.

Needs studies also make use of evaluation research methods, particularly in cases where studies can demonstrate a cause-and-effect relationship. For example, the development of needle exchange programs in Canadian cities was based on evidence linking the multiple use of needles to the spread of HIV. Needs studies are very important in policy analysis because a new policy initiative is seldom undertaken without demonstrable evidence of need.

While needs assessment studies are useful in policy-making, we argue that they reflect a deficit-oriented approach to analysis unless they are combined with an assessment of assets and capacities. Here again, a parallel between policy and practice can be drawn. In the human services, there is a growing awareness of the need to build on strengths at the individual, family, and community level in order to promote change, and this process begins with an identification of existing strengths and resources as an important aspect of the assessment stage. McKnight and Kretzmann (1992) apply a similar approach to policy-making at the community level in suggesting that needs-oriented assessments give us only half the picture. What is required to complete the picture is an identification of strengths and resources—a process described as 'mapping community capacity' or 'asset mapping'.

Using the community as an example, three types or levels of strengths and resources should be considered. First, there are the resources and strengths of individuals and organizations within the community that are largely subject to community control. Next are the assets located within the community that are largely controlled by outsiders. These assets may include both private and public institutions such as hospitals, schools, and social service agencies. Finally, there are potential building blocks that include those resources originating outside the neighbourhood that are controlled by outsiders. These may include actual or potential social transfer payments and capital improvement expenditures. With this kind of information, a policy analyst is in a better position to address existing needs by building both on identified strengths and on potential resources. While the principle of assessing strengths and resources is perhaps easier to apply in the case of a geographic community, it can also be applied to groups linked through affiliation or interest. In order to make a helpful contribution to the policy-making process, conventional approaches to needs assessment must be modified to incorporate procedures that develop an inventory of resources and capacities. Developing a resource inventory is not always a complicated process. For example, a matrix which lists potential resources and then assesses whether these are available and adequate, available but inadequate, or not available, can be quite helpful to the analysis of needs and resources.

## Formulation and Assessment

The second stage of the policy-making process—formulation—involves developing and analyzing alternatives. The methods used in policy analysis are particularly relevant to this stage of the planning process and a model for policy analysis is outlined later in this chapter. Policy analysis, as it is applied in the formulation stage of the policy-making process, is concerned with predicting the future consequences of different policy options. This requires a focus on both technical data and the political aspects of decision-making. Because policy analysis makes an effort to predict the anticipated outcomes of policy alternatives, it often considers evaluation studies conducted on similar policies that have been implemented elsewhere. Even though the major thrust or direction for change may have been set by the manner in which the problem has been framed, a number of different potential responses will still need to be considered. Thus, in formulating a response to delinquency, policy-makers may want to consider whether expanding the number of police and probation officers is preferable to an increase in the number of juvenile detention facilities, or whether more community-based responses are preferred over either of these options.

Formulation is the stage in which techniques from the rational model of planning become most useful. Formulating alternatives may begin in brainstorming sessions in which no suggestion, however improbable, is rejected. Once all possible alternatives have been identified, research may be conducted to anticipate consequences, and criteria may be identified to assist in the selection process. Considerations may include the anticipated cost, the feasibility of implementation, the implications for the political party in power, and possible outcomes for beneficiaries. As will be obvious from this beginning list, criteria are not of the same order or importance. Do benefits to the party in power outweigh financial costs? Does the flexibility of a new service take precedence over ease and simplicity in implementation?

Special commissions and task forces are favourite vehicles for dealing with complex issues at the formulation stage. These structures have a number of advantages to those in power: they give the appearance of action while buying time before a decision is required, and they assure everyone that the problem is being studied in depth by experts. While special commissions can be a means of postponing a policy response they can also draw attention to the need for a significant policy response. One example is the *Romanow Commission on the Future of Health Care*, which released its report in November 2002. This raised expectations for both reform of medicare and new investment in health care by the federal government.

The *Royal Commission on Aboriginal Peoples* (RCAP) (1996) is perhaps the most comprehensive study of any policy field ever conducted in Canada. Although it formulated a variety of recommendations to address the rights of Aboriginal peoples in Canada, there has been only limited progress in responding to these findings. Nevertheless, the Commission's findings have provided evidence that has been used to frame the 'problem' of underdevelopment and colonization in Aboriginal communities.

An integral part of special commissions and task forces is inviting the public to attend hearings and to submit briefs. These invitations are often taken up by a large number of individuals and groups. For example, the community panel that reviewed child welfare in British Columbia prior to the formulation of the *Child, Family and Community Service Act* (1994) 'heard 550 presentations in more than 23 communities and received over 600 written briefs from individuals and groups' (Durie and Armitage, 1996: 19). In such circumstances a vast amount of information is gathered, organized, and classified according to the themes that have emerged; analyzed to permit the identification of findings and recommendations; and, finally, translated into policy and/or legislation by analysts and legislative drafters.

While governments that follow this approach can claim that they consulted the public prior to making a choice among competing options, there is, nevertheless, no way to assure the public that all views have been represented in the final report in an equal and fair fashion. For example, governments may select those views that are more consistent with their particular perspective. The consultation process itself is open to even more criticism when, as in the case of the 1994–95 review of Canada's social security system, the nature of the inquiry was carefully orchestrated by policy-makers, including the selection of who was to be allowed to present briefs.[1] In this example, the nature and scope of public input begins with controlling who can provide this input.

One useful way of analyzing the extent of the influence of citizens in the policy-making process is provided by a framework called 'a ladder of citizen participation'. The ladder has eight rungs (see Figure 4.2). The top three rungs—citizen control, delegated power, and partnerships—represent differing degrees of citizen power. The next three, which include placation, consultation, and informing, symbolize degrees of tokenism. Consultation, the middle rung of this group, allows 'the have-nots to hear and have a voice, but . . . they lack the power to ensure that their views will be heeded by the powerful' (Arnstein, 1969: 217). The two bottom rungs refer to processes that do not enable participation; they include therapy and manipulation. We refer again to this useful conceptualization in the discussion of community governance in Chapter Six.

Like their policy counterparts, professionals in direct practice must develop an intervention plan, and tasks undertaken in completing an assessment provide the basis for such a plan. As in policy formulation, this phase may be extensive and elaborate, involving a number of people and generating several alternative

**Figure 4.2    A Ladder of Citizen Participation**

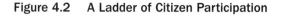

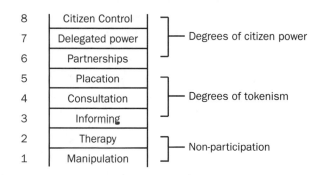

Source: Reproduced from Arnstein, 1969, p. 217

strategies. In some cases, the phase may be brief and yield only one plan. The latter is likely to occur when the medical model holds sway and a plan is developed by the practitioner or by an external expert. On the other hand, if a partnership approach exists, intervention plans will be developed jointly by the practitioner and the service user, perhaps with the input of additional experts. In these circumstances, it is more likely that a wider range of options will be considered.

## Execution and Contracting

At the execution stage, choices are reviewed and a decision is made. In federal and provincial policy matters, recommendations involving major changes and/or a substantial increase in resources will be reviewed by analysts from a standing committee of the cabinet and/or Treasury Board before being forwarded to cabinet for a decision. When the policy takes the form of new legislation or changes to existing laws, the cabinet will review and approve these plans prior to sending the draft bill to the legislature for debate and a decision.

In a voluntary agency, the board of directors will decide whether to proceed with the plans. Prior to doing so, it may refer recommendations made by committees comprising board and staff members to outside consultants or to standing committees of finance and personnel.

The execution stage in practice rests essentially with the practitioner and the service user. This is most often referred to as the contracting stage, in which goals, objectives, tasks, and activities for ongoing work are outlined.

## Implementation and Intervention

Implementation is the fourth stage of the policy-making process, and as noted earlier, the next chapter is devoted to this topic.

The parallel stage in practice is intervention. A wide range of intervention models exists in practice. Intervention, like the assessment stage in practice, will be shaped by several factors. These include the mandate of the agency, the nature of the problem, guidelines provided in the practice theory used in this particular situation, the service contract that has been established, and the nature of the relationship that evolves between the practitioner and service user.

Two general distinctions can be made and these are largely shaped by the mandate of the agency and the nature of the problem being addressed. In the case of voluntary contracts where the service user exercises a choice to receive service, more mutuality in the working relationship that evolves can be anticipated. In the case of non-voluntary situations where service is a requirement—whether or not the service user agrees—more difficulties in establishing a mutually acceptable approach to intervention may be anticipated. This is often true in fields such as child welfare and corrections although resistance to intervention may characterize other fields of practice as well. On the one hand, the intervention phase in voluntary service contracts may be compared to the implementation phase of policies where there is a high degree of acceptance of these policies by both service users and providers. On the other hand, the intervention phase in non-voluntary service contracts may reflect problems that are somewhat similar to those that arise in the implementation of policies that do not seem to match the particular needs of service users. While this comparison of practice intervention and policy implementation is of interest, one should not underestimate the differences. First, not only is intervention shaped by policies, but also in a very real way it is an extension of the implementation phase of the policy-making process. Second, because policy implementation is generally mediated by a larger number of political and bureaucratic decision-makers, and it is designed to meet the general needs of a target population, there is a greater likelihood that policies may fail to match the specific needs of an individual service user. In these circumstances it is often the ability of the practitioner to modify and adapt policies that will determine the extent to which service users' needs are met.

## Evaluation

Case-oriented practice evaluation involves both ongoing monitoring and the assessment of outcomes achieved by service users during the intervention process. Most often, this assessment of progress is connected to goals and objectives set during the contracting phase. A variety of methods may be used to assist in evaluation including standardized instruments, outcome measures, and ongoing feedback on the work or intervention stage. Evaluation is an interactive process and feedback from this stage will influence ongoing adjustments to the problem definition, contracting, and intervention stages.

Evaluation is the final stage of the policy-making process, but all stages should be subjected to evaluation in order to improve the process as it unfolds.

Evaluation results from policy implementation are particularly important, and this information may cause us to alter our understanding of the problem, to modify goals, or to include new activities in the implementation stage.

It is not always easy to distinguish between program and policy evaluation, and this is because there may be considerable overlap. First, a new policy often leads to one or more programs that may be established to carry out the policy. For example, changes to child welfare legislation that incorporate both mediation and family group conferencing as alternative methods of dealing with child protection concerns will lead to the development of programs to promote these approaches. And even if family group conferencing is identified as a separate policy under a new legislative framework that includes several new policy initiatives, there may be a variety of family group conferencing programs set up across the province. Second, most of the methods used to evaluate programs will be used to evaluate the impact of more general policies. However, the term 'program evaluation' is generally used to refer to measuring the effects from a specific program, whereas 'policy evaluation' is concerned with the broader assessment of a general course of action, a framework, or a piece of legislation.

A policy study may involve a large-scale study of multiple sites, or a review of program evaluation results from studies of individual programs. In addition, a policy study often involves a review of research or evaluation studies on the topic, which have been conducted in other jurisdictions. As indicated, policy evaluation studies often combine direct research with secondary analysis of research that has been conducted in the area. In the example noted above, a specific program evaluation might be conducted on the family conferencing initiative launched by a particular agency. However, government may be interested in whether family conferencing, in general, is an important policy initiative and whether it should be expanded to new sites. Thus, a more general policy evaluation of all sites might be commissioned with specific guidelines to examine effectiveness and efficiency on a province-wide basis. As well, specific policy questions pertaining to the feasibility of expanding this policy initiative may be included as part of the evaluation.

In Canada, research to inform social policy development often receives limited attention, and we have much to learn from the approach that led to the development of the Children Act (1989) in Britain (see Box 4.2). While the use of government-funded research for policy development is somewhat less evident in Canada, this is beginning to change and studies have been commissioned to examine specific policy issues (see the example in Box 4.3). From a provincial perspective, Quebec—more so than other provinces—appears to take a more systematic approach to using evaluation research in policy-making in that it funds a wide range of research that involves close collaboration between researchers and practitioners.

An important consideration is the extent to which policy is shaped by research and evaluation information about what works. Too often we have contradictory knowledge about what works in the social services or our evidence is limited to results from small studies that are unable to accurately predict the long-term effects

## Box 4.2  Using Research and Evaluation for Policy Development

The adoption of the Children Act (1989) in the United Kingdom was widely recognized as the culmination of a decade-long process that included systematic consideration of research and evaluation findings documenting the effects of various types of social care arrangements on children and their families. This process resulted in legislation that places increased emphasis on partnerships with parents, even when children are removed from their homes. For example, guardianship options provide for a continuing role for parents whenever feasible, and there is a great deal of emphasis on family visiting and connections while children are in care. New provisions also place increased emphasis on service options designed to support children in their own homes. Subsequent to the legislation research has continued to inform policy and practice. For example, service planning now includes more emphasis on the needs of the child and the outcomes that result from the services provided. New systems have been designed to focus attention on these aspects of the case planning process, including assessment and the development of an integrated service response for children and families in need. As well, new resources have been invested to ensure the implementation of these systems within local authorities throughout the United Kingdom.

## Box 4.3 Using Policy Research to Provide Information for Policy Analysis

The lack of national information on the incidence of child abuse and neglect in Canada led the federal government to provide funding for a national study on this issue that was completed in 1998 (see Trocmé et al., 2001). This study used a cluster sampling design that included a sample of 7,672 child maltreatment investigations conducted in 51 child welfare sites across the country. A common classification for types of maltreatment was used to avoid the definitional and tracking problems that characterize information systems within the provinces and territories. By applying weights, a national picture of the nature of child maltreatment, worker characteristics, placement patterns, and factors associated with maltreatment and placement was obtained. More important, the *Canadian Incidence Study* (cis), as it is known, was repeated in 2003 and then again in 2008. Comparative data provide policy-relevant information on a number of issues but one finding from the second cycle indicates a significant increase in the rate of child maltreatment referrals and the rate of substantiated cases of child maltreatment, particularly in relation to neglect, physical abuse, and exposure to domestic violence (Trocmé, Fallon, and MacLaurin, in press). These findings can be used to shape policy responses within the child welfare field and to provide some support for the growing interest in differential response, which focuses on providing supportive responses to families prior to the need for placement.

of new initiatives. The uncertainty of social service knowledge has produced an increased interest in outcome-based research and evidence-based practice.

The adoption of new initiatives is encouraged when evaluation is able to influence a shift in public opinion; in these circumstances government is more likely to respond. More attention to the use of evaluation research to shape policy is an important way of connecting policy to practice. While this requires a greater commitment on the part of government to fund applied research, the growing interest in evidence-based practice may help to encourage this trend. Recognition of the multiple roles of research suggests the following different types of use:

- research is used to provide the essential information to make a policy deci-sion or influence an orientation towards an issue;
- research is used to refine a position or understanding; and
- research is used to justify a position or orientation that has already been adopted.

It is self-evident that the use of policy-relevant research will be enhanced if the research provides credible evidence and is based on sound methodology. And while utilization is shaped by a number of other factors such as political context, timing, and the presence of leaders or champions who promote the use of findings, Nutley, Walter, and Davies (2007) suggest a number of strategies that can help. These include the following:

- tailor dissemination to potential users and provide support for the discus-sion of findings;
- include interactive approaches wherever possible, such as partnerships be-tween researchers and practitioners, and promote the testing of findings within the local context; and
- offer technical, financial, organizational, and emotional support for the implementation of research based protocols, tools, and programs.

It should be recognized that all governments do not react in the same fashion to social science information. While government responds to shifts in knowledge or public opinion, there are what may be termed 'early' and 'late movers' on policy initiatives. These differences are shaped by several factors. The most important of these are the availability of resources and whether the evidence from policy or program evaluations is consistent with existing government priorities. If the results from evaluation studies are consistent with a government's general priorities or its ideology, it is more likely that these results will be used to help shape specific policies; conversely, those that contradict a government's general policy direction or its ideological stance are more likely to be ignored.

At a general level, program or policy evaluation involves the systematic collection, analysis, and reporting of information about a program, service, or intervention for use in decision-making. While this identifies evaluation as a technical process, it has been noted that contextual, resource, and political factors also affect use. These issues blur the lines between tasks within policy and program evaluation in suggesting that evaluation involves activities that are partly social, partly political, and only partly technical. Evaluation in policy-making, then, reflects an action orientation, that is, it is concerned with the adjustment of policy goals, approaches to implementation, or the decision to either extend or terminate a policy.

Program or policy studies make use of methods associated with different approaches to evaluation; Herman, Morris, and Fitz-Gibbon (1987) distinguish between formative and summative approaches. Whereas a formative evaluation examines program or policy processes and is designed to produce information to assist a program in its development, a summative evaluation examines the outcomes, the impact, and the efficiency of a policy.

Formative evaluations—sometimes referred to as process evaluations—are concerned with the components of a policy or program, what services are being provided, and whether the policy or program is reaching those for whom it was intended. Implementation studies involving an assessment of policy processes are particularly relevant to new policies because they attempt to describe the details of the policy in order to ascertain what is causing certain effects or whether the policy is being implemented as planned. Two major sets of issues are considered: (1) coverage or actual participation in the program by the intended target population; and (2) service delivery, including the sequence of activities undertaken to achieve policy objectives. If a policy or program is not operating effectively, an implementation evaluation can help to determine what has gone wrong and what improvements can be made. Often these problems exist in one or more of the following areas: (a) a policy approach or design that fails to meet the needs of service users; (b) a lack of program acceptance caused by the attitudes of staff members or administrative policies that create barriers to access; (c) program management; and (d) program costs (Love, 1992).

Summative evaluations concentrate on policy or program outcomes and efficiency. An outcome study is concerned with the extent to which a policy meets its objectives, and, where those objectives involve changes for service users, how long those changes last. Efficiency evaluation is concerned with the ratio of benefits to costs; various forms of cost–utility analysis may be performed, including benefit–cost and cost-effectiveness studies. Box 4.4 summarizes how evaluation has been used to assess program outcomes and costs in a particular policy field, and some of the difficulties that can arise. As this example from the family preservation field demonstrates, a narrow focus on efficiency may divert attention from a more comprehensive review of outcomes. This example also illustrates how multiple evaluations of a new policy may highlight differences in the outcomes that may be experienced during implementation.

Formative and summative approaches to policy evaluation have been discussed as separate strategies; however, most studies combine these approaches. For example, an evaluation may be concerned with whether the policy is being implemented as intended and what the effects of the policy are on service

Box 4.4   Assessing Conflicting Results in Policy Evaluation

Evaluations can produce contradictory results, as indicated in the field of family preservation. Early research of the Homebuilders model—a social support program developed in the state of Washington—suggested that there were significant cost savings to a service model that included short-term intensive services to families where the children were at risk of out-of-home placement. These results encouraged new legislation and significant investment in these programs throughout the United States and Canada. Subsequent evaluations suggested that many of the short-term benefits reported in early evaluations were not sustained over time. Two important implications are apparent. First, major policy initiatives that are promoted on the basis of preliminary results may fail to live up to expectations. Second, even when program outcomes are positive, policy evaluation requires us to consider a wide range of studies, assess these results critically, and consider their relevance to our particular policy environment

users. However, we stress that the evaluation of new policies requires a special focus on formative issues; that is, the activities and the organizational processes associated with implementation. While both quantitative and qualitative methods are relevant to such studies, the collection of data often involves qualitative interviews with key informants, service user feedback, and a review of documents. Triangulation, which involves collecting data from more than one source using different data collection methods or different investigators is recommended in such studies.

A primary focus on outcomes may become the purpose of evaluation in mature programs, and in such studies the use of control or comparison groups can provide additional evidence of whether the policy or program is responsible for observed changes in behaviour or outcomes. In recent years, computer-based monitoring systems that incorporate outcome measures have become quite popular, and such systems have the advantage of providing ongoing feedback to program managers and service providers. While these systems are intended to be helpful, certain disadvantages exist. These systems may not be designed to incorporate feedback from service users, and they focus largely on recording and retrieving quantitative information. In addition, they often fail to promote community and service-user empowerment because institutions, such as government agencies, control both the technology and the information.

The evaluation dilemma posed here is not easy to resolve. Information on needs and resources, program design, activities, effectiveness, and costs are essential requirements for good policy-making. Methods for program and policy monitoring, as well as carefully designed outcome studies, can help to provide this information. But these approaches are not sufficient. We argue that such approaches must be accompanied by more participatory methods if we are to generate the kind of evaluation information needed to design programs and policies that respond most effectively to the differing cultural and social needs of service users.

Participatory evaluation methods are not new but there is a growing interest in these approaches. One of the authors was involved in a community-based research project that featured two rounds of focus group discussions which began to identify culturally appropriate standards for child welfare practice for eight First Nations communities (McKenzie, 1997). There is a wide range of literature which focuses on the use of participatory research and empowerment oriented evaluations (see for example, Fetterman and Wandersman, 2007). The principles and methods discussed in these approaches should be carefully considered because they promote greater community and service-user control over both the evaluation process and results. For example, a number of research studies conducted in Aboriginal communities now incorporate the principles of Aboriginal ownership, control, access, and possession (OCAP) sanctioned by the Assembly of First Nations (First Nations Centre, 2007).

To this point we have described policy analysis and evaluation as if all activities were carried out in relation to a single policy. In fact, policy-making often involves the development of several policies embedded within a more general policy direction. This requires the coordinated assessment and development of several policies at different levels, often simultaneously. For example, a new general policy in health care designed to integrate community and institutional-based services is likely to require a new role for hospitals, as well as several new policies that might affect training, use, and expenditures within hospitals. For community-based health care services there will also be a number of new policies, such as an increased emphasis on home care, that may emerge from this more general policy change. In circumstances such as these, policy analysis and evaluation must be concerned with both the actual and the anticipated effects of several different policies. Different methods and sources of data as well as different approaches to analysis should be used in more comprehensive policy studies, and multiple policy recommendations that reflect a more coordinated approach to policy development in a particular field of practice is the desired goal. Unfortunately, this more integrated approach to policy evaluation and reform is all too rare in the human services.

The remainder of this chapter focuses on policy analysis. As noted in the introduction to the chapter, policy analysis focuses in more detail on tasks to be undertaken in analyzing the problem at the initiation stage of policy-making and the assessment of policy alternatives at the formulation stage.

## Using Special Lenses in Policy Analysis

Approaches to policy analysis can be distinguished by the relative emphasis placed on 'content' or 'process' issues. A content approach stresses the actual ingredients of a policy, that is, the substance of the policy, its goals and value preferences, and the types of benefits it provides. We provide an example of this approach to policy analysis in the next section. The contents of policies are important because these are related to actual or anticipated results. However, content approaches do not focus on how policies emerge and why they are developed in a particular fashion. For example, content approaches pay little attention to the political processes that shape policy-making and the trade-offs and compromises that may characterize the policy development stage. As noted in Chapter One, this is one of the appealing attributes of the garbage can model of policy-making. A pure content approach to policy analysis may also tend to reinforce an elitist approach to policy analysis in that the policy expert, as an 'armchair critic', gathers data on the policy issue, subjects these data to critical scrutiny, and draws conclusions about the potential effects of the policy.

Without minimizing the importance of analyses of policy contents, we argue that process considerations must also be included as components in a preferred model for policy analysis. A process approach to policy analysis pays more attention to who influences the development of policies, how action is generated, and who makes decisions (Flynn, 1992). Additional considerations include questions of feasibility and how the implementation stage will affect the intent of a new policy on the ground. These considerations demand that policy analysts get out of their offices and discuss some of these issues with service users and staff responsible for delivering new programs. From a process perspective, policy analysis and policy-making are understood as an ongoing set of activities that involves creating and adapting policies and programs. This approach is consistent with efforts to encourage ongoing inclusiveness and connections between practice and policy. As well, process questions such as who influences policy development and how policy provisions are implemented enable the use of this information in trying to influence changes to particular policies or programs. Process considerations, then, place an emphasis on policy analysis as an exercise in information-sharing as well as information-gathering; in addition, activities may include negotiation and partisan-based advocacy. At the end of the day, any analysis of a policy must be designed to make a contribution to policy-making or policy change. If policy analysis is not undertaken with this goal in mind, it will remain aloof from practice and disconnected from the change process.

One approach that attempts to integrate content and process concerns is the identification of a special lens or focus, often framed as a series of questions, to assess the particular impact of a policy on special groups in the population. Special lenses have become quite popular in policy analysis but one of the earlier versions of this approach was the family impact model (Spakes, 1984). In this approach, policies are assessed for their impact on the membership function in families, the economic function, and the socialization/nurturance function.

The identification of special effects can help to focus policy attention on traditionally neglected aspects of the policy-making process. For example, health and social service policy questions that focus on impacts related to women, minority groups, and front-line service providers can be routinely incorporated as components of policy analysis if this approach is adapted to reflect such considerations. Three illustrative examples of special lenses are identified below.

Anti-racist and anti-colonial lenses are identified in the literature, and an Aboriginal framework for social work practice that includes five core elements has been proposed by McKenzie and Morrissette (2003). These are: (a) recognition of a distinct Aboriginal worldview; (b) recognition of the effects of colonialism; (c) recognition of the importance of Aboriginal identity or consciousness; (d) appreciation of the value of cultural knowledge and traditions in promoting healing and empowerment; and (e) an understanding of the diversity of Aboriginal cultural expression. These elements do not constitute a fully developed Aboriginal lens for policy analysis, but they do highlight some considerations that can be used for this purpose. For example, the substance or contents of a policy affecting Aboriginal people needs to be designed to respect the distinct world view of Aboriginal people as well as the cultural diversity among Aboriginal people.

Because policy analysis is also about process considerations, methods of analysis in an Aboriginal context should include a commitment to collaborative, community-based strategies for data collection; the promotion of indigenous knowledge and methods, where appropriate; and a requirement that culturally appropriate responses will be determined by Aboriginal people.

A framework for assessing the impact of a policy on women's equality was developed by the British Columbia Ministry of Women's Equality in 1994. This framework identified an analytical lens, which included questions about whether knowledge, ways of working, and consultation processes were inclusive of women and women's perspectives. A second lens, identified as a factor lens, focused attention on outcomes and their impact on equality for women.

A more gender inclusive framework was later developed that outlined a more comprehensive approach to analysis incorporating eight phases of work (British Columbia Ministry of Community, Aboriginal and Women's Services, 2003). A summary of these phases is provided in Table 4.3, and it is noted that these stages are generally consistent with those outlined in the gender-based guide for policy-making developed by the Status of Women Canada (1998).

The disability lens is a third example and one model is that developed by the Government of British Columbia (n.d.). In this model a checklist has been developed which includes questions relevant to the following considerations in the design of services for people with disabilities:

- consultation and data collection;
- accessibility and appropriate accommodation;
- discrimination and legal implications;
- economic status, education, training and development;
- communication;
- safety and protection from victimization; and
- health and well-being.

**Table 4.3**    **Steps in Integrating Gender Analysis within the Policy and Program Development Cycle**

| | |
|---|---|
| **Phase 1** | **Identify and Define the Issue** <br> • Consider the key factors affecting men and women (e.g., income levels, family responsibility, diversity). |
| **Phase 2** | **Define Goals and Outcomes** <br> • Determine the gender composition of people to be affected by the policy and anticipated outcomes for women and men. <br> • Consider gender-specific factors that could affect outcomes and whether goals of the policy need to be modified to address barriers. <br> • Review any evaluations or data that exist on policies or programs which goals and target populations are similar. |
| **Phase 3** | **Define Inputs** <br> • Determine whether relevant information is available by gender and, when consultations occur, include women and men. |
| **Phase 4** | **Conduct Research** <br> • Consult women and men in the design of research and ensure gender specific data can be collected. <br> • Collect both quantitative and qualitative information. |
| **Phase 5** | **Develop and Analyze Options** <br> • Consider how each option will affect women and men as a key element in analysis. <br> • Consider how each option can be monitored and evaluated to determine the impact on women and men. |
| **Phase 6** | **Recommendations** <br> • Review recommended options in light of legal, economic, social, or cultural constraints to the full participation of women and men in society and identify these impacts in any decision-making documents (e.g., briefing notes, policy documents). <br> • Outline methods to ensure the recommended policy or program is implemented in a manner that considers gender. |
| **Phase 7** | **Communication** <br> • Use communication strategies that will reach women and men from diverse communities. |
| **Phase 8** | **Assess Quality** <br> • Design, implement, and interpret evaluations that assess the impacts on both women and men. |

**Source:** Adapted from British Columbia Ministry of Community, Aboriginal and Women's Services (2003), *Guide to Best Practices in Gender Analysis.*

Special lenses may be used as a supplementary policy analysis tool, although some, such as the *gender inclusive lens* outlined in Table 4.3, include many of the basic requirements of a more generic model for policy analysis. The use of special lenses may not always be appropriate or necessary and, if used, guidelines and questions need to be adapted to the particular policy context or issue being considered.

# Models for Policy Analysis

One should consider whether a special lens is required in policy analysis, however, the analytical process is generally located within a framework that enables application to a wide range of policy issues. There are a variety of models for policy analysis and we draw brief attention to three examples before outlining our preferred model.

Policy analysis is not without certain limitations and we note four of these, as outlined by Westhues (2006), prior to further discussion of models for policy analysis. First, the policy analysis process can be exceedingly slow. Second, efforts to make changes in policies can be resource intensive and involve a considerable commitment of time, money, and energy. Third, even with the investment of resources it may not be possible to affect changes that are consistent with social justice principles. Finally, the policy analyst in government or in an organization often faces a dilemma about how political factors affect the presentation of proposals. Although these realities are important to consider, they should not prevent the adaptation and use of policy analysis as an essential method in promoting progressive changes.

Chambers and Wedel (2005) outline a model that can be described as a content approach to policy analysis. Two general components to the analytical process are described. One is the problem analysis component, including considerations related to definition, causal analysis, ideology and values pertaining to problem definition, and gainer and loser analysis. Results from the problem analysis stage influence policy and program elements related to the mission and goals, forms of benefits or services, eligibility rules, administration and service delivery, and financing arrangements (see Table 4.4). Value criteria are proposed for evaluating policy and program elements and these may emerge from three different sources. First, they may arise from analysis of the social problem and questions about whether the policy or program has any potential for making an impact on the social problem it is intended to solve. Second, evaluation criteria may be based on traditional value perspectives such as adequacy, equity, and efficiency. Finally, evaluation criteria may arise from the policy element itself and be reflected in objectives which have been translated into performance targets.

A second model outlined by Majchrzak (1984) includes steps based on principles of research design, such as operationalizing variables, developing the methodology, collecting data, analyzing data, and proposing tentative recommendations. However, there are several adaptations to the traditional research design phase which make this model more applicable to policy analysis. For example, a first

Table 4.4     Relationship between Problem Analysis and Policy
              or Program Elements

| Problem Analysis Component | Policy or Program Element |
|---|---|
| 1. Problem definition and quantification | Influences eligibility rules, specifies target population, and can influence priorities in goal selection. May also help to estimate resources needed. |
| 2. Causal analysis | Specifies particular types of benefits or services that must be delivered. Specifies types of service providers required to deliver services or benefits when causal factors suggest particular expertise, experience or background. |
| 3. Ideology and values | Can determine type of eligibility rules and goals. Influences amount of financing to be provided. |
| 4. Gainer and loser analysis (e.g., who loses and gains, the kinds of gains and losses and how much value is involved). | Often related to the method of financing and any restrictions (e.g., insurance principle, direct payment, fees for service, service or training funding to third parties). |

Source:  Adapted from Chambers and Wedel (2005): 24

stage is introduced that requires the analyst to develop an understanding of the sociopolitical environment. This stage includes the following steps:

- Clarify the social problem.
- Identify the key policy issues.
- Analyze the legislative history, if applicable.
- Identify results from previous research or change efforts.
- Obtain organizational charts of decision-making bodies.
- Draw a model of the policy-making process.
- Interview key stakeholders.
- Synthesize the information.

In addition, she proposes a stage at the conclusion of the research process which involves an analysis of potential implementation processes, relevant organizational variables, and the political consequences of recommendations emerging from the study. Based on this analysis one can estimate the probability of implementation and determine whether any adaptations to recommendations are required to increase the likelihood of implementation without sacrificing the major benefits to be gained by policy adoption.

The two content-oriented models just described can be contrasted with a process model like the action system model. Doing policy analysis within this model involves assessing factors that might lead to a convergence of interest and then to the initiation stage where goals, means, and access to resources are considered. A third step involves considerations of how the action system can be expanded to gain legitimacy and sponsorship.

# An Integrated Model for Policy Analysis

We remind readers of the advantages in including both content and process factors, as summarized in our introduction to the use of special lenses. First, a content approach directs attention to policy outcomes: who benefits and who loses and to what extent. But process considerations are also important because they help us to understand the factors that will influence policy change and direct attention to how these must be managed to influence policy-related outcomes. Thus, we prefer an integrated value-critical model of policy analysis that includes both content and process factors and permits the inclusion of special criteria to assess the effects on diverse populations. It has been noted that process models encourage a more inclusive approach to policy analysis; thus, we include specific guidelines in the *Integrated Model for Social Policy Analysis* to reinforce the importance of this approach.

Our proposed model is accompanied by the following qualifications. First, policy analysis, like policy-making, is not a linear process, and related tasks must be approached with adequate recognition of this fact. Second, the tasks in policy analysis are affected by the scope of the problem or issue being considered. For example, estimating the policy effects from major changes in legislation is a more complex undertaking than an analysis of program options for adolescent sex offenders in a particular community. Nevertheless, the general process is similar. Third, supplementary questions or considerations should be incorporated whenever necessary, but this is particularly true when assessing small-scale policies at the organizational level. The proposed model has five stages: (1) problem identification and goal specification, (2) selection of value criteria, (3) assessment of alternatives, (4) feasibility assessment, and (5) recommendations. As this outline indicates, the model is applied to both problem analysis and policy analysis tasks in the policy-making process.

## 1. Problem Identification and Goal Specification

Policy analysis begins with an examination of the problem or need, and several key questions are important to consider:

1.  What is the nature of the problem?
2.  Who are the people experiencing the problem, and what are their characteristics?
3.  How does the problem affect individuals, the community, and society?

4. What are the barriers to services at this time for the particular group of people most affected by the problem?
5. Who recognizes that the problem exists?
6. What are the causes of the problem, including relevant theoretical considerations and historical factors?
7. Are there ethnic, gender, and class considerations in identifying the problem?
8. What previous strategies have been tried and what has been their level of success?

There is some overlap between these questions and results that might be obtained from a needs assessment study. However, information on needs is used to begin to identify solutions or possible responses to a problem. In addition, a comparative study of needs may help to support the development of a policy response to the problem. As noted earlier, a needs assessment should be accompanied by the development of an inventory of strengths and resources, particularly when any new policy is directed at a community or special group. It is particularly important to identify those likely to be affected by the policy change, how service users are expected to respond to the new policy, and the desired outcomes. Relevant actors and interest groups—and the extent of their power and influence—should also be identified at this stage. A related consideration is the salience of the issue. *Issue salience* refers to the ability of the issue to give rise to group action; thus, it is relevant in assessing the potential strength of interest group influence that might be mobilized around the issue. It is also particularly important to review data on policies or programs where the goals and target populations are similar to those outlined in the policy issue being considered.

In examining an existing policy at the agency or program level, there are some additional questions to consider:

1. What is the basis for policy legitimacy and where does this authority or responsibility lie?
2. Does the desired outcome require system change or system maintenance?
3. What is the level of agreement regarding the policy?
4. What is the nature of linkages between the agency and other relevant systems in the policy environment?

Although we distinguish between policy analysis—completed prior to the implementation of a new policy—and policy evaluation—completed after the execution or implementation stage—this model can be used in both situations. When policy evaluation is involved, students frequently ask whether to focus on the problem that the existing policy was designed to address or whether they should focus on the problems apparent with the existing policy response. In general, we advise limiting the problem analysis stage to an assessment of the problem as it is currently being experienced.

## 2. Identification of Value Criteria

The second stage in this model is the identification of relevant value criteria. Like the value-criteria model for policy-making, we include the identification of both general criteria and selective criteria that are specific to the policy issue under consideration. Effectiveness and efficiency are essential criteria, and efficiency assessment may include strategies such as cost, cost-effectiveness, or benefit–cost analysis. Another consideration is adequacy. Adequacy and effectiveness are related concepts, yet it is sometimes important to distinguish between the two. Adequacy can be defined as *the extent to which the provision of benefits or services meets the identified need for particular target group members or the group in general.* Effectiveness, on the other hand, is directly related to the outcome goals and objectives of the policy.

Two other general value criteria we include are (1) the policy's impact on rights, statuses, and social justice, and (2) the ability of the policy to promote self-determination among service users.

Special or selected value criteria may be identified based on the policy issue under consideration. One example of special criteria that may need to be considered is whether or not service users and front-line staff have had opportunities to participate in shaping the policy response under consideration. This participatory element is often omitted from general policy-making models although, in practice, efforts are sometimes made to elicit some input from these constituencies.

Another important consideration is what Flynn (1992: 90) refers to as the SCRAPS test. This test is designed to focus special attention on issues of sexism, classism, racism, ageism, and poverty; the acronym is intended to remind the policy analyst that those who are the victims of such discrimination are likely to receive only 'scraps' without any compensatory attention paid to these issues. Other types of discrimination, such as heterosexism and ablism, should also be added to this list. During this second step, one can also adopt a special lens that focuses attention on cultural, gender, or other issues. For example, policies that are likely to have a particular impact on women might be assessed by questions emerging from the gender-lens perspective.

The specification of value criteria is included at an early stage in the policy analysis process, although it should be noted that values can also be examined later, particularly in assessing an existing agency policy or in completing an evaluation study of a policy. It is worth repeating that any approach to policy analysis that gives limited attention to values will be incomplete.

Three issues are particularly relevant to the value criteria stage in policy analysis. First, the model of policy analysis outlined here requires the explicit identification of criteria to be used in assessing alternatives and identifying your preferred policy choice. There is an advantage to being explicit about value criteria because these will have a major impact on the policy decision, and their identification supports the goals of transparency and accountability in policy analysis.

Second, value criteria are often used to assess both the existing policy response and alternatives that are generated to respond to the problem. This may be required if policy analysis tasks involve the assessment of different policy options where a policy response already exists. There are two approaches to consider in completing your policy analysis study where a policy already exists. One is to assess the status quo as one of the policy options and apply value criteria at this stage of the process. A second option is use value criteria to assess the existing policy response prior to identifying and assessing alternatives. It is difficult to provide advice on which approach is preferred because this is somewhat dependent on context. If the status quo can be considered a viable option we prefer applying value criteria at the stage of assessing alternatives. On the other hand, if the existing policy response is recognized as so inadequate that any type of change from what exists is needed, a preliminary review of this response may be considered in the problem analysis stage or prior to the specification of new alternatives.

Finally, as noted in Chapter One in our discussion of the value criteria model of policy-making, it is important to recognize that the selection of value criteria is not intended to be an arbitrary exercise that allows analysts to simply impose their particular values on the policy under consideration. Like the conclusions emerging from other types of data, most value criteria should be logically defended as important to the policy question under consideration. Part of this justification may emerge from the problem analysis stage in that these results may foreshadow values to be considered in the assessment stage. Some value criteria, such as effectiveness and efficiency, are likely to be considered in most policy reviews and it is not necessary to defend these choices. Others will be selected based on the issue being considered and a rationale for these becomes more important. Examples of value criteria are illustrated in Table 4.5, but these should be selected for their relevance to the policy issue, and it is not necessary to use all of them.

We have argued earlier that policy-making in the human services imposes a professional responsibility to address issues pertaining to social justice. In spite of this ethical obligation, it is apparent that differing interpretations of value criteria can arise. However, explicit attention to values will, at least, permit more open dialogue and debate about the normative aspects of the policy issue being considered. While we stipulate this as an obligation in an ethical approach to policy analysis, we are also aware of the fact that this is often not done. In fact, new policy proposals often contain language designed to obscure rather than clarify underlying values. For example, the language of community partnerships and decentralization is often used to disguise a government's intent to off-load service responsibility to community groups and organizations. Another job in analyzing public policies, then, is distinguishing between rhetoric and reality!

## 3. Assessment of Alternatives

The third stage in policy analysis involves collecting data on alternatives to be considered to meet specified goals, which address the problem and respond to selected value criteria. Here one is estimating both the anticipated and unanticipated effects of policy alternatives. Both quantitative and qualitative data collection approaches are relevant, and techniques such as cost–benefit analysis, cost-effectiveness analysis, forecasting survey research, and other types of evaluation data may be used. Consultation with representatives of the key populations affected by the policy should also be undertaken.

New policies often emerge without adequate attention to the lessons that can be learned from research studies of various aspects of the policy or similar policies adopted elsewhere. This may be a result of strongly held political or ideological beliefs, which lead either to the selective use of research which reinforces their ideology or the complete disregard for research evidence. In these circumstances, policy-makers may omit the policy analysis stage of policy development entirely, or use it narrowly to justify a policy decision that has already been made. For example, many critics felt that the federal government's 1996 reforms to EI, which restricted benefits and increased the time periods of work required to qualify for benefits in many areas of the country, followed a process of analysis, including public consultation, that served primarily to justify a decision that had already been made rather than to identify and consider seriously a range of options for policy reform. In cases such as these, research studies or consultation processes have little integrity and even less influence. Given this scenario, what are the options? One alternative is to encourage external groups to complete an analysis of such policies. These may provide one or more alternative viewpoints on possible effects.

At a general level, policy analysis tasks pertaining to the assessment of alternatives may conclude with a clear identification of anticipated consequences. If policies pertain to agency-level issues or require a careful consideration of service delivery questions, this will be insufficient, however. In such cases, an additional concern will be the effects of policy change on organizational functioning. This may require an assessment of the nature of authority, influence, and leadership; patterns of communication; and constraints on policy adoption, including any anticipated resistance to change.

## 4. Feasibility Assessment

Feasibility assessment is identified here as a fourth stage in policy analysis. It is included as a separate stage because of its particular relevance to analysis in agency or program-level policies, and its importance to implementation issues. However, it is not a substitute for the detailed planning and preparation that must occur at the implementation stage of policy-making. In assessing feasibility, it is important to consider the type of policy instrument to be used. For example, is legal compliance required or is compliance optional? Will change be accomplished by the provision of information and increased public awareness or are new regulations, services, or benefits required? An early step in this process should involve consultation with key implementing officials and, wherever possible, with service users. Resource requirements and their availability are also key considerations at this stage.

Two other questions may be important. First, does the policy give rise to newly perceived self-interests that might mobilize opposition to the policy? Second, is there a logical link between policy options and the original problem as defined, including research or theoretical support showing that the intervention is likely to achieve the intended results? This question involves examining whether new policy options are likely to address the problem, and, if so, to what extent.

## 5. Recommendations

The final stage in policy analysis involves recommendations that may include support for, or criticism of, a particular strategy and the specification of anticipated or realized effects of particular policy. The strengths and weaknesses of a limited number of policy options may also be summarized at this point if the intent is to present a range of options to senior policy-makers for final selection. If this approach is taken, selected alternatives should be considered in relation to value criteria and their ability to address the policy problem.

Table 4.5 summarizes the integrated model for policy analysis. Although this model provides only general guidelines for application, it includes elements that encourage connections between the realities of practice and the more general policy questions confronting policy-makers. The addition of a feasibility assessment stage directs attention to the implementation stage in the policy process, and it is at this stage that the interests of policy-makers and practitioners are most likely to either collide or to coalesce in rolling out the new policy.

**Table 4.5  An Integrated Model for Social Policy Analysis**

**Stage One: Problem Identification and Goal Specification**
1. Describe the nature and scope of the problem.
2. Identify needs and strengths.
3. Identify causal factors, including assumptions, theories for explanation, and key historical factors.
4. Identify targets for change and expected outcomes (goals).
5. Identify key actors and interest groups that shape problem recognition and definition, including their power and influence.
6. Review data on the policy issue and responses where program and goals are similar, and consider diversity dimensions of the issue.
7. Consult with key stakeholders, including service users, wherever possible.

**Stage Two: Identification of Value Criteria**
1. General criteria to be considered may include:
   a) Effectiveness
   b) Efficiency
   c) Adequacy
   d) Impact on rights, statuses, and social justice
   e) Impact on service user self-determination

**Table 4.5    An Integrated Model for Social Policy Analysis (cont'd.)**

2. Special criteria specific to the policy under consideration should be identified along with a rationale for their inclusion. Special criteria may include such things as:
   a) Level of staff and consumer involvement
   b) Elements related to an adaptation of the SCRAPS test
   c) Application of elements of a special lens.

**Stage Three:  Assessment of Alternatives**
1. Consult with populations affected by the policy and ensure assessment considers these perspectives.
2. Identify alternatives to be considered.
3. Collect quantitative and qualitative data on alternatives to be assessed in relation to problem analysis, goal selection, and relevant value criteria.

**Stage Four:  Feasibility Assessment (especially for agency- or program-level policies)**
1. Identify the type of policy instrument to be used (e.g., education and awareness campaign, voluntary service option, new benefit or incentive, or regulation requiring compliance).
2. Consult with implementing officials and service users on implementation.
3. Identify the resource requirements and availability.
4. Consider whether the policy gives rise to newly perceived self-interests that need to be considered.
5. Examine whether there is a logical link (theoretical or otherwise) between the policy and the problem or goals initially identified.

**Stage Five: Recommendations**
1. Specify the policy choice and its relationship to intended goals and the identified means for goal achievement, and/or specify anticipated or actual effects flowing from a particular policy.
2. If requested, summarize the strengths and weaknesses of optional policy choices in relation to value criteria and the extent to which each option addresses the nature and scope of the problem.

# Summary and Conclusion

The stages of the policy-making process including initiation, formulation, execution, implementation, and evaluation were defined, discussed, and compared with their parallel stages in social work practice in this chapter; however, a more comprehensive discussion of the implementation stage occurs in the next chapter. Although the presentation of the stages in a linear fashion reflects a rational approach to policy-making, the process of policy-making is anything but rational and activities associated with more than one stage may be occurring at the same time; alternatively, one may go back and forth between stages. Thus, information gained in the formulation stage may alter the framing of the problem as established in the initiation stage, and the lessons learned from evaluation may well lead to modification in policy formulation or implementation after a new policy is adopted.

The importance of convergence of interest and problem definition was emphasized at the initiation stage. It is the convergence of interest or 'window of opportunity' that will determine whether a policy issue gets on the policy agenda of decision-makers, and this element is much more complicated and infused with politics than the parallel stage in practice. We substituted the notion of problem framing for problem definition in the initiation stage, because the framing of the problem draws attention to both the definitional aspects of the problem and the related need for an understanding of causality and the values that influence our understanding of contributing causes. Although we do retain the use of the term 'problem definition' elsewhere in the chapter it includes requirements to identify causal factors and the values that shape these factors.

The evaluation stage in policy-making is a critical stage and in this discussion, we explored approaches to evaluation, the overlap between policy and program evaluation, and some of the difficulties surrounding the utilization of evaluation findings in the development of new policies or in making policy changes. We also distinguished between policy analysis activities which are conducted at the formulation stage in policy-making and policy evaluation which is conducted following the implementation stage.

Considerable emphasis was placed on the development of a model for policy analysis. In this section of the chapter we explored the use of special lenses in policy analysis and identified some examples of models which can be used for policy analysis. Although the approach outlined by Chambers and Wedel (2005) incorporates value criteria, we outlined a general model that integrates content and process considerations as well as value criteria in the analytical process. This model contains some core considerations, including a critical approach to problem analysis and the specification of value criteria that can highlight social justice goals, which permit its application to a wide range of policy problems. However, it can also be supplemented by specific considerations and questions that may originate with other models or special lenses. Policy analysis is, after all, part science and part art, and applied policy analysis often uses the knowledge and skills from different perspectives and different disciplines.

# Recommended Reading

Status of Women Canada (1998). *Gender Based Analysis: A Guide for Policy-making*. Available at http://www.swc-cfc.gc.ca/pubs/gbaguide/gbaguide_e.html. This website provides a comprehensive outline of gender-based considerations on policy-making.

P.M. Kettner, R.M. Moroney and L.L. Martin, *Designing and Managing Programs: An Effectiveness-Based Approach*, 3rd edn (Thousand Oaks, CA: Sage, 2008). This book provides a step-by-step approach to program design. It includes particularly useful coverage of needs assessment, setting goals and objectives, and budgeting systems.

D.E. Chambers and K.R. Wedel, *Social Policy and Social Programs: A Method for the Practical Public Policy Analyst* (Boston: Pearson Education, 2005). This book provides comprehensive coverage of a content approach to policy analysis which incorporates value criteria as a central feature of the analytical process.

## Critical Thinking Questions

1.  Consider the policy issue of poverty for a particular target population such as children, Aboriginal people or newcomers. Apply Steps 1 and 3 of Stage One (Problem Identification and Goal Specification of the *Integrated Model for Social Policy Analysis*).

2.  Poverty reduction strategies have been proposed in some provinces, including Ontario and Quebec. Review the *Integrated Model for Social Policy Analysis*. What value criteria would you propose for strategies that might be designed to reduce poverty? Consider both general and special criteria in your answer and provide a rationale for your choices.

3.  Framing a problem is different than simply identifying a problem. What are these differences?

4.  Four different types of perspectives on need were identified in this chapter. Select a policy issue and review how these different perspectives on need might be applied to your policy issue.

5.  Think of a policy issue that affects Aboriginal people or another group of special interest to you. Design some questions or guidelines that you might use to create a special policy lens which could assist you in conducting a policy analysis study of this issue.

## Note

1. In 1994, the federal Minister of Human Resources introduced a Green Paper on social security reforms, and a parliamentary committee held public hearings in major centres across the country. However, groups and individuals wishing to make presentations had to apply in advance to be heard, and government staff and politicians reviewed these applications and selected those who would be allowed to present briefs at these public hearings.

# Chapter Five

# The Implementation Stage

As indicated in the previous chapter, there is a compelling reason for devoting a separate chapter to implementation: it is the stage of the policy process where the connections between policy and practice become virtually inseparable. Whether policies have been developed in a hurried fashion in response to a crisis or whether the process has been long and laboured, policies eventually result in programs or services provided by practitioners. At the point when practitioners become responsible for putting these programs into place they have a variety of options: they can implement the policy as intended by head office, they can improve certain provisions within their span of control to enhance benefits for service users, they can adapt procedures to better fit with existing practices without major changes to the policy, or they can resist policy implementation through non-compliance or other means.

In some circumstances policies leave head office only after a great deal of time and attention has been given to planning for implementation. The more changes required by the new policy, the more complex and larger in size the organization, the more issues and problems will occur as the policy is rolled out. Thus a provincial department of social services that has passed new legislation in child welfare will have to take into account how the changes will affect the judicial system, other departments, and community organizations. In addition, field offices across the province will react differently to the introduction of new programs and to the prospect of changing practice.

That said, we recognize that in many instances head office staff have insufficient time to devote to implementation. Initiation and formulation are the most creative and exciting stages in the policy process. Once a new policy has been approved, new opportunities or crises may demand the attention of policy-makers. Alternatively, having experienced the adrenalin rush of policy development, policy-makers may lose interest in what often seems to be the tedious work of implementation.

In this chapter, we address both the head- and field-office responsibilities for the implementation process, giving proportionately more time and attention to the field office. We begin by reviewing the literature and then turn to a consideration of more recent experiences in Canada.

## What the Literature Reveals about Implementation

The vast majority of the scholarly literature on implementation is confined to the US and contained within a fairly brief period of time. Its beginnings can be traced to the early 1970s with the publication of *Implementation: How Great Hopes in Washington are Dashed in Oakland* (Pressman and Wildavsky, 1973). Its demise occurred some 20 years later. The Pressman and Wildavsky book described the implementation of an economic development program funded by the federal government and implemented in Oakland, California. As the subtitle indicates, the story is one of disappointment not because of any wrongdoing or incompetence, but mainly because of the many and largely unanticipated difficulties encountered between the ideas identified in Washington and the realities experienced in Oakland.

A notable contribution of this book was the concept of 'clearance points'. Like a barge passing through a number of locks where the water has to be raised in order to allow it to continue, policies encounter crucial junctures where opportunities exist to alter direction. The longer the chain from head to field offices, the vaguer the statement of policy objectives, the more clearance points in place, the less likely the policy will be implemented as intended. The authors of *Implementation* argued that in order to improve implementation the number of clearance points should be kept to a minimum, objectives should be stated clearly and precisely, and the head office should take charge of the process. As the research on implementation continued, this message came to be known as the top-down approach to implementation.

After considerable experience, researchers using the top-down approach concluded that there are a number of conditions necessary for effective implementation. The conditions are summarized as:

a)   clear and consistent objectives;
b)   an adequate causal theory;
c)   a structured implementation process to ensure compliance by implementing officials;
d)   committed and skillful implementors;
e)   the support of interest groups; and
f)   a stable environment (Sabatier, 1986).

Although theoretically appealing, these conditions are rarely evident in practice. Thus, many years later, a review of the literature on the implementation of innovative in child welfare programs found that the above conditions had seldom been in place (Cameron, Karabanow, Laurendeau, and Chamberlain, 2001). In addition, the top-down approach was severely criticized for its overly optimistic assumption that the implementors would be both skillful and committed. This assumption failed to recognize the realities of the work life of front-line practitioners who, in many instances, regard new policies as unnecessarily adding to and complicating a crisis-ridden work environment.

A different perspective on implementation emerged with the work of Walter Williams, the director of the research and evaluation section of the Office of Economic Opportunity in the United States in the 1960s. During this period, Williams came to realize that many programs introduced by the Office of Economic Opportunity had not been implemented as intended and thus it was difficult, if not impossible, to determine program outcomes. Together with Richard Elmore and other colleagues at the Institute for Research on Governmental Affairs at the University of Washington, Williams focused attention on identifying the complexities inherent within implementation and cautioned that while useful, implementation research 'should not become the new hope for technical ascendance. It should not become the new bandwagon seeking the sure technological fix' (Williams, 1976: 292). In his later work Williams came to the view that front-line practitioners in field offices were the most important people in determining whether a policy would be implemented as intended:

> The main message of the implementation perspective is that the central focus of policy-making should be on the point of service delivery. . . . After the big decisions get made at the highest levels, what is done by those who implement and operate programs and projects has the critical impact on evolving policy. (Williams, 1980: 5)

Elmore carried the case further by arguing that policy-making should be turned on its head. Rather than emanating from the top (i.e., the head office), policy should be made in a 'backwards mapping fashion': 'The closer one is to the source of the problem, the greater is one's ability to influence it; and the problem solving ability of complex systems depends not on hierarchical control but on maximizing discretion at the point where the problem is most immediate' (Elmore, 1982: 21). This perspective came to be known as the bottom-up or backwards mapping approach to implementation. Chapter Six includes a recent example of the use of backwards mapping in the development of a new policy.

By the 1980s several scholars concluded that neither approach was satisfactory. Two attempts to combine the best of both are briefly noted here. Elmore converted his notion of backward mapping to forward mapping in which he acknowledged that leadership in policy-making usually emanated from politicians and senior bureaucrats. However, these policy-makers neglect field offices at their peril, and meshing the interests and commitment of both those at the top and the bottom of the organization is essential for effective implementation.

Another attempt to synthesize the approaches came from Sabatier:

In short the synthesis adopts the bottom-uppers unit of analysis—a whole variety of public and private actors involved with a policy problem—as well as their concerns with understanding the perspectives and strategies of all major categories of actors (not simply program proponents). It then combines this starting point with top-downers' concern with the manner in which socio-economic conditions and legal instruments constrain behaviour. It applies this synthesized perspective to the analysis of policy change over periods of a decade or more. . . . Finally the synthesis adopts the intellectual style or methodological perspective of many top-downers in its willingness to utilize fairly abstract constructs. (1986: 38)

Sabatier also concluded that the support of an advocacy coalition was a key component for effective implementation; indeed the combination of champions within an organization and influential supporters in the policy environment can go a long way to ensuring that a policy is adopted. But even this combination is not a sufficient guarantee that front-line staff will be committed to implementation.

Another important contribution to understanding the implementation process came from Paul Berman at the Rand Institute. Berman focused attention on the kind of policy being implemented and argued that there is a distinct difference between policies that demand a programmed approach and those requiring *adaptation* during implementation. Essentially, the argument is that some policies can be prescribed from head office while others must be adapted to the needs of local communities and different types of service users. According to Berman (1980), the differences between the two approaches are determined by assessing the following factors:

1.  scope of the change;
2.  soundness of the theory or technology underlying the change;
3.  amount of agreement among those affected as to the desirability of the change;
4.  degree of control over clearance points;
5.  availability of resources; and
6.  stability of the environment.

Analyzing the policy using these criteria determines whether it can be implemented in a rather mechanistic, rule-bound fashion or whether a considerable amount of discretion must be left to the implementors. According to Berman, policies that must be implemented in an adaptive fashion are characterized by one or more of the following characteristics: radical and/or extensive change, a tentative or weak theory underlying the change, disagreement regarding objectives of the change by those affected, limited control over clearance points, inadequate or inappropriate resources, or a turbulent environment. In the human services, implementors are primarily practitioners and they are integral to the implementation process; it is their judgment and the use of discretion that has a major impact on implementation outcomes.

By the late 1980s, the interest of the social scientists in the study of implementation had waned considerably. Peirson's (2002) search of the literature revealed that 90 articles and books on implementation were published in the 1970s and 1980s, but from 1990 to 2002 only 31 could be identified. Williams had warned that implementation should not be seen as a technological fix, but some researchers pounced on it in the hopes that it would point the way to effective policy-making. Some promising leads were discovered. For example, research revealed what should have been clear all along, namely, that a policy announced is not a policy implemented and that implementation is a neglected but crucial stage of the policy process. The research also pointed to the complexities involved in implementation and the notion of clearance points provided policy-makers with an opportunity to reduce complexity by eliminating some of these junctures. Above all, the bottom-up studies identified the pivotal significance of the field office.

Whether these insights proved to be useful to policy-makers is a moot question. One scholar argued that the research had contributed little in terms of developing 'a coherent, systematic body of knowledge or identifying strategies for effective policy implementation which would be of practical assistance to policy-makers' (Palumbo, 1987: 91). A similar view came from Alexander (1985: 411) who asserted studies of implementation had lacked 'an integrating framework' and 'if we continue to pursue this multiplicity of approaches without any integrating framework we cannot expect anything but the lack of convergence that has characterized the field to date.' In response to this multiplicity of approaches, Alexander proposed a 'conceptualization of the policy implementation process [that] sees the transformation of intent into action as a continuous interactive process' (1985: 412). The proposed *policy-program-implementation-process* consists of the development of a policy in response to a problem, the translation of the policy into specific programs, and the implementation of these programs. One contribution of this conceptualization was the recognition that what happens in each stage affects other stages in a reciprocal fashion. Thus, the experience gained in the implementation stage may result in altering the design of programs and indeed the premises underlying the initial policy stage. Despite its promise, this integrative model did not attract the attention of policy-makers, and Alexander noted in 2002 that he was not aware of where/when the model has actually been applied in empirical studies nor of other efforts made to further refine the model.

There are many things that can go wrong in implementation, as illustrated by the example of gun control in Box 5.1. Although this example highlights the problems that can plague implementation, it is also interesting to note what happened to the gun registry after the federal Conservatives were elected in 2006. The Conservative Party had been opposed to the gun registry but once in power there was concern that repealing the legislation might trigger a firestorm

## Box 5.1 An Implementation Disaster

A conspicuous and highly controversial example of implementation gone awry is the attempt of the federal government to establish a gun registry. The Act, which requires owners to register all guns, was passed in 1994 but owners were given until 1 January 2003 to complete the registration process and pay the fee. Only two-thirds of the guns in the country had been registered by that time. While some gun-owners objected to the Act on the grounds that it was an unnecessary infringement of their rights, others, including the Canadian Association of Chiefs of Police, supported the Act on the grounds that it has the potential to reduce crime. Both critics and supporters were disappointed, if not enraged, by the difficulties in implementation that plagued the Act and caused the costs to escalate from the 1994 estimate of $2 million to $860 million in 2004–05. One of the chief difficulties was the failure to develop and maintain the computer program to record the registrations. A long list of changes in the contracts to outside companies to develop appropriate software was not only responsible for increasing costs, but also caused endless frustration for owners trying to register their guns. The goal of this policy may have been sound but implementation was a disaster.

Adapted from 'Can the Gun Registry Be Saved?' (2003).

of opposition for the new minority government. Instead, the government has limited funding to this program and, starved for cash, the registry has lacked the ability to fully implement the legislative intent of the 1994 Act. Although the gun registry is still regarded as a valuable tool by police and now costs only $2.9 million a year to operate (Russell, 2009), the government has recently introduced a bill to eliminate long gun registry requirements and weaken a number of other provisions in the legislation. Fortunately, implementation does not always lead to the collapse of a new policy or program, and research on the policy process in child welfare in Manitoba and British Columbia more than two decades ago provide some lessons on implementation that remain relevant today. We review these examples next.

# Implementing Policy in Child Welfare: The Experiences of Two Provinces

McKenzie's (1989) study of the implementation processes in the decentralization of child welfare services in the city of Winnipeg during the 1980s provides some insights into the complexities of the implementation stage in policy-making. In 1982, the Manitoba government made a decision to dissolve the Children's Aid Society of Winnipeg, an agency criticized for its highly centralized and specialized approach to service. Six new, community-based child welfare agencies located in the voluntary sector were established, each governed by board of directors. The policy intent was to establish a more responsive, accessible service system that would include an increased emphasis on early intervention and family support. An implementation-planning phase, which included a central coordinating committee, was established and by April 1985 the six new agencies opened their doors.

As documented by McKenzie, within two years the number of service-delivery sites had increased from 6 to more than 20, and community advisory committees within a number of agencies had been established. These committees played a prominent role in promoting prevention programs, including resource centres and community development initiatives. There was a dramatic increase in outreach programs even though the nature and scope of these programs varied significantly across agencies. Increased service accessibility arising from this policy change also resulted in an increase in service demand; there was an increase in requests for voluntary services and an increase in child protection referrals. For example, the number of children in care increased by more than 60 per cent, and the number of family service cases almost doubled in the two-year period following decentralization (McKenzie, 1989: 153). Although the rate of change also increased in other areas of the province during this time period, Winnipeg's increase was approximately three times that of the rest of the province.

While the increased number of children in care was disconcerting to policy-makers, it is a matter of debate as to whether this indicator reflected a positive change in service quality and outcomes. It is of some interest to note that the increase in caseloads experienced in the initial stage reached a plateau and changed only modestly over the next 15 years. There is much less doubt about the influence of the policy change on outreach, prevention, and the involvement of the community in child and family service issues. All increased significantly, and these results occurred because agencies were given significant autonomy to develop initiatives that reflected local needs and priorities.

Closer analysis of this policy and the approach to implementation gives rise to some interesting observations. First, policy-makers underestimated the extent to which the demand for services would increase, and a subsequent review of workloads demonstrated the need for additional funding. Second, the coordination of services within agency boundaries increased with decentralization because staff was more visible and connected to other service providers in their neighbourhoods. However, service coordination across agency boundaries was more problematic. This problem had not been fully anticipated, and community-wide responses to issues such as child abuse were criticized as being inconsistent and somewhat worse under the new decentralized system. Third, the effects of the policy change on front-line staff were somewhat contradictory. Staff experienced higher workloads and relatively high stress levels between 1985 and 1987. At the same time, they had a relatively positive view of the policy change because they were able to participate in shaping service-delivery approaches in their local units.

These results tend to provide some support for the position that a synthesis between a more centralized and adaptive approach to implementation is required. A more centralized response is required to affect changes in resources, system-wide coordination, and compliance with general standards although even at this level a commitment to make these adjustments must be present. More responsive, effective services are also encouraged if implementing officials at the local level are given enough autonomy to develop their own approaches to service provision, within general guidelines, including the development of working relationships with other community service providers.

In British Columbia, the *Child, Family and Community Service Act* and the *Child, Youth and Family Advocacy Act* were passed by the provincial legislature in June 1994 but were not proclaimed by the lieutenant-governor until January 1996. The period between passage and proclamation (the date that the Acts became law) was devoted to planning for implementation. The Acts were the consequence of two comprehensive community-consultation processes into child welfare conducted by the Ministry of Social Services in 1991 to 1992. One consultation was devoted to the needs and views on child welfare by the First Nations people of BC and it culminated in the report *Liberating Our Children, Liberating Our Nations* (Report of the Aboriginal Committee, 1992). The opinions of other citizens were expressed in Making Changes: A Place to Start (Report of the Community Panel, 1992). Both community panel reports concluded that child welfare in BC required fundamental reform and that the welfare of children should be seen in a societal and community context that recognized that poverty, inadequate housing, and the lack of supports to families severely impacts the ability of parents to care for their children. In addition, the reports criticized the 'social cop' approach to practice that restricted the role of child welfare staff to intrusive investigations.

The process of planning for the development of the new Acts and for their implementation consumed the time and attention of head-office staff for four years. Our attention here is focused on the two-year period between 1994 and 1996, and our sources of information include *Planning for Implementation of B.C.'s Child, Family and Community Service Act* (Durie and Armitage, 1996), and interviews with a senior staff member of the ministry who was a key member of the head-office implementation team.

If time, conscious attention to planning, and resources could ensure smooth implementation, the experience in BC exemplifies such a process. A beginning list of the painstaking efforts made during the process were:

- appointment of a head-office steering committee chaired by an assistant deputy minister and staffed by two staff members in the ministry who had extensive experience in child welfare;
- forming regional committees to gain the input of front-line professionals; the regional committees were staffed by facilitators seconded from other positions in the region;
- attending to the concerns of community organizations, sister ministries, the judicial system, and the BC Employees Union, all of which would be affected by the new legislation; and

- establishing training sessions on a regional basis to acquaint staff with the objectives and provisions of the *Child, Family and Community Service Act* and the *Child, Youth and Family Advocacy Act.*

The primary reason for this careful planning was that these Acts were dedicated to changing the culture of the ministry. The plan sought to change, in a very fundamental fashion, the day-to-day practice of staff: from adversarial and intrusive to respectful and courteous approaches; from working with individuals on a one-on-one basis to group and community approaches; and from investigation and referral to purposeful planning for change.

Yet, despite this care and attention, the legislation, as eventually implemented, departed in substantial ways from the vision outlined in *Making Changes: A Place to Start* (Report of the Community Panel, 1992). For example, the section calling for family conferences as a way of making plans for children in a collaborative fashion was not implemented until 2002. What happened?

Without doubt, the most important factor was the formation of a judicial inquiry in 1994 and its subsequent report one year later (Report of the Gove Inquiry into Child Protection, 1995). Given that the ministry had just concluded two substantial reviews of child welfare, that it had followed the recommendations of the reviews and developed two new Acts, and was heavily involved in the process of implementing these Acts, it is perplexing why a minister would decide to launch a judicial inquiry into the middle of this complex and demanding process. The answer is, of course, to be found in politics and the media. A child had been killed by his mother in a small northern community and the report by the then-Superintendent of Child Welfare into the circumstances of the death was deemed to be too defensive of the performance of staff. Although the minister and the premier at first found the report quite acceptable, it was severely criticized in the legislature and in the press. Bowing to the pressure, the minister sought to deflect attention from the ministry by firing the superintendent and launching an inquiry headed by Judge Thomas Gove.

Had the preliminary and final findings of the inquiry corresponded with those of the community panels, the only effect on the work of the ministry, and in particular on those charged with the responsibility of implementation, would have been the time and energy required to attend hearings and to respond to the many demands from the inquiry for information. But from quite early days it was evident that this was not to be. As noted above, the new Acts promoted a preventive, family support approach to service provision, while the inquiry came to favour a more narrow emphasis on protecting children. Hence, conflicting messages began to swirl about the ministry and its objectives—messages that culminated in changes to the *Child, Family and Community Services Act* and in the establishment of a comprehensive, rigorous, and intrusive risk-assessment process.

This rather extensive discussion of the Gove Inquiry is important because it draws attention to the salience of the policy environment as a significant factor in implementation. Clearly, the turbulent environment disrupted the plans and painstaking efforts of policy-makers. In an interview, a senior official in the ministry who had been heavily involved in both the development and implementation stages of the legislation, identified two revealing criticisms of the process. First, he and other architects of the Act did not realize the extent to which the culture of the 'social cop' approach to practice was embedded in the ministry. Front-line staff knew how to investigate, how to interview individuals preferably in their office, and how to refer families needing counselling or other services to community agencies. Although some had experimented successfully with group and community approaches, the majority clung to the practice with which they were familiar. In spite of this, more staff might have been excited by the new approaches called for in the new legislation had not the messages emerging from the Gove Inquiry quickly dashed interest in new approaches. As Smale (1996) has noted, when all about them is changing, when organizational structures are being reconfigured, and when their practice is being scrutinized in the media, practitioners will remain committed to present modes of practice and shy away from ones that are unknown and risky.

The second criticism concerned the environment. In retrospect, the senior official noted that when major changes are involved, when the environment cannot be anticipated or controlled, the most effective strategy may well be to restrict detailed planning in head office, proclaim a new Act or new policy, and deal with difficulties as they arise—in short, to proceed more quickly with the execution stage and incorporate an adaptive approach to implementation. Although some planning is required, a lengthy drawn-out process allows resistance to mount and to magnify proposed changes to the point that they seem undesirable. After all, it is human nature to stay with the known, and as the literature on the planning of change has revealed, it will often be resisted unless incentives and rewards are provided to smooth the path of acceptance (see, among other sources, Marris, 1986).

The example of the gun registry described in Box 5.1 also supports the case for combining programmed and adaptive approaches. In that example, the federal government failed to take into account the reactions of gun-owners and the limitations of computer systems to register the estimated 7.9 million guns in the country. Careful attention to aspects of a programmed approach could have resulted in well-thought-out publicity releases that included the support of the Canadian Association of Chiefs of Police. The complexities involved in registration might have also pointed to more emphasis on an adaptive approach whereby implementation would have occurred on a province-by-province or regional basis in order to ensure that the volume of registrations could be handled, and to allow for adjustments to the system. With a more effective implementation process, it may have been much more difficult to restrict the scope of this new policy after 2006.

Two strategies for smoothing the path of resistance are noted here. First, in situations that require an adaptive approach, the involvement of front-line staff and service users at the outset of the policy process is essential. If they bring their experiences and knowledge to the policy table in the early stages of the process, the likelihood of their cooperation in the implementation stage is substantially increased. We give further attention to the contributions of front-line staff and service users in the following section and in Chapter Six. A second strategy is to incorporate the role of a 'fixer' (Bardach, 1977) within the implementation process. Fixers play precisely the role that the title implies. They anticipate difficulties in the implementation process and they find ways to eliminate or reduce the impact of these barriers. They provide information to allay worries about the new policy, referring to the experience of other jurisdictions in the implementation process and securing new funds or personnel.

## The World of the Front-Line Practitioner

Our discussion now turns to a review of the capacity and commitment of practitioners to the policy process. In theory, one would assume that because policies affect their work-life and the quality of the services to be provided, practitioners would be keenly committed to the policy process. But such an assumption ignores the fact that front-line practitioners often feel as badly treated by their employing agency as do the users of service. They feel—in many instances rightly so—underpaid, overworked, and undervalued by their employers.

The discussion is based on a number of studies of the work-life of front-line practitioners and begins with the classic book, *Street Level Bureaucracy* (Lipsky, 1980). Although Lipsky's research took place in Boston, Massachusetts, in the late 1970s, his observations are as pertinent today in many public service jurisdictions as they were almost 40 years ago. Lipsky's street level bureaucrats worked in the most difficult of circumstances; they served the poor, those who had committed crimes, and people who were mentally and physically ill. Both the street level bureaucrats and those being served were enmeshed in crises on a daily basis:

> Street level bureaucrats spend their work lives in a corrupted world of service. They believe themselves to be doing the best they can under adverse circumstances and they develop techniques to salvage services within the limits imposed upon them by the structure of their work. At best street level bureaucrats invent benign modes of mass processing that more or less permit them to deal with the public fairly, appropriately and successfully. At worst they give in to favoritism, stereotyping and routinizing. (Lipsky, 1980: xiii)

Lipsky argues that from the perspective of service users, practitioners make policy: 'The decisions of street level bureaucrats, the routines they establish and the devices they invent to cope with their uncertainties and work pressures effectively become the public policies they carry out' (Lipsky, 1980: xii). Although some service users might have recognized that policies were made by the state legislature and the Boston city council, they interacted daily with practitioners and the decisions that affected them were made by practitioners. In addition, service users were well aware that street level bureaucrats could and did exercise discretion. Thus practice varied in such matters as whether to grant emergency assistance and whether the assistance would be in cash or by voucher.

Discretion is an important but neglected concept in the human services, and it is important to recognize that it can be exercised either to enhance or limit services. Essentially, discretion involves the exercise of judgment in situations where the policy is not clear and where the circumstances of a service user is unique. Some examples illustrate the pervasiveness of discretion in the lives of all citizens: a clerk in a department store decides to answer the phone in the midst of discussing the availability of stock to a customer; a police officer pulls over a motorist and issues a ticket despite the driver's pleas that others had been travelling at far greater speed; a teacher issues a formal warning to a student for misbehaving in class but merely reprimands another for similar behaviour. Discretion is welcomed when it is applied in our favour. It is seen as unfair and capricious when we are singled out for treatment that in our opinion we do not deserve.

Policies represent the intent of organizations to ensure equity, but even the most comprehensive set of policies and attendant procedures cannot cover all situations. Inevitably, practitioners will find it necessary to exercise discretion. For example, a child welfare worker in a rural office visiting a home in response to a complaint of child neglect cannot depend completely on the policy established in legislation and regulations. The policy manuals will be back in the office, the supervisor and other senior officials may not be available for consultation, and the circumstances may be unique and outside the rubric of established policy. On the other hand, a staff member in a social assistance office will be more closely bound by policy and a supervisor will likely be available for ready consultation. Yet even such tightly regulated situations cannot prescribe what should be done in emergencies. In the ideal, discretion represents an exercise in balancing equal treatment for all and giving special attention to the unique circumstances for some. Practitioners want to act in a fair and open fashion. Although they recognize the compelling need for preferential treatment in some situations, they are fully aware that such treatment can be seen as favouritism and, in some instances, as failing to comply with policy. In the past decade the balance has swung towards policies and procedures that restrict the use of discretion. Instruments such as risk assessments and computerized reporting mechanisms require practitioners to comply with standards developed by head offices, often without input from the local level. Writing more than two decades ago, Elmore's (1982) comments on the connections between implementation and discretion foreshadowed the trend toward standardized approaches to practice:

The dominant view that discretion is at best a necessary evil and at worst a threat to democratic government pushes implementation analysis toward hierarchically structured models of the process and toward increased reliance on hierarchical control to solve implementation problems. . . . Nowhere in this view is serious thought given to how to capitalize on discretion as a device for improving the reliability and effectiveness of policies at the street level. (Elmore, 1982: 26)

Lipsky's street level bureaucrats were seen as powerful by service users; however, these same street level bureaucrats viewed themselves as oppressed and as having no capacity to contribute to or influence the policy process. In these circumstances, Lipsky argued, discretion was often used by the street level bureaucrat to maintain some degree of personal control within an alienating work environment. Support for Lipsky's findings comes from a study carried out in the Corrections Branch of the Attorney General's Ministry in British Columbia (Wharf, 1984). The study sought to identify the level of participation of field-office staff in the policy-making process of the branch. The head office of the branch was located in the provincial capital of Victoria and field offices were scattered across the province. The branch created policy advisory groups that included representation from all ranks—probation officer, district supervisor, regional director, and a policy analyst from head office. This vertical slice arrangement was developed in a deliberate attempt to gain a perspective from each level of the organization, and to use these perspectives in the policy-making process.

Despite this attempt to secure involvement, the consistent message from front-line staff was that 'policy comes from head office to regulate and to control practice' (Wharf, 1984: 24). Policy was seen by staff as out of touch with the realities of life in the field, and the constant revisions to policy manuals were viewed with amusement and as the product of head-office staff with nothing else to do.

The only exception to this view came from the staff of a newly created program in family court counselling. These counsellors worked out of field offices, but they came together on a regular basis to develop policies. This example suggests that if newly recruited and eager practitioners are given the opportunity to participate in the policy-making process, they will do so. Support for this finding also comes from Sabatier's (1986: 27) review of successful examples of implementation, which pointed to 'the importance of selecting implementing institutions supportive of the new program, and creating new agencies as a specific strategy'. It does appear, then, that in organizations where the arteries have hardened or even closed, front-line practitioners will feel oppressed and uninterested in policy and those who make it. However, newer organizations or units are more likely to be receptive in actively participating both in policy development and the design of implementation strategies.

# Centralization and Decentralization: The Variable of Distance

A final variable in their discussion of implementation relates back to the notion of clearance points but is more explicitly revealed by examining the centralization of authority. Kernaghan and Siegel (1995: 55) pose the dilemma in the following way: 'A responsive bureaucracy clearly ought to concentrate on transferring authority down the hierarchy and out in the field; yet the historical claims for a responsible bureaucracy can best be met by retaining authority close to the top where it can be used by the Minister and scrutinized by parliament.' Governments have struggled with this dilemma for decades.

At one point, the complaint will be heard that field offices have too little discretion. They cannot adapt programs to meet local needs and cannot take a leadership role in activities such as connecting with community partners. If these complaints are seen as valid, head offices may reduce their control and enhance the autonomy of field offices. However, when a different set of complaints emerge—that programs are too uneven, that programs available in one office are not provided in other locations—and when issues of incompetence arise, head offices are quick to pull in the reins and develop centralizing measures, including central agencies, restrictive regulations, and close surveillance of performance.

A further complication occurs in countries such as Canada, where governments are responsible for services to communities differing widely in terms of culture, history, and size. Head offices attempt valiantly to develop policies and programs that will be implemented in a consistent fashion across jurisdictions, but in many ways their efforts are doomed to fail. Urban neighbourhoods differ considerably from rural and remote communities. There are also other diversity-related characteristics to consider. It is self-evident that the provision of counselling services, day care, specialized health programs, and other services is heavily affected by issues such as diversity and distance.

Our discussion of the centralization–decentralization dilemma is further illuminated by the findings of a national study of front-line public servants (Carroll and Siegel, 1999). These researchers interviewed 97 federal and 123 provincial civil servants during a two-year period from 1993 to 1995. The study sought to collect information about the work-lives of civil servants in field offices: what do they do, how, and under what conditions? In particular, the study focused on the relationships and interactions between head- and field-office personnel. The authors claimed at the time that the study represented 'the first broadly based study on the function of civil servants and in particular the vast majority of those who work in field offices delivering services to the public' (1999: 27). As they noted, 'Field people felt that head offices believe that field officers do not know what to do or how to do it. This perception existed almost everywhere but varied in intensity by province, department and functional areas' (1999: 203).

The study concluded that the greater the geographic distance between head and field offices, the greater the autonomy of field offices. As long as they perform their responsibilities in an appropriate and adequate fashion, as long as no serious complaints of incompetence are heard, and as long as troublesome personnel issues do not arise, field offices in remote locations exist in relative isolation from the head office. This finding is similar to that observed in the Corrections Branch study cited earlier. In that study, a probation officer in a small BC office captured the point succinctly: 'We are on the periphery and we like it that way. We just purr along and no one bothers us' (Wharf, 1984: 39).

Both positive and negative consequences can accrue from the autonomy afforded by distance. An example of positive consequences comes from the examination of a child welfare office in northern British Columbia in 2002. Like a pendulum, policy directions from head office in Victoria have swung over time from a very residual approach to child welfare to an approach focused on early intervention and supporting families and back to the 'social cop' style of work. Regardless of these policy shifts, the Hazelton office had carved out its own mode of practice. In the words of a long-time community resident, '[T]he community makes the office' (Wharf, 2002: 51). Implied in this remark was the fact that the child welfare workers in Hazelton had tuned their practice to the culture and traditions of the communities they served. Staff saw themselves as members of the community; they were open to the community by listing their phone numbers and by responding to after-hours requests. They involved family members, other professionals, and concerned citizens in determining plans for a particular child. This style of work enabled the staff to win the respect of the surrounding communities and to be able to call for help when they required it. To illustrate, from 1998 to 2003 the Hazelton office took 225 children into its care, but parental consent for this action was given in all but two cases.

We need to note that isolation also affords an opportunity for the development of the condition of 'acute localitis' (Montgomery, 1979), whereby standards and practices that are at variance with those outside the community can occur. Acute localitis allowed the conditions of incest and child abuse to continue over a period of years in the isolated community of Kings County, Nova Scotia (Cruise and Griffiths, 1997). Clearly, the autonomy afforded by distance provides an opportunity for innovative staff to exercise their creativity and to adopt an adaptive approach to implementation. Just as clearly, staff who feel overwhelmed by their responsibilities, who are worried about making independent judgments, who, in short, are not well trained or experienced, require more supervision from a central or regional office to ensure adequate and effective services.

## Summary and Conclusion

Since implementation is an integral part of the overall policy process, suggestions for improvement are best left to a discussion of reforming the entire process, and these reforms are discussed in more detail in subsequent chapters. Nevertheless, it is useful to pave the way for these discussions by summarizing some of the main points identified in this chapter.

In our view, the distinction between programmed and adaptive approaches to implementation is extremely useful. The implementation of the *Child, Family and Community Service Act* in BC affords a very compelling example of the frustrations encountered when a prolonged programmed planning approach to implementation was taken. In that example, earlier implementation coupled with a more adaptive approach during the field implementation stage might have been more effective.

Carroll and Siegel's (1999) study of front-line civil servants also reinforces the case for adaptive approaches. Not only does effective implementation rest in the hands of staff in local or field offices, but these individuals are also described as 'the most important people in government' (1999: 3). These authors ask, 'Why can't policy and administrative changes originate in field offices? After all, if they are going to be implemented in field offices eventually why not allow them to flow from the field offices in the first place?'

The phrasing of these questions reinforces the findings of earlier researchers who argued for closer attention to bottom-up approaches to implementation. The need for more attention to an adaptive or bottom-up model of implementation should not be interpreted to mean that central office is off the hook. In fact, an adaptive approach to implementation requires that central office staff respond in a positive way to the problems identified by front-line practitioners during the implementation process. In effect, an adaptive approach calls for inclusiveness in policy-making. In the next chapter we present a number of these approaches and assess their potential for improving the policy process.

# Recommended Reading

E. Alexander, 'From Idea to Action: Notes for a Contingency Theory of the Policy Implementation Process', *Administration and Society* 16, 4 (1985), 403–6 and P. Sabatier, 'Top-Down and Bottom-Up Approaches to Implementation Research: A Critical Analysis and Suggested Synthesis', *Journal of Public Policy*, 1, 1 (1986), 21–48. These two articles provide critical appraisals of theory and research on implementation.

M. Lipsky, *Street Level Bureaucracy* (New York: Russell Sage Foundation, 1980). This is one of the most influential studies of policy-making and direct practice.

B. Carroll and D. Siegel, *Service in the Field* (Kingston, ON: McGill-Queen's University Press, 1999). This Canadian study of the relationship between field and head offices provides a useful critique of the traditional bureaucratic model of operations.

W. Williams, *The Implementation Perspective* (Berkeley, CA: University of California Press, 1980). This book provides supporting evidence for a bottom-up approach to implementation.

# Critical Thinking Questions

1.  Top-down or *programmed* and bottom-up or *adaptive* approaches to implementation were described in this chapter. Identify some policy examples where it might be appropriate to place more emphasis on top-down approaches and some examples where more emphasis on a bottom-up approach is required. Defend your choices.

2.  A synthesis of programmed and adaptive approaches to implementation was suggested as having some advantages in implementation. How might front-line practitioners and supervisors be involved in this model?

3.  Most literature on implementation neglects the role of service users. How realistic is it for service users to become involved in shaping implementation? How could they be more involved and on what issues might their involvement be most critical? What barriers exist to greater involvement of service users and how might these be overcome?

4.  The concept of discretion can be used to enhance or restrict benefits and services to those who require these. Identify examples of each from a field of practice with which you are familiar.

5.  In some cases new policies impose increased costs on service users, and the exercise of discretion by front-line service providers might involve ignoring these policies or undercutting these policies in certain ways. Can you identify some of the factors that might either increase or minimize the degree of personal risk to the front-line practitioner in these circumstances?

# Chapter Six

# Inclusive Approaches to Policy-Making

In this chapter we identify both models and processes that can promote more inclusive approaches to policy-making. We begin with a brief discussion of citizen participation, and then provide a brief summary of approaches to planning and policy analysis that may promote increased participation if there is a genuine commitment on the part of policy-makers or policy analysts to respect this fundamental principle. We examine several specialized approaches or models that can be deliberately designed to incorporate the principle of inclusivity. These are backwards mapping, which was discussed in Chapter Five as an approach to implementation, shared decision-making, policy communities, and community governance. In each case, examples are identified in an effort to critically examine the potential of these models to improve the policy-making process. In Chapter Ten more detailed case studies of shared decision-making, policy communities, and community governance in an Aboriginal context are presented. We need to remind ourselves that a more inclusive or participatory approach to policy-making also carries two somewhat interrelated risks. First, it does not always lead to policy-making that might be defined as progressive in social justice terms. Citizen movements reflecting a 'tough on crime' approach to criminal justice reforms reflect one such example. Second, and somewhat related, is the ability of those with greater privilege to exercise more control over participatory processes and to shape the outcomes of these processes in their interests. Thus the outcomes from inclusive models need to be critically examined to ensure that processes are managed in a way that permits the voices of all groups to be heard and considered. If this occurs then the results need to be respected even though they might not reflect everyone's first preferences. Central to this process is the principle of affected interests which is discussed in the next section.

# The Case for Citizen Participation

The literature on citizen participation in social policy is voluminous and our discussion is brief in the extreme (see among other sources, Phillips and Orsini, 2002, and Wharf-Higgins, Cossom, and Wharf, 2006). We simply wish to establish that there has been a long-standing debate in representative democracies about whether citizens should participate in making social policy and if so, how. Is it sufficient to rely on those elected to the various levels of government to make policy? David Zussman, an advisor to Jean Chrétien, when he was prime minister and a former president of an Ottawa think tank, the *Public Policy Forum*, answers the question in the affirmative: 'I think a majority of Canadians say to themselves, "Look, I sent you to Ottawa, so do your job and don't keep asking me what the right answer is. Go ahead and do it yourself "' (Zussman, quoted in May 2002: A15). We disagree, and our position was outlined earlier in the book where we have argued that such an arrangement results in domination of the policy process and its outcomes by elite members of society. Moreover, this approach to centralizing policy-making authority leads to the loss of civil society where citizens become too accepting of the authority of those in power to make decisions for them. In the extreme this leads to a loss of civil society, a decline in 'active citizenship' and an increased acceptance of 'feelings of disempowerment'. This process can be understood by examining the long term effects of oppression in a number of countries, including the contemporary responses of many citizens in Eastern Europe to the highly centralized decision-making apparatus that characterized the Communist era. In these countries there are incredible acts of bravery in contesting corruption and the abuse of centralized authority but there is also deference to authority among many that leads to complacency and resignation.

Closer to home, the long-standing debate on the continuing concentration of power in the office of the prime minister reached crescendo proportions in the latter months of 2002. In the words of former Prime Minister Paul Martin: 'We have permitted a culture to arise that has been some 30 years in the making, one that can be best summarized by the one question that everyone in Ottawa believes has become the key to getting things done: "Who do you know in the PMO (The Prime Minister's Office)?"' (quoted in Clark, 2002: 1). Martin focused his campaign for the leadership of the Liberal Party on the case for overcoming the 'democratic deficit'. Although he succeeded Jean Chrétien as prime minister in 2003, he remained in power only until 2006 when he was replaced by Stephen Harper and the Conservatives. Although some efforts were made to extend more power to back-benchers, Paul Martin was prime minister for too short a period of time to assess whether his commitment to more democracy at this level would have made much of a difference. The present Conservative government retains the old pattern of concentrating power in the PMO.

Selective reforms to the centralized representative style of governance that exists in Canada were identified in Chapter Three, including an increased emphasis on information sharing, relaxing the rules on charitable donations so that such organizations could speak out on issues without fear of jeopardizing their funding, and promoting the responsibility of public and community organizations to build more approaches that involve service users and community members in policy design. Other suggestions include electing rather than appointing members to the Senate and vesting some authority with that body, giving more power to backbenchers and allowing them to vote according to their conscience rather than having to toe the party line and referenda. These suggestions merit further consideration; however, there are important implications to consider. For example, Senate reform would require significant modifications to our current governance model in which authority rests primarily with the House of Commons. However, we are quite wary of using referenda to settle contentious public issues. Such issues require careful study and debate and the members of the public are rarely provided with both adequate information and the opportunity for full study and reflection on these issues. In addition, as a referendum held in BC in 2002 on Aboriginal treaty claims clearly showed, the wording of referenda can be slanted in such a way as to make it much more likely that a state desired outcome will receive approval. As noted in Chapter Three, we are supportive of some form of proportional representation as a way of giving voice to minority viewpoints, but note that this is likely to result in a need for coalition governments in many jurisdictions, including the federal level.

All of these suggested reforms focus on general models of governance rather than approaches to making decisions on the ordinary issues of social policy. Our case for the use of more specialized approaches introduced in this chapter is anchored in the principle of *affected interests* as outlined by Dahl (1970: 64) and summarized in the Introduction: 'Everyone who is affected by the decision of a government should have a right to participate in that government.' Dahl concedes that the principle lacks specificity and gives rise to some thorny issues. He suggests that the criteria of *personal choice, competence*, and *economy* can be helpful in applying the principle. Personal choice refers to the right of individuals to choose to participate or to opt out. Competence suggests that not all individuals can tackle situations requiring advanced skill and knowledge. The criteria of economy mean that in issues where a large number of people are affected, some means of representation must be established.

The principle of affected interests has particular relevance to social policy and to models of policy-making. For example, most parents are deeply concerned about the well-being of their children, and often become active participants in school-based activities, including parent councils or School Board meetings, day care centres, or community recreation centres. Given the opportunity to participate many parents meet the criteria established by Dahl: they are knowledgeable about the needs of children and are prepared to contribute. We do acknowledge that not all citizens have the time or the inclination to participate in matters that affect them, and we are also aware that one of the reasons for this lack of participation is that opportunities have traditionally been restricted to meetings held in locations and at times that are inappropriate for many. We are also aware that as governments assume more and more control over local matters, such as school boards, the interest in local participation tends to decline. That is, as the opportunity to exercise influence in decisions that affect our interests declines so too will the commitment to engagement. If this is true, then the converse also applies: if local decision-making will affect the nature and scope of the human services, then given opportunities citizens will engage in activities to affect these decisions.

Prior to discussing our list of inclusive models or approaches we note the following observations. First, these approaches respect the principle of affected interests by including at least representatives of those affected by policies in the policy-making process. Second, and somewhat paradoxically, the adoption of any of these models requires a commitment by senior policy-makers, whether these are Ministers and CEOs in public sector organizations or boards of directors and CEOs in voluntary agencies, to relinquish some control and facilitate meaningful participation. Third, all contain limitations and we note these in the concluding section of the chapter.

# Enhancing Participation in General Models of Planning and Policy Analysis

A strategy that is sometimes used as a means to secure involvement from those affected by policies within an organization is to create a policy group composed of representatives from different levels of the organization. We refer to this as the *vertical slice approach* because it often includes representatives from front-line service providers, supervisors, program managers, and senior policy-makers. This model may also include service users, and although we advocate the inclusion of service users this does not always occur. Policy groups structured in this way can be assigned responsibility for developing, reviewing, and changing policies within the organization whether these pertain to substantive issues or more functional matters. Such groups can be quite effective in implementation planning, particularly if an adaptive approach to implementation is being used because participants understand the special needs and issues that that exist at different levels of the organization.

The vertical slice approach can allow both service users and front-line staff opportunities to learn about budgets and the political aspects of policy-making while at the same time providing senior level policy-makers with much needed information on the realities experienced by service users and front-line staff. Based on our experience this approach is likely to be most effective in organizations where there is some level of commitment to and experience with a more participatory style of decision-making. As noted in the previous chapter, the vertical slice approach enjoyed only limited success in integrating field office input within the policy-making process of the BC Corrections Branch (Wharf, 1984). This strategy was less effective when applied to ongoing policy changes, such as reviewing and updating policy manuals, but was more highly valued where policies for implementation in a new program were being developed. When using a vertical slice approach, it would appear that two factors help to encourage meaningful participation. One is a commitment by senior staff to treat suggested changes seriously and be accountable in responding to recommendations emerging from such a policy group, and a second may be the need to ensure that those who are recruited as members are committed to the process.

The vertical slice approach is not a panacea for organizational reform or major policy change. In circumstances like these the approval of recommended policies often lies some distance from the policy group; their ability to influence these decisions may be quite limited. There is also a membership accountability issue with the vertical slice approach. Are participants accountable for the views they express to their peers who come from different levels of the organization or do they exercise their own judgments as individuals once they are selected?

# Backwards Mapping

In Chapter Five we noted the salience of the backwards mapping approach to implementing policy and here we argue that the approach has merit in the development of new policies. The approach essentially requires that policy development begin by going back to identify the problems and their characteristics as these are being experienced by service users and practitioners.

A recent initiative of the Ministry for Children and Family Development in British Columbia provides an example of backwards mapping in creating a distinct policy for kinship care. By way of background it should be noted that children have been placed in the care of extended family members in a number of ways: by purely informal arrangements between parents and relatives; in a more formal way by the Ministry under the provisions of the *Child, Family and Community Service Act*; and through the Child in the Home of a Relative (cihr) program provided by the Ministry of Employment and Income Assistance. Each of these alternative placement arrangements differ in terms of the amount of resources provided to caregivers, the kind of assessment undertaken prior to placement and the on-going support provided by the state.

These arrangements have been in place for many years and may well have continued had they not come under scrutiny during the development of the Ministry's new action plan, *Strong, Safe and Supported: A Commitment to B.C.'s Children and Youth*. This plan contains several 'pillars' each devoted to improving services to children and youth: prevention, early intervention, intervention and support, the Aboriginal approach, and quality assurance. In reviewing the early intervention pillar it became quickly evident the current arrangements for kinship care were inadequate and should be revised. The interest of the Ministry in undertaking the review received support from a report by the Provincial Child Advocate. Following an inquiry into the death of a First Nations child who had been placed in kinship care, the Advocate strongly recommended the Ministry develop a policy for kinship care that would formalize all aspects of these previously rather haphazard arrangements.

Although the Ministry has on many occasions solicited the advice of service users, staff, and community members, consulting front-line staff and service users has by no means been a constant and regular feature in creating policy. In this particular instance the Ministry made a formal commitment to an extensive process of consultation. Without explicitly acknowledging the principle of affected interests as a well known concept in the political science literature, it essentially adopted it as the guiding principle for the process. For example, the draft report summarizing the results of the consultations noted that 'it is important that those who are directly affected by policy, including service providers who use it in their practice, as well as children, family and community members who receive services, have a voice in the development of policy. When practice informs policy we can expect policy to be effective in achieving the expected results' (Ministry of Children and Family Development [MCED], 2008: 17). For a number of reasons, including the need to pay attention to the criteria of economy, the consultations were restricted to the Vancouver Island Region of the Ministry. However, the number of consultations was extensive. According to the MCED: 'Close to 250 people were involved, including 70 staff members of the Ministry, 30 foster parents, 50 other service providers, and 95 kinship care givers' (2008: 18).

Incorporating an evaluative component to this backwards mapping initiative was made possible by a rather fortuitous meeting between the Regional Director for Vancouver Island and one of the authors (i.e., Wharf). During the meeting the Director noted that before proceeding to obtain approval for the draft report from other regions and from head office, he wanted to know if it fairly represented the views of those who had been consulted. Because of his interest in learning whether the backwards mapping approach could be used as an inclusive approach to new policy development and be effective in promoting change, Wharf agreed to undertake this review. While it was impossible to meet with all who had participated, a day-long meeting was held with 10 staff members of the Ministry and a representative from a First Nations child and family services agency.

The participants were unanimous that their views were adequately represented in the draft report and that it represented the essential components for a new policy on kinship care. Furthermore, they urged that such a policy be developed and implemented as soon as possible, and that if other regions in the province expressed reservations about the report, it should be implemented on a pilot basis on Vancouver Island. Nevertheless, several concerns were expressed, and most centred around one central issue: the need to end the tradition whereby new policies prescribe how policies are to be carried out but neglect to provide the resources required. The resources required for kinship care include remuneration for caregivers and medical coverage for children. Greider (1992) notes that policies which fail to include necessary resources are 'empty policies'.

At the time of writing, the draft report had not yet been approved; thus, the utility of using the principle of affected interests cannot be fully assessed, nor is it an integral component of the work of the Ministry. Nevertheless, the initiative was well received by participants and does represent an example of progressive policy development—perhaps an exception from prevailing practice but one which should be recognized for its potential in breaking with tradition.

# Shared Decision-Making

One example of shared decision-making comes from the work of the Commission on Resources and Environment (CORE) established by the BC provincial government in 1992. CORE was given the responsibility of developing land use plans in four regions of the province that had been characterized by intense conflict between the forest industry, local communities, and environmental groups. 'The key challenge was to develop a participation process that would enable strongly opposed and politically influential public interest groups to reconcile their differences in a manner that would permit the government to act decisively on many highly controversial land use issues. CORE proposed round table style decision-making (shared decision-making) in which all affected parties would participate in the development of regional land use plans' (Owen, 1998: 83). At first glance, it may seem curious to feature an example concerned with environmental issues in a book focused on the human services. We include CORE for two reasons. First, reaching agreement on land use plans has been extremely difficult, marked by hostile relationships and even violence. If land use plans can be developed, there may well be hope for resolving other issues. Second, CORE represents a particularly sophisticated example of shared decision-making and therefore there is much to learn from its experience.

Although government participated in the roundtables, it did so as one participant, not as the ultimate source of authority. It was made clear at the outset that if agreement could be reached by the roundtables, government would approve these decisions. If not, government would use the insights and lessons learned from the roundtables.

Some of the important lessons from the CORE experience make the rather obvious point that resolving contentious policy issues takes time. Many rounds of discussions and negotiations are required to reach agreement by participants who have markedly different agendas and objectives. Second, the process requires skilled facilitators who can bring participants together and ensure that, although disagreements will occur, these need not sabotage the process. Perhaps the most significant lesson is that shared decision-making results in shared learning. All the participants came to the roundtables not only with their own strongly held opinions, but also with equally firm views on the opinions of the other participants. Intense discussions conducted over a period of months allowed both sets of perceptions to change. Participants distinguished between their absolute priorities and other less important matters Participants also learned where their views of others had been incorrect and were able to alter these. The learning lasted after the termination of the CORE process and was a major legacy of the project.

While consensus was not reached by any of the roundtables, there was a sufficient level of agreement for CORE to develop land use plans for each of the regions, and with modifications, these plans were approved by government. Following the submission of the plans, CORE was disbanded: 'It was appropriate that the lead land use planning function be reassumed within government following the developmental phase of CORE. Government works best when it assumes responsibilities directly and delivers services in an unambiguous and accountable way' (Owen, 1998: 95). At the same time, we need to recognize that governments do not always work well in carrying out these functions and their ability to broker agreements in many aspects of public policy is limited. There may well be a compelling case for the establishment of shared decision-making mechanisms as a more frequently used option in major policy-making initiatives.

# Policy Communities

Policy communities are loosely knit groups of individuals interested in and knowledgeable about a particular aspect of public policy. Membership varies depending on the issues. In the human services, membership may include politicians, senior civil servants, and representatives of community agencies. In policy arenas such as banking, the representatives from outside government will be presidents of banks and insurance companies. Policy communities are not usually registered as voluntary organizations and their activities are most often conducted in a rather informal fashion. At times they may meet on a regular basis and at other times slip into periods of inactivity.

Some policy communities have been extremely influential in shaping public policy, yet they typically receive scant attention in the public policy literature. In our survey of some of the most widely used Canadian social policy texts, there is almost no attention to the role of policy communities. The only book that has given comprehensive treatment to the contribution of policy communities is *Policy Communities and Public Policy in Canada* (Coleman and Skogstad, 1990). As might be expected, the book concludes that the women's movement and the poverty policy community exercised little influence on the policies of the federal government from 1970 to 1990, whereas the banking and forestry policy communities were extremely influential. Two of the examples discussed below—the poverty policy community and the financial community—illustrate these findings.

## The Poverty Policy Community

This community is of particular interest because it has gone through several stages ranging from an early period where it wielded considerable influence, to the present time where it carries little weight in the Ottawa corridors of power.

The first period occurred during the 1950s when, under the auspices of the Public Welfare Division (PWD) of the Canadian Welfare Council (now the Canadian Council on Social Development or CCSD), senior civil servants from the federal and provincial departments of social services and staff of the Council met on a regular basis. The original reason for the establishment of the PWD was to identify and discuss common problems, but under the leadership of several key individuals, it became a vehicle to plan major changes in public assistance programs. As Haddow (1990: 25) points out, 'The PWD gave senior public assistance officials an opportunity to reach agreement on policy reforms and to camouflage their activity as the product of a disinterested and prestigious non-governmental organization.' The executive secretary of the division was even more blunt: 'Members of the PWD most of whom are appointed officials, would be placed in an awkward position by having to take responsibility for recommendations which might be considered policy matters and as such more appropriately the responsibility of elected officials.' The work of this policy community culminated in the publication of Social Security for Canada in 1958 that laid the groundwork for the Canada Assistance Plan (CAP) enacted by the federal government in 1966.

Wanting to take a more holistic approach to its research and policy-related activities, CCSD dissolved the PWD and other divisions in 1969. Even without the structure of the PWD, cordial and supportive relationships between senior staff of the Department of Health and Welfare and the Council continued until the mid-1970s. However, in 1976 both the department and the Council issued reports recommending reforms in income security. The Council attacked the departmental report on several occasions, the latter responded in kind, and the long record of support and cooperation between the two collapsed: 'The Council's capacity to participate in social reform depended on the cogency and originality of its research and policy analysis and on its capacity to serve as a forum for welfare state clients. . . . [But] neither its research results nor its efforts to mobilize program clients gave it access to government decision-making' (Haddow, 1990: 181).

This point is important. In order to influence government polices, it is not sufficient that voluntary agencies produce sound research and timely proposals. Such organizations also require the connections that will ensure their proposals will receive attention. Although a number of policy organizations and think tanks now exist in Ottawa, and although staffs of some of these organizations have good connections with senior civil servants, a policy community of reform-minded civil servants and community representatives does not exist. The scene has shifted dramatically. Instead of a policy community dedicated to improving Canada's welfare state, there is a different, more powerful policy community dedicated to dismantling it. Rather than a social policy community consisting of representatives of agencies like the CCSD, the Centre for Policy Alternatives, and the Caledon Institute, there is now a financial policy community led by the Canadian Council of Chief Executives. We take up the story of this policy community next.

## The Financial Policy Community

Although many policy communities struggle because of insufficient resources, the same cannot be said of the financial policy community summarized in this section. This community consists of politicians and senior civil servants in the Department of Finance, Treasury Board, and representatives from the Canadian Council of Chief Executives (CCCE).

As noted in Chapter Two, the CCCE, which was formerly known as the Business Council on National Interests, was initially formed in 1976 to represent the interests of the financial and business community in Canada. It is described on its website as 'Canada's premier business association' made up of the 'chief executive officers of some 150 leading Canadian corporations' whose companies administer C\$3.5 trillion in assets' and 'have annual revenue in excess of \$800 billion' (Canadian Council of Chief Executives website, 2009).

In some ways, the CCCE could be considered an interest or pressure group committed to pushing the state to adopt policies favoured by the financial community. It is seen here as the business partner of a policy community because of its close contacts and relationships with officials in the federal government. In his analysis of the Council in 1998, Peter Newman documented just how close these connections were. Paul Martin, former minister of finance and prime minister, was a member of CCCE prior to his entry into politics, and when he was minister of finance, Jean Chrétien acknowledged 'that I don't do my budgets without consulting with the Council on Business Interests' (as quoted in Newman, 1998: 157). Although these and other connections exist between the two partners, perhaps the most significant reason for achieving ready agreement on policy issues is that they share common backgrounds, ideologies, and commitments to a neo-liberal agenda.

The CCCE has been remarkably effective in influencing the policies of the federal level government. The president, Thomas D'Acquino (as quoted in Newman, 1998: 159) summed up its achievements in the following quotation: 'If you ask yourself, in which period since 1900 has Canada's business community had the most influence on public policy I would say it was in the last twenty years. Look at what we stand for and look at what all the governments, all the major parties including Reform have done and what they want to do. They have adopted the agendas we've been fighting for in the past two decades.' The successful outcomes of this policy community include the dismantling of the National Energy Program, persuading the federal government to give priority to reducing the public debt using as one rationale the high cost of social programs, and becoming the pivotal advocate in the Free Trade Debate, 'spending \$200 million in the largest and most powerful lobby effort in Canadian history' (Newman, 1998: 156).

Given the commitment of the authors to a social justice agenda, it is difficult to pay tribute to an organization that has done so much to concentrate power in the hands of so few for their private interests, yet the strategies employed by the

CCCE have been nothing short of brilliant. Rather than waiting for government to enact legislation and policy and then complaining if these measures do not suit the interests of the business community, the CCCE has anticipated the agenda of government and developed carefully worked out proposals that, just coincidentally, support and enhance the cause of business. The *strategy of anticipation* works for CCCE because it has excellent sources of information within government, and it has enough resources to prepare proposals that resonate with the requirements of government.

## A Disability Policy Community in British Columbia

The story of the efforts of the staff of the provincial government and community agencies coming together to reform guardianship legislation for vulnerable adults in BC provides a textbook example of the workings of a policy community. The story reveals both the advantages and some of the inherent difficulties in policy communities where one partner, usually the state, has access to more resources both in terms of funds and people than the community partner.

In addition, this example provides an apt illustration of the concept of the policy window noted in Chapter One. In the garbage can model of policy-making a policy window opens when problems, politics, and policy solutions—the three key components of the policy process—come into alignment. As described by Kingdon (1995: 165), 'a problem is recognized, a solution is developed and available in the policy community, a political change makes it the right time for policy change and potential constraints are not severe'. With the exception of the policy solution, all the other components were present in the example under discussion. A reform-minded government had just been elected. As well, the relevant community organizations and the newly appointed public trustee were keenly aware of the inadequacies of the existing *Patients Property Act* and committed to developing new, more progressive legislation.

The initiative for change came from community organizations, and a consortium of five agencies launched a province-wide survey to document problems resulting from the outdated Act. Sometime later, an interministerial committee was formed within the provincial government, and the two groups came together to form a joint working committee. Over a two-year period, 1991 to 1993, this committee worked at a frantic pace: it sought further information from concerned individuals and disability organizations, it prepared a framework document setting out the direction for the new legislation, it provided extensive opportunities for reviews of the document, and it developed new legislation and again sought consultation. In 1993, a new Act was passed in the provincial legislature that 'was heralded by many within both government and community as the best and most innovative legislative framework focusing on the rights of the disabled in vulnerable circumstances in North America. The process of its development and passage— the process of community driven legislative reform—is certainly just as unique' (Rutman, 1998: 104).

Yet all the provisions of the new legislation were not proclaimed until 2000. What happened to delay final approval for seven years? The essential reason was that the policy window began to close. The resources required to implement the new legislation were deemed too expensive and the attorney general, who had supported the involvement of the disability community and was committed to reforming the legislation, resigned. Political crises, which garnered daily media attention, effectively diverted the government from tending to substantive policy responsibilities. Finally, the disability community simply ran out of funds and energy.

The lessons from the experience of this policy community are instructive. First, the two partners did not have access to equal funds and staff skilled in research and policy analysis; hence, the partnership was an unequal one. Second, the insistence of the community partners that their participation should not be limited to a few advisors, and that wide-ranging consultation with disability organizations was essential in all phases of the process, appeared to government to slow down the pace of reform. Indeed, some government officials simply did not understand why community partners should be part of drafting legislation. After all, legislation is a state responsibility! Only direct intervention from the attorney general saved the day on this issue.

In spite of these difficulties, assigning policy reform to a policy community has considerable advantages. It encourages the collection of comprehensive information, it secures the cooperation of community agencies that in the last analysis will be responsible for at least some aspects of implementation, and it meets the challenge of transparency on key matters of public interest.

# Community Governance

## Overview

We devote the major section of the chapter to a more extensive discussion of community governance. This discussion is more extensive because devolving responsibility to community bodies—be they school boards, health councils, or child and family service agencies—has been the most frequently used approach in securing the involvement of those affected by these programs.

Community governance brings policy-making and the management of the outcomes of that process to the level of local communities. It is an attractive strategy to both those on the left and on the right of the political spectrum, but this very quality suggests that the concept contains a basic contradiction. Thus, for neo-liberals, community governance often means reducing the size and significance of governments by returning the responsibility for helping individuals and families to churches, neighbourhoods, and charitable organizations. For those who believe in democratic socialism, community governance does not represent an abandonment of state responsibility for the human services, but rather affords an opportunity to involve more citizens in governance issues. It is a policy direction that has the potential to create small, user-friendly agencies. Although our resolution of this issue will appeal most to those of this political persuasion, we recognize that some on the left favour the centralization of power in the hands of senior policy experts. Our resolution will offend these left-leaning central planners just as thoroughly as it will those in the neo-liberal camp who favour centralized control of decision-making.

We begin by describing what we mean by 'community' and 'governance' and then identify both the advantages and disadvantages of community governance. We note some examples and conclude the discussion by presenting our approach to community governance.

## What Do We Mean by 'Community'?

Although 'community' can refer to communities of interest without geographic boundaries, we are primarily concerned here with communities in the geographic sense. Thus, 'community' is defined to mean a group of people having common interests and sharing a particular place. But this definition is still imprecise with respect to size since it can refer to neighbourhoods, municipalities, and regions. For our purposes this is not a vexing issue because we argue that the concept of community governance can apply to all these geographic units.

It is important to clarify that our arguments for community governance do not apply to all health and social policies. Some programs such as income security and medicare coverage must be provided at provincial or federal levels. Here, the principle of equity is paramount, and equity demands that all citizens regardless of residence are entitled to the same level of benefits whether these are provided through a pension, social assistance, workers' compensation, or employment insurance. We agree with Piven's trenchant criticism of calls to delegate responsibility for income support programs to communities: 'The most serious problems in these programs—of inadequate benefits and demeaning treatment of beneficiaries—are surely not likely to be solved by decentralization or community participation. To me such proposals are exasperating for their pig-headed rejection of either history or analysis. No one seems to remember the local and private tyranny that bedeviled relief programs for the poor before they were at least partially nationalized in the 1930s' (1993: 69).

Leaving aside medicare and social policies pertaining to income security, the issue of which services and programs are most appropriately dealt with at what level is a contentious and slippery one. While it is apparent that the issue cannot be resolved by unambiguous formulas, some clarity can be obtained by examining four principles: affinity, affected interests, accessibility, and a low level of bureaucratization.

The *principle of affinity* suggests that people from diverse groups, including those with significantly different faith or cultural traditions, have a right to receive services from agencies and practitioners who are also committed to these values. Examples of the principle of affinity include church-sponsored agencies, First

Nations agencies, and ethno-cultural agencies. People coming to these agencies know in advance that they will receive counselling and other services consistent with their values and belief systems. 'Affinity is the perception that a provider possesses a unique set of characteristics which are important to the consumer' (Social Planning Council of Metropolitan Toronto, 1976: 106).

The *principle of affected interests* was discussed earlier in this chapter, and this principle is a common rationale for the development of programs and agencies by groups with a particular interest or cause. Some examples include Associations for Community Living, transition houses, women's centres, and antipoverty organizations. And in order for the principle of affected interests to work, the remaining two principles come into play.

The third principle is that of *accessibility*. In his contributions to the Seebohm report on the reorganization of health and social services in the United Kingdom, Roy Parker captured the essence of accessibility by the phrase 'pram-pushing distance' (Report of the Committee on Local Authority and Allied Services, 1968). Such services include daycare; meeting places for children, youth, parents, and seniors; and neighbourhood-organizing activities. Although the principle of accessibility must be operationalized differently in urban and rural areas, the experience of neighbourhood houses and community schools is that accessibility— both in terms of location and a welcoming, user-friendly philosophy of service— is a determining factor in the use of services. One of the few empirical studies of the effects of decentralization in child welfare demonstrated that accessibility was directly associated with service use:

> To summarize, service demand as reflected by caseload increases in child abuse, family service, and children in care increased at a much higher rate in Winnipeg following the transition to decentralized, community-based services than elsewhere in the province. These data along with the evidence of increased activity in prevention and early intervention demonstrate that regionalization led to significant increases in the utilization of child and family services. (McKenzie, 1991: 61)

Finally, the *principle of a low level of bureaucratization* calls for a flat, rather than a hierarchical, structure in organizations. Flat structures provide an environment for human services that is more conducive to collaboration between the executive and front-line staff, and between organizational staff and service users.

These principles provide guidance rather than precise direction and require an adaptive approach to implementation. Taken together they make a convincing argument that governance should be suited to the geographic area and the people to be served. Thus, neighbourhood houses should be governed by residents of the neighbourhood since services are available only to these residents. However, services such as mental health and child welfare, which affect a large number of people, may need to be organized on a regional basis and governed by an elected board that is representative of the citizens in the area.

## What Do We Mean by 'Governance'?

A number of attempts have been made to clarify the meaning of 'governance' at a community level. Basic to the concept is the delegation of authority and responsibility from senior levels of government that traditionally have authority over the delivery of health and social services. Rein (1972) distinguishes among political, geographic, and administrative decentralization. Geographic decentralization consists of the establishment of local offices without any transfer of power. Political decentralization delegates policy-making authority to the local unit, while administrative decentralization is more restrictive and grants autonomy only with respect to specified tasks.

A more elaborate and better-known framework is the ladder of citizen participation referred to in Chapter Four (Arnstein, 1969). Arnstein developed the framework in an attempt to clarify the levels of engagement of citizens in the Model Cities programs in the United States in the 1960s. While the ladder refers to citizens rather than communities, the basic intent of the framework— to distinguish between differing levels of control—applies just as clearly to communities as to citizens. It will be clear as the discussion proceeds that our view of community governance involves the top three rungs of the ladder: citizen control, delegated power, and partnership arrangements.

Before proceeding to the discussion of advantages and disadvantages of community governance, we note that neither of the above frameworks speaks to practice, and in our view a community work approach to practice is an essential component of community governance. The discussion of the work of the Hazelton office in Chapter Five captures the essence of community work, but it is appropriate at this juncture to describe the approach in a more explicit fashion.

A community work approach to practice contains the following characteristics. The people being served:

- become partners in developing and managing programs that affect them,
- become partners in identifying and then taking action to change harmful and negative conditions that are present in their neighbourhood, and
- have reserved seats at policy-making tables to ensure that not just the professionals and other experienced volunteers participate.

This collaborative approach to service provision may be reflected in an agency's overall service model and, under these circumstances, the agency can be considered to have adopted an inclusive approach to policy-making and practice. Over time we have identified a number of examples of schools, as well as health and social service agencies that focus most of their attention on providing effective, high quality services through building partnerships with the community and developing staff who are committed to this way of working. Much less time is often spent on larger systemic issues outside the local community or matters of concern to central authorities; indeed, a relatively high degree of autonomy from central office is preferred, as was the case in the Hazelton office, because it enables more attention to local innovations. These agencies, which can be thought of as *Islands of Excellence*, are almost always associated with some form of community governance or a level of autonomy that permits a significant degree of local control.

A community work approach to practice is the antithesis of the current and strongly held view in which, in the guise of attempting to coordinate services and ensure accountability, people being served are cast as 'cases' and professionals as 'case managers'. This 'solution' has arisen because many individuals are buffeted by problems such as poverty, inadequate housing, unemployment, unsafe neighbourhoods, and difficulties in marital and parent–child relationships. But unlike the interconnectedness of these issues, programs have been developed on a specialized basis and are offered by agencies with specific functions. Since these agencies are often located in different areas, people must travel from one area to another, and not infrequently they receive different responses to questions and conflicting advice and opinions.

This scenario is described in detail in the first volume of the Gove Inquiry into Child Protection in British Columbia (Report of the Gove Inquiry into Child Protection in British Columbia, 1995). This inquiry made 116 recommendations, and pertinent to this discussion is the following recommendations: that services should be integrated, provided in a common location, and governed by regional boards of elected citizens; and that a system of case management be developed and implemented. The inquiry concluded that case management is required to ensure that clients do not fall between the cracks of programs and providers.

In our view, the recommendation calling for service integration and community governance was sound and progressive, but it was ignored by the NDP government in power at the time and, after an initial spurt of interest, by the succeeding Liberal government. However, there is a revival of interest in service integration in a number of other provinces, including Alberta, Manitoba, and Ontario; Quebec has always retained some level of commitment to service integration through its Locaux de Services Communautaires (CLSC) which have now been reconfigured as Health and Social Service Centres (CSSS).

Community governance must not provide an excuse to off-load resources. Being close to and aware of community needs and resources, community governance has the potential to come to grips with the multi-agency problem described in the Gove Inquiry. It might reduce the number of agencies and thereby the number of service providers involved with any one family; it might organize common sites of operation, and, as a radical innovation, install citizens as the managers or co-managers in the planning and implementation of the services that affect them. In brief, it can lead to more effective services; it may, in time, also result in more efficient services.

## The Advantages of Community Governance

The case for community governance is summed up in three propositions:

1.  People respect more those laws on which they have been consulted.
2.  People identify strongly with programs they have helped plan.
3.  People perform better in projects they have assisted in setting up. (Bregha, n.d.: 3)

Simply put, community governance provides more space for more people to participate, to develop a constituency for the human services, and to increase the sense of participants' self-worth. The advantages have been identified in greater detail by many authors (see, among others, Cassidy, 1991; Clague, Dill, Seebaran, and Wharf, 1984; Pateman, 1970). They can be enumerated as follows:

*   Community organizations are connected to local customs and traditions. They are intimately aware of the history of issues and of what has been done in the past to resolve these issues.
*   Action on community issues is likely to be faster if the decisions are made at a local level rather than at senior levels of government.
*   Community governance provides an opportunity for people to learn about the process of governing; thus, it serves as a training ground for engagement in other political arenas.
*   Community governance affords an opportunity for social learning, for individuals to become knowledgeable about social issues and the complex interplay between personal troubles and public issues.
*   Community governance contains the potential for building a constituency for the services being governed. Thus, a constituency for education has been built through citizens participating on regional school boards and parent advisory committees.

All of the above advantages occur because community governance structures are small and accessible. It is easier for citizens to be involved in, to have contact with, and to influence small governing units as opposed to regional and provincial governments. The experience of the Greater London Council, which experimented with various kinds of both functional and geographic structures, was that 'the smaller the unit, the more effective was its attack on hierarchy, fragmentation of services and the deskilling of professional talents' (Murray, 1993: 61).

However, the advantages of small governing structures are countered by the claims that they are costly and inefficient. We discuss these claims next.

## The Disadvantages of Community Governance

Earlier we referred to one significant disadvantage of community governance—the condition of 'acute localitis' (Montgomery, 1979). Acute localitis refers to the potential for communities to become closed and intolerant of diverging patterns of behaviour. Although the rural community of old is often romanticized today as a place of support and mutual affection, we often forget that these were also often places of intolerance and even cruelty. As a consequence, many individuals fled to the anonymity of cities, where their views and behaviour were accepted or at least tolerated.

A second disadvantage noted above is that community governance affords an opportunity for neo-liberal governments to reduce costs. Critics of community governance and, indeed, of most forms of participatory democracy often claim that these structures waste time and energy. They argue that community governance represents yet another layer of government in our already complicated government system. The development of a New Directions policy for health care in British Columbia provides an instructive example of the potency of this argument. This policy was established by an NDP government following a Royal Commission initiated by the previous government. The Commission recommended that funding and the delivery of health services be placed under regional control 'closer to home'. New Directions proposed implementing this reform by establishing regional and community health boards composed of elected citizens. From the outset the policy was hailed by the advocates of community governance as innovative and imaginative. It was also severely criticized by opponents on the grounds that it would create an expensive and bureaucratic form of governance. Attempts to implement New Directions consumed the better part of three years and, in the end, the critics won. The initiative was discarded as too 'expensive and bureaucratic'!

Similar arguments were made in 1991 when community-based child and family service agencies in the city of Winnipeg were disbanded and organized under one administrative authority. However, despite predictions of cost savings there was no evidence that a return to a more centralized structure with a reduced level of community control realized this goal. In fact, costs continued to escalate.

## Examples of Community Governance

Several examples of community governance come to mind. Voluntary agencies have traditionally been governed by their communities, whether these are geographic or interest communities. Agencies such as transition houses, child sexual abuse centres, child and family services agencies, Associations for Community Living, and social planning councils are governed by boards of directors. Since the elections of these boards are generally confined to members of the society legally responsible for the agency, and since many members come from the middle- and upper-income classes, charges of elitism are not uncommon. Indeed, some of these agencies have become closed to all but the members of the society and their friends.

Other examples include regional school boards and community health centres. While elections to these agencies can be contested by any citizen, the charge of elitism is still relevant. As we noted earlier, the ability to participate successfully in the electoral process depends on the availability of financial resources and influence, and this tilts the scale heavily in favour of middle- and upper-income earners.

In a very real sense, particularly in small communities, municipal governments can be considered examples of community governance. Voter turnout for municipal elections is lower than for provincial and federal elections, perhaps reflecting a commonly held view that the most important decisions are made by the senior levels of government. Nevertheless, some of these elections are hotly contested affairs, and the controversial issues of policing, housing, recreation, and zoning that confront municipal councils involve difficult policy decisions. While arguments for the amalgamation of contiguous municipalities and school boards are frequently heard, citizens are often resistant to these initiatives because of the loss of local autonomy. In the last analysis, people prefer organizations that provide important community services to be located in or near the community, to be subject to local accountability, and to be managed by people who are widely known in the community.

## The Effectiveness of Community Governance

The effectiveness of community governance is difficult to establish. The first question is, 'effective compared to what'? Other levels of government? Business corporations? What are the indicators of effectiveness? While the effectiveness of the ministries of provincial and federal governments is occasionally evaluated, we rarely venture into the daunting task of an evaluation of an entire government.

As noted earlier, voluntary agencies, such as those financially supported by the United Way, represent a form of community governance. These agencies occasionally experience management difficulties stemming from conflicts between members of the board, or between staff and board members; however, the structure of local governance has generally remained in place. This long-standing record is a remarkable testimony to the salience of the principles of affinity, affected interests, and a low level of bureaucratization. Other successful examples of community governance come from the establishment of Health and Human Resource Centres in British Columbia (Clague et al., 1984), from the regionalization of child welfare services in Manitoba (McKenzie, 1991), and from Shragge's (1990) review of alternative service organizations in Montreal. Unfortunately, some of these structures have been discarded by governments ambivalent about community empowerment. Nevertheless, Shragge's conclusions provide an apt summary of the case for community governance:

> The community-based option has shown itself to be responsible and innovative, creating new approaches and service delivery at a level that can respond directly to a range of community needs and problems. One critique of the post-war welfare state centres on its bureaucratic structure, overreliance

on professionals, and the fact that planning and control of services are remote from the local community. Clearly, alternative service organizations are able to address these problems even with their chronic underfunding. (Shragge, 1990)

Finally, some insights into effectiveness can be gleaned from the studies of well-performing organizations. Building on the work of Peters and Waterman (1982) and a study by the Auditor General of Canada (1988), Brodtrick (1991) developed a set of criteria that exemplify well-performing organizations in the public sector. These criteria are.

- An emphasis on people. People are challenged and developed; they are given power to act and to use their judgments.
- Participative leadership. Leadership is not authoritarian but participative whenever possible.
- Innovative work styles. Staffs reflect on their performance and seek to solve problems creatively.
- Strong client orientation. These organizations focus strongly on their clients and derive their satisfaction from serving the client rather than the bureaucracy.
- A mindset that seeks optimum performance. People hold values that drive them to seek improvement in their organization's performance. (Brodtrick, 1991: 18–19)

There are many similarities between the characteristics of well-performing organizations and the type of community governance we have in mind. The common characteristics include inclusiveness, valuing individuals, flat rather than steep organizational structures, and small in scale and size.

## Towards a Resolution

We argue that community governance is the model of choice for many, although not all, programs. Indeed, a very short program ladder consisting of only three rungs can be identified. The first rung consists of those programs that are purely local and, here, community governance or control should be the rule. The second rung refers to delegated power whereby legislative authority and all or most of the responsibility for funding rests with the federal or provincial levels but operating responsibilities are delegated to communities. Education, child welfare, and health services fall on this second rung. In a delegated model there is likely to be tension around how policy-making authority and accountability is shared between the local and central governance structures in that both levels may wish more authority than they currently hold. It is not unreasonable that the senior governance structure should exercise a certain amount of authority over general policy-making priorities and accountability given the role of government in funding such services and its general responsibility for ensuring service adequacy and quality. However, in our view this requirement is best met through a partnership model which ensures as much local control as possible over the policies, programs, and services that must be adapted to meet local needs and priorities. The third rung is concerned with programs in which the principle of equity is of fundamental importance. This requires an arrangement between community and a senior level of government whereby government has more control over the policies and programs to be provided but local citizens have mechanisms that permit local feedback and influence. Examples of these programs include social assistance, employment insurance, and pensions for the elderly. Here, community groups and organizations can make an important contribution by evaluating the outcomes of these programs and communicating the results to senior levels of government. Although these organizations will not be primarily responsible for setting policy or delivering services, they provide essential information about the contents of these policies and the nature of the services that should be provided.

As we note throughout this book, the effectiveness of policy is ultimately determined by the capacity of the local service delivery unit and the relationships that prevail among staff members and those being served. Unfortunately, efforts to reform the human services usually concentrate on changing structures and rarely on redistributing some of the power from politicians and bureaucrats to service providers and users.

In the last analysis, the resolution of the issue depends on whether one favours the centralization or the dispersal of power. Centralists point to the advantages to be gained from governing structures that enable decisions to be made quickly, with a minimum expenditure of time and energy. They view the work of committees— especially meetings that are long and inconclusive—as a waste of time.

For their part, the proponents of a dispersed power model base their arguments, in part, on the axiom of Lord Acton: power corrupts and absolute power corrupts absolutely! From this perspective, power-sharing reduces the chances of a few people governing in their own interests and contributes to the development of a more informed and more responsible citizenry. The concern about wasted time and energy is countered by the response that participation is cost-effective because it avoids mistakes in implementation that frequently occur when those who must implement a policy have had no part in its development.

The dilemma is summed up by the observation that 'the real debate is not about cost savings; it is about the nature of local territorially-based communities and about their potential for democratic self-governance within the complex political and economic environment in which we find ourselves' (Sancton, 1997: 286). Community governance of the human services represents an essential addition to the limited range of opportunities for citizens to contribute to democratic self-governance. As we have emphasized, full reliance on the representative model of governance is open primarily to those with the financial resources, time, and self-confidence to participate. In the human services in particular, the policy priorities of these individuals are often quite different from those who receive the services. Community governance would pave the way for some improvements in an otherwise severely restricted form of democracy.

## Summary and Conclusion

We have made a strong argument for the establishment of more inclusive approaches to policy development. However, we acknowledge that the backwards mapping and vertical slice approaches require the support of reform-minded policy-makers and managers and that this essential ingredient is often not present.

Policy communities can be effective in some circumstances but as our discussion of this approach demonstrates, policy communities in the human service sectors experience more difficulty in maintaining access to government decision-makers and in sustaining their activities due to resource constraints. The issue of the poverty policy community is an interesting one in that our assessment demonstrated both early successes and then failures later on as the collaborative engagement of federal government officials turned to resistance and non-co-operation. However, advocacy on child poverty under the auspices of Campaign 2000—a coalition of organizations from across Canada—remains very active in keeping this issue on the policy agenda. We discuss this coalition in more detail in Chapter Seven.

Although most approaches to inclusive policy-making discussed in this chapter are designed to answer more specific policy questions, community governance is a more difficult proposition because it involves surrendering power to local authorities for long-term policy and program development. To ensure that service users and front-line staff can participate, seats at the policy table need to be reserved for members of these groups, and other means to ensure ongoing participation need to be considered. Community governance is associated with the decentralization of power, and new relationships between government and these local organizations must be developed to make this arrangement work.

In our view, the concept of shared learning is perhaps the most important contribution of inclusive approaches. Shared learning breaks down misconceptions that often stand in the way of reaching agreement, it brings in the perspectives of the front-line practitioners and of service users, and in so doing enriches the information at the policy table.

Two disadvantages of inclusive approaches have been noted. First, they involve more people in the policy process and in turn this can extend the time needed to reach a decision. Second, decentralization and community governance can provide an opportunity for neo-liberal governments to off-load responsibilities and reduce resources for the human services. But, to emphasize again, the primary problem preventing more widespread use of inclusive approaches is that they require those who hold power to transfer some of that power to those who lack power. Surrendering power does not come easily and for many, including senior bureaucrats, it represents an option they will not willingly accept. Yet transferring power is essential if human services are to be responsive to the needs of service users and we return to this complex issue in the final chapter.

# Recommended Reading

P. Newman, *The Titans: How the New Canadian Establishment Seized Power* (Toronto: Penguin, 1998). This book provides an entertaining and illuminating account of the influence exercised by elites in Canadian society.

R. Haddow, 'The Poverty Policy Community in Canada's Liberal Welfare State', in W. Coleman and G. Skogstad, eds, *Policy Communities and Public Policy in Canada: A Structural Approach* (Toronto: Copp Clark Pitman, 1990), 213–37. This chapter provides a historical review of the poverty policy community in Canada.

S. Phillips and M. Orsini, *Mapping the Links: Citizen Involvement in Policy Processes* (Ottawa: Canadian Policy Research Networks, 2002). This review examines the level of citizen participation in policy processes, notably at the federal government level, and includes suggestions for reform.

Institute on Governance Website. Available at http://www.iog.ca. This website includes position papers and reports published by the Institute on Governance regarding the role of the public and other sectors in policy development.

# Critical Thinking Questions

1.  Select a policy problem that requires assessment using one of the models for policy analysis discussed in Chapter Four. Outline how the tasks to be undertaken in the analysis of this policy can be made more inclusive.

2.  Review the strengths and weaknesses identified in this chapter for any one of the following approaches to inclusive policy-making: backwards mapping, shared decision-making, or policy communities. What additional advantages or risks can you think of?

3.  Community governance is different than decentralization. Define these concepts and identify the differences. What type of decentralization is similar to community governance?

4.  When we think of services or programs that are subject to community governance we often think of local boards or committees that have decision-making authority as the primary method of ensuring local governance. However, as noted, citizen participation must go well beyond participation in these structures. Making the most of local governance also requires a community-oriented approach to local policy-making and practice where engaging service users and other community members is an ongoing priority. Select a community-based program with which you are familiar and identify other ways of encouraging community engagement in this program, in addition to the development of a local board or advisory committee.

5.  If the program you selected in answering Question 4 has a community board, assess the extent of its power to make policy decisions. Does the central authority still exercise certain controls over local decisions? If so, what are the advantages and disadvantages of this arrangement?

# Chapter Seven

# Influencing Policy from Outside the System

This chapter focuses primarily on ways of influencing policy from outside government. Included in this discussion are the roles that can be played by unions and professional associations, think tanks, and social movements and advocacy groups. Strategies that emerge from the activities of these groups often involve the media in an effort to mobilize public opinion.

Staff working inside organizations may also adopt strategies designed to change seriously flawed policies that they feel will have adverse effects on service users or their own capacity to provide quality services. Both individual and group advocacy activities may be used, including such low risk efforts as identifying the unanticipated consequences of a policy to more assertive objections which carry somewhat greater risks. Staff inside an organization may also adopt actions designed to subvert a particular policy that has been adopted. And when all else fails, staff may conclude that they have no option but to disclose issues involving fraud or bad practice to the public by 'blowing the whistle'. We identify a number of examples of 'whistle-blowing' and discuss some of the implications related to this strategy choice in the final section of this chapter.

It is important to underline the context that faces those who attempt to influence policy, a discussion that has been foreshadowed in many of the previous chapters. In previous chapters we have emphasized that government policies represent the concrete expression of the ideology of the government in power. Thus neo-liberal governments in several provinces have reduced the nature and scope of social programs and have transferred many services to the private sector. Other governments, with more moderate tendencies, have made some efforts to maintain and extend social programs, although the scope of these improvements has been modest at best over the past two decades. We have only to look at the actions of previous governments in Ontario and Alberta and their neo-liberal agenda of cutbacks in the fields of social assistance, daycare, and education to find evidence of these strongly held convictions.

## Unions and Professional Organizations

Most human service agencies in the public sector and in larger non-government sectors, such as child and family services and regional health authorities, are unionized and human service workers in these organizations can rely on unions not only to negotiate collective bargaining agreements but to act on their behalf on issues that affect them personally and have broader implications for service quality and effectiveness. Unions have played important roles in advancing concerns around pay equity and working conditions, including high caseloads that have an impact on the quality of services that are provided. Each province has unions representing nurses and teachers and these unions have been prominent in advancing interests that represent the broader policy agenda of health care and education as well as the self-interests of their members.

Professional organizations can be a vehicle for change, although most professional organizations are somewhat pre-occupied with regulating their profession and acting on allegations of unprofessional practice. Legislation regarding the licensing of social workers has now been enacted in most provinces in Canada, but in most cases membership remains voluntary among practitioners in the field. Those professions that require membership in their professional associations as a condition of practice (e.g., teachers, doctors) tend to have stronger voices but critics often assert that these bodies are more interested in self-protection than the advancement of progressive reforms. Nevertheless, most of the human service professions have supported policies such as public rather than private health care, progressive approaches to taxation and more adequate income support programs. And the social work profession, despite its limited power, has a record of engaging in progressive advocacy work on social issues (see Canadian Association of Social Workers [CASW] website for an outline of its social policy principles and examples of the policy positions taken by the profession on issues such as the federal budget, child welfare programs, and amendments to the Criminal Code). On occasion, professional associations also sponsor research projects. For example, in 2002, CASW undertook a survey that documented the inordinate amount of time child welfare workers were forced to spend on paperwork, and the effects this had on limiting direct service contacts with families and children.

Individual engagement with unions and professional associations not only provides opportunities to engage with colleagues in collective action on policies affecting staff and service providers in their workplace settings but also enables individuals to advance their views on policy reforms within an environment that protects the right to voice these concerns. Of course, convincing others that your issue is a priority requiring collective attention and action may be another matter.

# Think Tanks

The label 'think tanks' applies to organizations established for the purpose of doing research on public issues. The largest and best known on the international scene are located in the United States and include the Brookings and Hoover Institutes, and the Rand Corporation. In Canada there are more than 100 think tanks, ranging from the Conference Board of Canada, with a staff of more than 200, to the Caledon Institute of Social Policy with only a few staff.

Although all think tanks are committed to research, some place their research in an ideological frame and use the findings to advance this ideology. For example, the Fraser Institute clearly states its frame of reference in its letterhead and publications noting that it has been committed to 'offering market solutions to public policy problems since 1974' (personal communication). Regardless of the problem being studied, the Fraser Institute seeks to find remedies that will reinforce the contribution of the private market sector and reduce the size and scope of government. By contrast, the research inquiries of the Centre for Policy Alternatives will most likely lead to solutions in the form of expanded public policies with a focus on social justice. Think tanks seek to influence government in a number of ways. They bring the results of their research studies to the attention of senior officials in government in an effort to convince these officials of the validity of their research and the importance of their proposals.

The influence of research findings on public policy decision-making is quite difficult to assess; this was discussed in some detail in Chapter Four. A similar observation can be made about the research findings of think tanks. Although good quality research is essential there is no guarantee that quality will ensure utilization. Other factors, including the presentation style (i.e., clear and easily accessible), whether results are straightforward, whether guardians or advocates are available to influence utilization, and whether the agency or department has the authority to make use of the information and make a difference (Davies, 2003). A more important factor may be timing and political factors, including the resonance of findings with the values and priorities of decision-makers. Abelson (2002: 161) in seeking to answer the question 'Do think tanks matter?', concluded that 'depending on the specific policy issue that is under consideration and the particular stage of the policy-making process that one is focusing on, scholars may walk away with the impression that think tanks are either extremely influential or entirely irrelevant. Both impressions would be right.' Returning to the Lemann observation about the importance of 'what we believe', it seems reasonable to argue that conservative governments will favour the research and the findings of conservative think tanks. By the same token, social democratic governments will look to think tanks that reflect their commitment to social reform.

Finally, we note that in their day-to-day work some think tanks resemble policy communities: 'Although Maxwell [a former President of the Canadian Policy Research Networks (CPRN) at the time] does not downplay the importance of media exposure, she maintains that think tanks exercise the most influence working with key stakeholders behind the scene, not by discussing policy issues with reporters. Maxwell believes that part of CPRN's role is to bring together senior bureaucrats, academics and representatives from the private and not-for-profit sector in closed door meetings to discuss social and economic policy issues' (Abelson, 2002: 68).

And like the example of the Canadian Council of Chief Executives discussed in Chapter Six, think tanks such as the Canadian Policy Research Networks and the Caledon Institute on Social Policy use their contacts in government and their accumulated knowledge of the workings of government to anticipate issues on the government's agenda and to offer proposals to address these issues.

# Social Movements and Policy Advocacy Groups

Social movements and advocacy groups have played a prominent part of the social policy scene in Canada for many years. For example, first wave feminism and the social gospel movement were influential in the development of some of Canada's earliest social policies such as 'Mothers' Allowances'. In our discussion of shared decision-making in Chapter Ten, we suggest that federal government action on funding in First Nations child and family services appears to have been influenced, at least in part, by the actions of the First Nations Child and Family Caring Society and the Assembly of First Nations in filing a complaint under the Human Rights Act and the later report on this issue by the Auditor General of Canada. In this section we focus on the Independent Living (IL) movement in the disability community as an example of a social movement and Campaign 2000 as an example of an advocacy group or coalition.

## The Independent Living Movement

In Chapter Six we considered the disability community in BC as a partner in a policy community dedicated to changing guardianship legislation for vulnerable adults. But parts of the disability community have also acted as a social movement by significantly influencing the policies of the state with respect to conditions for persons with disabilities. This is particularly evident in the disability community's efforts to promote the independent living paradigm as an approach to service delivery.

In Chapter Three, we defined social movements as a broadly based network of people, groups, or organizations that share a common characteristic that unites them, at least in a loose-knit fashion, in collective action for social change. The history of social movements since the last half of the twentieth century includes feminist organizations, the civil rights movement, and welfare rights coalitions. One of the seminal texts on social movements is Piven and Cloward's (1977) text on poor people's movements in the United States. Fagan and Lee (1997: 151–3) identify some of the characteristics of social movements and the extent to which the disability movement can be classified as a social movement:

- *Social movements embrace alternative forms of political action.* Disabled people have done this through self-organization and control by disabled people of the organizations representing their interests.
- *Social movements advance a critical evaluation of the values and structures of dominant society.* The disability movement has done this by highlighting the denial of citizenship rights arising from practices and policies that define disabled people as dependent and in need of care based on a medical model of rehabilitation.
- *Social movements promote collective action to achieve goals in both a national and international context.* A disability movement based on the independent living philosophy has developed in many countries and has international links through cross-national cooperative endeavours and organizations such as Disabled People's International.

In brief, the disability movement has taken direct action to challenge both the failings of the state and the public view of the disabled. In so doing it has built a sense of solidarity among the disabled people for social and economic reform. It is useful to consider the development of the disability movement as a social movement, with a particular focus on Canada, and our analysis pays particular attention to the Independent Living (IL) movement.

In a review of the Canadian IL movement, Valentine (1994) associates the rise of the movement in Western Canada with the values of consumer control and self-help in the early 1970s. Provincial organizations were formed in Saskatchewan, Manitoba, and Alberta; the momentum of these organizations and a national conference in Toronto in 1973 led to the formation of the Coalition of Provincial Organizations of the Handicapped (COPOH) in 1976 (now known as the Council of Canadians with Disabilities). COPOH, as a national consumer organization, focused its energy on human rights legislation, revision of building codes, establishment of public transportation services for persons with disabilities, and efforts to improve employment through job creation and policy change.

There was a rapid growth of the consumer movement at the local, provincial, and national levels, and in June 1980, COPOH held its third national conference in Vancouver. At this conference, Canadian consumers were introduced to an alternative view of rehabilitation—the independent living paradigm, a model consistent with the growing grassroots interest in consumer control and self-determination. This paradigm, posed as an alternative to the medical model reflected in rehabilitation programs of the day, identified the problems created by dependency arising out of the medical model and proposed solutions based on peer counselling, advocacy, self-help, consumer control, and the removal of barriers to independent living. This mantra quickly became the guiding philosophy of the emerging Independent Living movement in Canada.

Nyp (2002), who reviews the history of the Independent Living Centre of Waterloo Region, documents the growth of this consumer-based self-help organization over 20 years, from a fledgling organization operating out of a Sunday School room in a Mennonite church to a major consumer-based service organization with a budget of nearly $5 million and more than 300 staff. Operating four supportive housing units and a variety of other programs, including peer support and information and referral, the agency has become a model of a consumer-based organization that has successfully combined service with individual advocacy and self-help.

There are more than 25 Independent Living Resource Centres across Canada, and a national coordinating body known as the Canadian Association of Independent Living Centres (CAILC). Independent Living Centres emphasize consumer control, cross-disability issues, community-based approaches, and the full integration and participation of disabled people in Canadian society. Disabled people make up the majority of staff and board positions in these organizations, and their influence on disability issues with governments at all levels has been significant. With government assistance improved accessibility, supportive housing units, new legislation, public transportation for the disabled, and direct support and advocacy services have been established.

It is important to consider some of the reasons for the relative success of the IL movement. First, disability issues are perhaps less partisan in a political sense than many other social policy issues, partly because disabled people are likely to be seen as more deserving than some other groups. Thus government support, although never a guarantee for consumer-based initiatives, is somewhat more likely. Second, the IL movement benefited from growing national and international awareness of the need to address disability issues in a more responsive and respectful fashion. Finally, the movement quickly became a very effective lobby group. There is no doubt that this can be attributed to the effective leadership that was able to establish a broad base of support for a consumer-initiated approach to policy development.

There are also shortcomings within the IL movement that must be recognized. IL, as a consumer movement, is sometimes criticized for failing to represent the broad spectrum of disabled people (Lysack and Kaufert, 1994). For example, despite the commitment to cross-disability issues, the movement has often focused more directly on challenges experienced by those who are physically disabled. As well, the IL movement has remained largely an urban-based movement and its influence in rural and Aboriginal communities has been less profound. Despite these limitations, the accomplishments of the IL movement stand as a tribute to the vision of those who have been involved with this consumer-based movement.

## Campaign 2000

The impetus for Campaign 2000 came from a resolution in the House of Commons approved by members of all political parties to end child poverty by the year 2000. In a committed attempt to ensure that the government would live up to this promise, a number of social policy and advocacy organizations such as the Canadian Council on Social Development, the National Anti-Poverty

Organization, and the Toronto-based Child Poverty Action Group developed a national action plan. A cornerstone of this plan was that pressure could best be brought to bear by a network of local and provincial organizations dedicated to the elimination of poverty. The founding organizations sponsored a number of meetings across the country attended by members of anti-poverty groups, academics, and staff of human service organizations. At a national meeting and only after prolonged discussion and negotiations, the following goals for Campaign 2000 were approved:

- To raise and protect the basic living standards of all families in all regions of the country so that no Canadian child would ever live in poverty.
- To improve the life chances of all children so they can fulfill their potential and nurture their talent, and become responsible and contributing members of society.
- To ensure the availability of secure, adequate, affordable, and suitable housing as an inherent right for all children in Canada.
- To create, build, and strengthen family supports and community-based resources in order to empower families so they can provide the best possible care for their children. (Campaign 2000, as quoted in Popham, Hays, and Hughes, 1997: 254)

The principal strategy employed by Campaign 2000 has been to prepare an annual report card that displays changes in the number of children living in poverty by province since the House of Commons resolution. This report card highlights the consequences of child poverty and proposes strategies to eliminate, or at least reduce, poverty among children. The national report cards have been released on November 24, the anniversary of the all-party resolution, and have received considerable publicity. Campaign 2000 also produces discussion papers and lobbies all parties in both federal and provincial governments for improved social policies related to such things as the national child benefit, housing, and child care. Campaign 2000 is also dependent on a network of local and provincial organizations that participate in the development of provincial report cards, develop proposals for poverty reduction, and lobby governments at the provincial level.

Campaign 2000 is not without its critics. Not surprisingly, neo-liberal politicians scoff at the annual report card. Thus the former premier of Ontario, Mike Harris, contemptuously dismissed the 1999 report card saying, 'The report is hogwash. It's based on false data' (Campbell, 1999: A3). The accusation of false data is based on the use of Statistics Canada LICOs, which are often used by social policy organizations (the exception is the Fraser Institute) as the measure of poverty in Canada. And criticism has been voiced by some feminist scholars. For example, McGrath (1997) has claimed that the child-centred strategies used by advocacy groups have inadvertently played into the hands of business interest groups that support state intervention only when children are deemed to be at risk.

There is some legitimacy to McGrath's concern, and a focus on child poverty pursued in a very narrow way can obscure state responsibility for a broad range of social issues. However, we recognize that the focus on child poverty was originally selected by Campaign 2000, in part, as a strategic consideration in helping to mobilize broad public support. We also note that the report cards and other public positions advanced by Campaign 2000 are careful to connect the poverty of children with family poverty and related factors such as inadequate housing.

# Whistle-Blowing

The final strategy for criticizing policies that are seen as harmful is *blowing the whistle*. Although the use of the masculine pronoun is inappropriate in the following quotation—some of the most prominent whistle-blowers are women—the quote sums up the essence of the act of whistle-blowing: 'The message of the whistle-blower is seen as a breach of loyalty. Though he is neither coach nor referee, the whistle-blower blows the whistle on his own team' (Bok, 1984: 215). Although employees are often required to take an Oath of Office that forbids them to divulge information learned on the job (and certainly this is the case in government ministries or departments), those who blow the whistle are so convinced that the activities of their organization are harmful, they have no option but to disregard the Oath of Office. And, as will be evident in the following discussion, if an employee disregards the Oath of Office it can lead to ridicule and even dismissal.

Bok (1984) suggests there are three components that lead to the act of whistle-blowing. First is the presence of *dissent* which follows an awareness that the organization is engaged in wrong-doing. The second is a *breach of loyalty* where the individual breaks faith with employer–employee confidentiality provisions and makes a decision to go public with the complaint. Finally, there is the *accusation* stage where the whistle-blower registers a complaint with the public. But many people within organizations fail to take action even when faced with questionable organizational practices. Bok suggests that this reflects the predominant pattern of self-preservation and risk aversion that exists within organizations. Four different types of responses are hypothesized to clarify the range of possible responses by staff. One type of employee is the person who does not observe any wrongdoing or negligence and identifies completely with the organization. A second type is the employee who observes acts of wrongdoing but decides to take no action. A third type is the worker who observes wrongdoing and takes limited action by following established channels but takes no further action, even if the matter is not resolved. Finally, there is the person who takes action up to and including whistle-blowing stage to bring the matter to the attention of the public.

The person who gave real prominence to whistle-blowing is Daniel Ellsberg. Convinced that the US President and his Cabinet colleagues were not receiving accurate information about the war in Viet Nam, Ellsberg, a policy analyst, released 'the Pentagon Papers' to the *New York Times* in 1971. The papers consisted of a 7,000-word history of the Viet Nam War, which were published in both the *New York Times* and other newspapers (see Ellsberg, 2002). Once identified as a source of the information Ellsberg resigned and was charged with breaching confidentiality. Although he was eventually found not guilty, his career as a promising policy analyst with government and the Rand Corporation came to an abrupt end.

Loss of employment is a common consequence of high-profile whistle-blowing. Jeffrey Wigand blew the whistle on the Brown Williamson Tobacco company because, contrary to its public pronouncements, the company was deliberately increasing the amount of nicotine contained in cigarettes; he was fired. Wigand's story is told in a most compelling fashion in the movie *The Insider*. An equally engrossing film, *Silkwood*, reveals the whistle-blowing activities of Karen Silkwood. She became convinced of the health hazards involved in handling plutonium fuel rods in her place of employment. Both films provide some telling insights about the courage of whistle-blowers and the consequences of their actions. Wigand was fired, his pension and medical benefits were terminated, and he was harassed by Brown Williamson to such an extent that his mental health deteriorated and his marriage collapsed. However, Wigand subsequently overcame these difficulties and became an internationally known advocate for the antismoking cause. Tragically, Karen Silkwood was killed in a traffic collision that the movie suggests was far from an accident.

A Canadian example of whistle-blowing is that of Dr Nancy Oliveri, a medical researcher and adjunct member of the Faculty of Medicine at the University of Toronto, whose story is discussed in Box 7.1.

All the foregoing examples of whistle-blowing have received a great deal of public attention, but whistle-blowers in the social services have remained relatively unknown. The experiences of two Canadian social workers who blew the whistle are described below. The first is Bridget Moran, who was a social worker in the BC Ministry of Social Services in the 1950s and 1960s. Moran decided to blow the whistle on her ministry after years of attempting to change policies through the regular channels had failed.

Bridget Moran commenced her career in social work in Prince George, BC, in 1954. She describes her responsibilities in the following words:

> Starting in Prince George, my region extended sixty miles across dirt roads to Vanderhoof. West of Vanderhoof I travelled fifty miles and more to the settlements of Fort Fraser, Fraser Lake, Endako, and beyond. I drove south from those settlements over logging roads to reach a number of homes. North from Vanderhoof I covered the forty miles to Fort St. James again on dirt roads. . . . In that huge wooded territory which I reckoned to be about the size of Holland, I was responsible for the elderly, the poor, people of all ages with mental and social problems and the infirm. My area included one Indian residential school and five reservations, every one of them a text book study in poverty, disease and despair. (Moran, 2001: 29)

## Box 7.1  The Case of Nancy Oliveri

Nancy Oliveri was a medical researcher with the Hospital for Sick Children in Toronto and an adjunct professor of the Faculty of Medicine at the University of Toronto in the early 1990s. Oliveri became concerned about the potentially harmful effects of a drug she had played a pivotal role in developing. Despite the terms of a contract that allowed only the drug company, Apotex, to release results, she published her findings in a medical journal in 1996. The hospital promptly fired her but, because of widespread public indignation, subsequently revoked the firing.

Oliveri's findings were supported by some colleagues and peers but questioned by others. The dispute as to the accuracy of her findings and of her right to break the contract by blowing the whistle continued on both national and international fronts for six years. During this time, Oliveri was maligned both professionally and personally. She was accused of having dealt with patients in an unethical fashion and of having stolen from her research grants. In addition, Apotex lashed out by accusing her of rude and intemperate behaviour. In late 2001, the College of Physicians and Surgeons of Ontario fully vindicated Oliveri, indicating that she acted in a manner that was in the best interests of her patients ('College Vindicates Oliveri', 2002). A settlement between Oliveri, four colleagues who supported her, and the hospital was reached, and an agreement with Apotex regarding a defamation suit was reached in 2004. However, the battle did not end there and Oliveri was forced to go to court to enforce the agreement. In November 2008, the Ontario Supreme Court ordered Apotex to comply with terms of the 2004 agreement, including payment of $800,000 to Oliveri.

Instead of complying, Apotex has filed a further lawsuit alleging Oliveri has 'disparaged' Apotex contrary to the agreement because she has participated in conferences related to topics on such things as the relationship between universities, scientific research, and conflict of interest ('An Attack on Academic Freedom: Apotex vs Oliveri', 2009: A1). The circumstances facing Dr Oliveri have been extremely difficult. However, she has been somewhat fortunate to have the support of the Canadian Association of University Teachers (CAUT), and their academic freedom fund is enabling her to respond to the legal actions required against the hospital initially and then subsequently against Apotex, a pharmaceutical company with deep pockets.

At that time Prince George, like other Northern communities, was desperately short of resources to aid families and children. Not only were the social workers of the ministry overwhelmed by the size of the districts they had to cover and the enormity of the problems they encountered, but they were also in many ways the only source of assistance. Prince George lacked all the resources typically found in communities today: mental health services, transition houses for abused women, group homes for children, and neighbourhood houses for families. Unfortunately, the persistent efforts of Moran and her colleagues to gain additional staff met with little success. Faced with this lack of response, Moran decided to go outside the usual channels and to bring the situation facing her and the families she served to the attention of the Social Credit premier of the province as well as the public. In December 1963 Moran wrote to Premier Bennett, with copies to newspapers in Prince George, Vancouver, and Victoria, and to the leaders of the Conservative, Liberal, and New Democratic parties. Moran concluded her long and detailed letter with the following words:

> Every day here and across the province social workers are called upon to deal with seriously disturbed children. We have no psychiatrist, no specially trained foster parents, no receiving or detention homes to aid us. We place children in homes that have never been properly investigated, we ignore serious neglect cases because we have no available homes. Inadequate? Yes. Dangerous? Yes. . . . The group for whom I am begging help will continue to cost money, more and more money. So it becomes, does it not, a question not of whether we will spend money but of how that money will be spent? (Moran, 2001: 70)

Although Moran never received a reply from the premier, the letters to the opposition parties occasioned a veritable spate of questions in the legislature and newspapers gave extensive coverage to Moran's concerns. Within weeks she became a *cause célèbre* in BC, and gained considerable support from colleagues, from faculty members in the School of Social Work at the University of British Columbia, and indeed from the public. And initially it seemed as if the accusation of inadequate resources had produced the desired effect. Additional staff were promised to the Prince George Social Services office and there was a commitment to establish a mental health office. However, both promises faded quickly, and the predictable response of organizations confronting whistle-blowers occurred in Moran's case. She was accused of exaggerating the problems. For example, the member of the legislature for Prince George and the minister of finance dismissed her claims by saying 'she was only a part time social worker who became overwhelmed by her job' (Moran, 2001: 87). Finally, Moran was suspended from her position. Although the same suspension was later lifted for colleagues who had supported her, it remained in effect for Moran.

Some support for whistle-blowers may be available through the courts based on provisions in the Canadian *Charter of Rights and Freedoms*. For example, in 1998 Jason Gibson—a social worker employed by the Alberta Department of Family and Social Services—wrote a letter to a member of the opposition expressing his concerns about the planned redesign of services to children and families in the province. He sent copies to his own MLA, the minister, and the regional board responsible for social services. As a consequence, Gibson was reprimanded. He filed a grievance that was dismissed and the case was then reviewed by the Alberta Court of Queen's Bench. The court delivered a mixed decision, and both the government and Gibson appealed to the Alberta Court of Appeal. In its judgment, the Appeal Court agreed with Gibson. It cited the Canadian *Chapter of Rights and Freedoms* in finding that the reprimand of the social worker violated his right to freedom of expression. The Appeal Court also cited the Supreme Court of Canada in concluding that an employee's duty of loyalty needs to be balanced with the right of free expression, including the ability to criticize government, provided it is framed with restraint. In this instance, the concerns expressed related directly to the ability of social workers to effectively protect children from harm and the social worker's criticism had no adverse effect on his ability to perform his duties (Lancaster House, 2002).

It may well be that most front line practitioners are unaware of the Charter protections of freedom of expression. While the decision of the Appeal court based on the Charter of Rights does provide  protection for whistle-blowers, provided that they 'frame their concerns with restraint', it seems likely that the Charter is too remote and only tangentially connected to whistle-blowing for it to be a ready source of protection. Specific legislation and policies to protect whistle-blowers is an important consideration and one example is outlined in Box 7.2.

## Box 7.2 Whistle-Blowing Protection

Legislation and policies to protect whistle-blowers have been quite limited historically but there is more recent attention to this. Whistle-blowing protection exists in some form at the federal level and several provinces have enacted legislation in this area. Manitoba's *Public Interest Disclosure Act* (PIDA) received Royal Assent in 2006. It was developed in response to a review of the Workers' Compensation Board that substantiated allegations against the Chairman of the Board about highly questionable compensation and abuse of power. The *Act* applies to all government departments and agencies related to government, including child and family service agencies and regional health boards. It is designed to facilitate the disclosure of significant and serious matters related to public service which are unlawful, dangerous to the public, or detrimental to the public interest. The Act also serves to protect persons who make those disclosures, provided these are made in good faith. Whistle-blowers are protected in the following ways:

- Employees can make a confidential report about misconduct to a supervisor or union official within the department or agency or to the Ombudsman.
- Procedures to enable the confidential investigation of disclosures must be developed within each department or agency.
- When the information is provided to the Ombudsman, the Ombudsman may investigate the matter and make recommendations.
- A whistle-blower who is fired, demoted, or otherwise penalized can file a complaint with the Manitoba Labour Board.

Arguments supporting such legislation stem from a recognition that in-house whistle-blowing policies and procedures can be beneficial both to the organization and to service users. The Manitoba PIDA, like other similar Acts elsewhere, restricts the complaint process to internal government channels and does not offer protection to those who may go public with their complaint. In addition, such protection is restricted only to those working in government or related agencies. Nevertheless, these provisions offer an opportunity for whistle-blowers to report wrongdoing and questionable practices without having to risk public disclosure and discipline, including the potential loss of employment.

While the resource situation has improved in all communities across the country since Moran's days, there remains a continuing mismatch between the extent and severity of social problems and the resources available to respond to these problems. And there have been numerous efforts by social workers to bring attention to the gap between problems and resources.

With Gibson as a prominent exception, the recent calls for changes in child welfare do not rely on whistle-blowing by an individual. Rather, they have taken the form of group protests where a local office stages a day of protest, a union files a grievance on behalf of child welfare staff, or a provincial association of social workers registers its concerns with the minister and senior staff of the provincial ministries (Hart, 2001). While these advocacy efforts are to be commended, they are usually of short duration and too easily ignored by the minister in charge and his cabinet colleagues. More powerful advocacy campaigns could be launched if professional associations and unions collaborated, but to our knowledge such joint efforts have not occurred.

The influence of whistle-blowers in exposing punitive policies and outright wrongdoing in both the private and public sectors has been greatly aided by the media. Their actions have been described, often in sympathetic terms, in newspapers, magazines, and even in the movies such as *Silkwood* and *The Insider*. This supportive role differs dramatically from the one usually taken by the media in its coverage of the human services. For the most part, media interest is aroused by a tragedy: a child dies while in the care of a child welfare agency, a patient fails to recover from illness because of the negligence of nurses and physicians, or a person suspected of a crime is beaten while being taken into custody. And because all human service agencies are now subject to the scrutiny of review boards or agencies, the initial tragedy will be reviewed to determine where errors occurred and how these can be corrected. While some reviews are carried out without media attention, others become the source of continuing interest. It is worth noting that, at least in some matters, the tone of media coverage is set quickly and then maintained throughout subsequent reports. One example is the coverage by the *Vancouver Sun* of the Gove Inquiry, where a tone of blaming both the mother and the Ministry was established at the very beginning (see Callahan and Callahan, 1997).

The above should not be interpreted to mean that reviews and media attention are unnecessary. It is only suggested that public reviews and the media coverage need to be balanced and take into account all of the factors and conditions that resulted in a tragedy. Too often there is a tendency to blame individuals without considering the contributing factors of environment and the adequacy of resources available both to service users and practitioners.

## Summary and Conclusion

Progressive policy change does not come easily in a neo-liberal policy climate as noted by Steve Kerstetter, the former director of the National Council of Welfare. In discussing improvements to social security at the federal level he noted, somewhat pessimistically, that 'almost nothing works when the government is dedicated to paying down the debt, reducing taxes, and ignoring the poor' (Kerstetter, 2002: 1). And these comments were made when significant government surpluses were the norm—not during an economic recession with future budget deficits to look forward to! Indeed, federal social policy reforms since 1996 have been limited primarily to increases in health care funding, the development of the National Child Benefit as an income support measure for low income families, the National Child Care Benefit, and a few other modest income supplement or taxation reforms. But this does not mean one should give up in despair.

Three general strategies have had some success, and should be further considered. First, the general approach of Campaign 2000 has involved building support and common cause with groups and associations that would not automatically be clarified as 'soul mates'. This coalition building process and the activities emerging from this work have been invaluable in keeping the subject of poverty alive in the media and on the policy agenda of governments. Second, the work of the Caledon Institute indicates the usefulness of the concept of a policy window where a policy specialist, working in cooperation with like-minded government officials, established a policy community that was able to promote a significant policy response to the problem of child poverty. The result was the National Child Benefit, which reduces the size and severity of child poverty for low-income families based on eligibility established from filing one's income tax return. In this case, the ability to anticipate a policy gap that government was interested in addressing and be ready with a proposed solution was an element to success. A third strategy is whistle-blowing which involves public disclosure of wrong-doing. Whistle-blowing is a courageous act that needs to be carefully assessed by the individual. It becomes justifiable when all possible efforts to resolve matters through established channels have failed and when the issue should not be ignored.

The more general approaches summarized in this chapter, such as think tanks, social movements, and advocacy groups have been discussed in relation to government policy-making, primarily at the federal level. In addition, our examples in describing these approaches have focused largely on poverty reduction. We conclude with four important observations. First, the general approaches outlined here are easily adaptable to the provincial and local or organizational level.

Second, opportunities for influencing new policy development exist in a number of fields of practice besides income security and poverty reduction, including areas such as child welfare, health care, mental health, and criminal justice. Third, as noted above, timing matters and the ability to anticipate 'hot topics' or areas of potential priority is important to consider if one wants to influence change. For example, in the child welfare field new investment in differential response projects focusing on alternatives to taking children into care is a current policy priority in many provinces. This offers a 'policy window' in this field of practice where new policies and programs are more likely to be supported; however, this policy window may soon close and other priorities could emerge as more important to decision-makers. Finally individual opportunities to influence policy include policy advocacy from inside the organization and involvement in a professional association, union, or a community-based organization. Although individual advocacy work within a community-based context outside the system was not discussed in this chapter, an example of this was included in Chapter Two, when we described how a community activist worked both with community residents at the 'street level' and with authorities to address issues of neighbourhood safety and crime (see Box 2.1). Policy development at this level matters a great deal to local citizens and the benefits go far beyond the local community.

## Recommended Reading

N. Lemann, 'Paper Tiger: Daniel Ellsberg's War', *The New Yorker* 4 November 2002: 96–9. This article provides an insightful review of Ellsberg's book as well as the contribution of such information to policy-making.

B. Moran, *A Little Rebellion* (Vancouver: Arsenal Pulp Press, 2001). This autobiographical book provides an intriguing account of a social worker's experience as a whistle-blower.

R. Popham, D. Hay, and C. Hughes, 'Campaign 2000 to End Child Poverty: Building and Sustaining a Movement', in B. Wharf and M. Clague, eds, *Community Organizing: Canadian Experiences* (Don Mills, ON: Oxford University Press, 1997), 248–72. This chapter provides an early account of the work of Campaign 2000.

M. Callahan and K. Callahan, 'Victims and Villains: Scandals, the Press and Policy-Making in Child Welfare', in J. Pulkingham and G. Ternowetsky, eds, *Child and Family Policies: Struggle, Strategies and Options* (Halifax: Fernwood Press, 1997), 40–58. This chapter provides a careful analysis of the often contradictory role of the media in child welfare.

## Critical Thinking Questions

1.  Provide an example of where advocacy from inside the organization might be required in an effort to change a flawed policy developed by government or the organization. What strategies might be considered in order to change

the policy or mitigate its adverse effects? What are the risks, and how might these be managed?

2.  Several think tanks were mentioned in this chapter. Complete a search of their websites and provide a brief summary of their purposes. Can you identify the ideological orientation of each of these sites? What evidence can you provide to support your conclusions?

3.  What are the advantages of Campaign 2000's focus on child poverty? Are there any limitations in adopting this particular focus?

4.  Under what circumstances can whistle-blowing involving public disclosure of wrongdoing be justified?

5.  Examine the provisions of the Manitoba's *Public Interest Disclosure Act* (PIDA) identified in Box 7.2. Does this provide adequate whistle-blowing protection? Defend your answer.

## Chapter Eight

# Chalk and Cheese: Feminist Thinking and Policy-Making

*by Marilyn Callahan[1]*

This chapter reviews the particular contributions of feminist thinking to the central goal of this book: making connections amongst social policy, human service practice, and the lives of citizens. If I were writing this chapter a decade ago, I would take a very different tack than I will today. Much has changed in the past 10 years, including the vibrancy and currency of the women's movement. Further, issues of concern to feminists have been swept off the policy table in the rush to clean house of social programs and enhance the role of private interests in what used to be public responsibilities. There has been a sea change in expectations concerning the role of government in redressing inequalities (Bashevkin, 2002; Cohen Griffin and Pulkingham, 2009a). Even in academia, there is cold comfort. Some scholars claim that the women's agenda of the past 30 years has been largely accomplished now that women are occupying some of the key roles in academic administration and gaining proportional representation in many disciplines. Some fields, including social work, that were formerly sympathetic have turned their attention to perspectives (e.g., anti-oppressive practice) that subsume feminist perspectives under broader theorizing about oppression and race in particular. Feminism seems out of fashion in many quarters. Apparently we live in a 'post-feminist' era.

In this chapter, I take issue with these assertions and argue that now, more than ever, it is crucial to include feminist perspectives in dealing with problems, policy, and practice in the human services. Women still occupy most of the front line positions in human services and in many fields they make up the majority of the users of these services. While women may occupy significant posts in government and institutions, attend post-secondary institutions in equal or greater numbers than men, and work outside the home as well as within it, their overall economic status in Canada and other western countries still lags well behind their male counterparts (Dobson, 2002; Yalnizyan, 2008). Equality is far from accomplished. Feminist thinking has always focused upon the relationships amongst experiences in everyday life, the practice of professionals, and the policies which shape these practices. It has a rich legacy and pressing agenda to contribute to this enterprise.

## Feminist Thinking

Several years ago, I was involved in a research project examining policy alternatives to address the issue of women and substance use during pregnancy (Rutman, Callahan, Lundquist, Jackson, and Field, 1999). During the project, a team of Aboriginal researchers met with rural Aboriginal women to discuss whether women should be restrained or incarcerated if they continued to use substances during pregnancy. Initially, the Aboriginal women agreed with the idea, citing their own experiences within their families and voicing concerns about future generations of their people. However, as they considered the question, they thought about how such a policy would actually play out in their lives. Which women would be restrained? Mostly Aboriginal women, they predicted, even though more non-Aboriginal women use substances during pregnancy. Why? Because Aboriginal women are more visible to those in the helping and policing professions, because they have fewer resources to resist and challenge policies, because they frequently live in rural areas where treatment facilities are nonexistent, and because they are generally disregarded. The women reflected on the inordinate numbers of Aboriginal peoples in federal and provincial jails as a similar consequence of applying policies without regard to differing circumstances.

They also suggested that resources used for incarceration would continue to funnel funds away from helpful programs and that the policy would continue the stereotyping of Aboriginal people. They concluded that the policy could promote conflicts within communities already disadvantaged by historical, geographical, and economic realities. They gave examples of hardships that some women and their families would suffer.

Although they resisted an incarceration policy, these women proposed solutions of their own, which included reinstating the practice of traditional home visitors, usually senior women in the community; reforming health care funding policies so that funds could be distributed to women's organizations concerned with health and social issues; and dismantling the Band Council structures created under the *Indian Act*. To them, Band Councils reflected the colonizing aims of government policies and undermined the hereditary organization of communities, creating artificial elites within the community and disenfranchising many women. The women were also careful to underscore that their suggestions might work for their Tribal Council and communities but may not suit others.

Schroedel and Peretz (1994), reflecting on the same issue in the United States where several states have enacted policies permitting the incarceration of women using substances during pregnancy, raise another question. Why has the focus of media and research turned relentlessly on women's behaviour during pregnancy and not on other toxic hazards in the environment or to the effects of alcohol and drug use by men that can damage sperm and lead to violent behaviour towards pregnant women? They argue that there is no overt conspiracy among lawyers, medical professionals, and journalists to define fetal abuse in a manner that blames the woman while ignoring the man's role. Instead there is simply a pre-disposition to view the world through analytical lenses that replicate and reinforce the existing gender biases.

This discussion by Aboriginal women and American scholars illustrates several central planks of feminist theorizing. Although it is impossible to provide a thorough review of feminist thinking and its variations and controversies, a few essentials require mention. First, feminist thinking challenges the conventional wisdom that equality can be achieved by treating everyone the same. Clearly, passing legislation to allow the incarceration of women who use substances while pregnant would not play out equally amongst women. At the turn of the twentieth century when first wave feminists were fighting for the right to vote, many held the view that once women obtained suffrage they would be able to run for office and make significant strides in addressing inequalities. Yet in 2008 in Canada, fully 90 years after the passage of the federal *Women's Franchise Act* of 1918, only 27 per cent of the candidates in the federal election were female and women won 22 per cent of the seats (up one per cent from the election of 2006). In fact, the dismal record of electing women to government was the significant factor in Canada's score in a recent global gender gap index survey; Canada fell 13 points, is now ranked behind the United States and is 31st out of 130 countries (Hausmann, Tyson, and Zahidid, 2007). Universal franchise did not lead to equal opportunities in the political arena. For some, this is a problem for women to address by running for office. Feminist thinking underscores the reality that so-called equal treatment can maintain substantial disadvantages for groups while at the same time reducing sympathy for their circumstances. No one would argue that gaining the franchise was vitally important for improving the status of women. But it alone is insufficient.

Feminist thinking probes how inequality is maintained through everyday practices. Most institutions and policies have been designed and are controlled by middle-aged men, not by any conspiracy but by tradition and by the ongoing advantaging process within these patriarchal structures that maintain this tradition. How that advantaging process works is often unrecognized because it is so familiar, so accepted, and so normalized. One component of this process is the creation of knowledge: Whose way of perceiving the world becomes accepted knowledge and whose ways are ignored? For instance, the idea of reforming Band structures imposed on Aboriginal nations has not gained the same currency as incarcerating women who use substances during pregnancy. Feminist thinking seeks to disrupt that sense of normalcy.

Creating space for different ways of knowing is one way to challenge the status quo. From the experiences of women in daily life come the questions: How does this process affect me and how is it perpetuated? Why are things the way they are? This examination frequently reveals the interconnection between dichotomies—the economic and the social, the private and the public, the emotional and the rational—that frame our 'usual' thinking. Key to understanding how these dichotomies have disadvantaged women is the unwillingness to recognize women's work in social reproduction as making a central contribution to the economy of any nation. Instead, women's caring has been ignored as part of such calculations, as taking place in the private (non-monetary) rather than the public realm. Neo-liberal thinking has reinforced this dichotomy. For instance, instead of recognizing the need for public child care expenditures to support women's caring responsibilities, the Conservative government of Canada developed a policy to provide families with $100 monthly (amounting to about $85 after tax), an amount far short of the cost of child care, even if spaces were available.

A rallying cry of second wave feminist movement of the 1960s and 1970s—the personal is political—contains a key plank of feminist thinking. Each individual's experience of disadvantage reveals within it connections to formal and informal workings of power well beyond the individual. Making those connections does not come naturally. We are often inclined to personalize our experience and frequently blame ourselves for our failings. Instead, feminism has traced how what happens on the ground is connected to what happens beyond ourselves. Dorothy Smith, a Canadian sociologist, has made it her life's work to underscore these connections and her book, *The Everyday World as Problematic* (1987), informed by Marxist and feminist thinking, stands as a landmark. The Aboriginal women discussing substance use during pregnancy spoke about being marginalized within their communities and then connected this to the behaviour of some men and, in turn, related this male behaviour to the patriarchal systems imposed on the men by white government policies.

Feminist thinking exposes injustice in many quarters, working from the individual injustices experienced by women. And it benefits from other theories of oppression, such as those developed by Aboriginal peoples and others regarding colonization. It enriches these theories by exposing how gender interacts with other socially constructed disadvantages. Feminism is most misunderstood on this particular issue because there is a common misconception that it reveals the oppression of women only. The strength of feminism lies in its grounding in the everyday experiences of half the population and the movement beyond that to uncover how formal and informal systems work to perpetuate inequities for many.

This process of uncovering injustices reveals clearly that while all women are negatively affected by patriarchal values and systems, some women and some groups of both men and women are more harmed than others. Although those who feel the pain of oppression most severely are those most disadvantaged by race, class, gender, ability, sexual orientation, and other socially constructed categories of privilege, individual identities can change in different circumstances. In one group, for example, individuals can be privileged on some occasions and severely penalized in others (Yeatman and Gunew, 1993). Feminism 'has lost the moral high ground that comes with the depiction of all women everywhere as victims of patriarchy' (Brodie, 1995: 79).

Perhaps one of the most important advances in feminist thinking is that because of the differences amongst women it is important to break down such overarching concepts as feminist, oppression, patriarchy, organizing, and the state. Postmodern feminist theorizing has contributed significantly to understanding the many, often conflicting dimensions of these large taken-for-granted concepts and how power works well apart from formal structures (Nicholson, 1990).

Embedded in the notion of movement between privilege and disadvantage is another key plank of feminist thinking: Women are not only victims of oppression but also actors within oppressive systems who can both maintain and disrupt them. How these disruptions have and can occur is the subject of this chapter.

# Feminist Thinking and the Challenge of Connecting Policy and Practice

Earlier in the chapter, I indicated that feminist thinking has a rich legacy to offer to the challenge of connecting policy and practice. The following section highlights some of these contributions. While I illustrate these contributions with broad policy initiatives, it is also true that the same lessons can be applied at smaller group levels and by practitioners in their daily work.

## Making Connections between Policy and the Lives of Women

A significant strength of women's groups and feminist research is its focus on the realities of women's lives and then its commitment to making those realities heard in the public forum. This is the first connection: from private to public, personal to political. This has been the work of many women's groups that have successfully and continually kept the spotlight on injustices affecting women. Another process of connecting occurs as feminists analyze existing public policies and professional practices to demonstrate how they affect individual women in different circumstances, testing the impact of public policies on private lives. These two dialectical processes are ongoing. They may occur at broad national and international levels or within much smaller arenas such as an existing program or community. But the aim is the same: illuminating disadvantage and redressing it.

In the process of making these connections, feminist thinking directs policy-makers and practitioners to ask a few central questions: how will this particular policy or practice affect people differentially? Who will benefit, who loses out and how could these inequalities be mitigated? These are the same questions raised by Aboriginal women contemplating the introduction of incarceration of women who use substances during pregnancy discussed at the beginning of this chapter. It is first and foremost an analytical stance. 'Gender-based analysis challenges the assumption that everyone is affected by policies, programs and legislation in the same way regardless of gender, a notion often referred to as "gender-neutral policy"' (Status of Women Canada, 1996: 4).

One vehicle for analysis—gender lenses—has promise although there is no legislation in Canada requiring the inclusion of gender lenses in the policy-making process. Effectively, lenses pose a series of questions and actions designed to assess the differential impact of any one policy or program on the target population. The gender lens developed by the BC Ministry of Women's Equality (1997), the gender-sensitive model for policy analysis developed by Status of Women Canada (1998), and Health Canada's policy on Gender-based Policy Analysis (Health Canada, 2009) are examples of this approach. The lenses are based upon some fundamental principles related to feminist thinking and are concerned with both the substance and process of policy and program development and implementation (see Box 8.1).

While not widely embraced by government, gender lens analysis has found traction in quasi-government and not-for-profit organizations, and it is used to scrutinize initiatives both within a particular organization and by outside groups analyzing government policy. For instance, a gender analysis of the federal budget published by the Canadian Centre for Policy Alternatives (Yalnizyan, 2008) reveals some key findings largely ignored by popular media but crucial to advancing women's equality. Using the central question of 'What's in it for women?', Yalnizyan demonstrates that although women make up slightly more than half of the contributors to the tax system, they benefit substantially less from the fiscal policies that shaped the 2005–08 federal government budgets: tax breaks, smaller government, and debt reduction. Tax breaks overwhelmingly benefit higher income earners and women make up two-thirds of minimum wage

---

## Box 8.1 Principles of Gender-Based Analysis

- Every government policy has a human impact.
- Policies affect men and women differently.
- Women are not a homogeneous group.
- Policies must attempt to create equal outcomes for men and women.
- Equal outcomes will not result from treating everyone the same.
- Equal outcomes benefit everyone.
- Policy-makers bring their own biases to the job.
- The best policies are those where consultation has played a considerable role.
- Special measures are required so that those disadvantaged can make their views known.
- Consultation is ongoing and not a one-off business.

Source: BC Ministry of Women's Equality, 1997

earners. So-called smaller government policies have slashed the social programs of most benefit to women and redirected resources to those more focused upon surveillance and control. The federal government's debt reduction strategy has resulted in a hugely accelerated program to pay down the national debt and has provided a rationale for restricting social programs, although the reasons for such a massive debt reduction strategy are far from clear. This analysis reveals the importance of examining what government does in terms of policy and what it doesn't do, in the name of insufficient resources. While these policies disadvantage women overall, they have a differential impact on low-income women, many of whom are women of colour. The economic recession of 2008–09 has resulted in a return to deficit budgets on the part of the federal government beginning in 2009, and a similar analysis of the impact of expenditures under this scenario is warranted.

The case of Kimberly Rogers illustrates how the failure to evaluate the gender implications of policy can have devastating consequences. On 25 April 2001, Kimberly Rogers was convicted of defrauding Ontario Works because she was receiving benefits and also had a student loan. She was sentenced to six months of general house arrest and 18 months of probation with no right to receive further benefits for three months. (A lifetime ban has since been implemented for others who commit the same offence.) She lost her drug prescription coverage and, although she had no other income, she was required to make restitution of about $14,000. At the time, she was five months' pregnant. A law firm launched a Charter challenge and her benefits were reinstated pending the outcome of the challenge which was to be decided in September 2001. She committed suicide in August of that year during a heat wave in Sudbury.

The public debate was intense. The policy of a lifetime ban on benefits and house arrest was the focus of the debate. How such a policy affects men and women differently received less attention. As women are most likely to be the ones who care for children, their loss of benefits will affect their children (the regulations cut off the mother but continue payments for her children reducing family income overall). Further, women with children are more likely to remain longer on income benefits than their male counterparts, making it more likely that they will run afoul of regulations. Even if they find work after being banned from income support, women still earn significantly less than their male counterparts and have to cope with inadequate and expensive child care provisions. The distinct possibility that the lifetime ban contravenes the *Charter of Rights and Freedoms* was considered, although the Charter challenge was dropped with the death of Ms Rogers.[2]

The gender lens approach to policy-making demands a restructuring of policy-making processes so that it is focused less on the expertise of a few and more on different ways of knowing by many. It requires consultation on a broad and ongoing basis. While seemingly more cumbersome, this consultation also builds alliances that can protect practitioners and policy-makers from egregious errors that erode their own credibility.

## Making Connections between Feminists and Those Who May Share Common Cause

The history of women influencing policy and practice to improve their status in Canada is illustrious. Some examples at the national level include the following:

- The work of early feminists who fought for the franchise resulting in federal legislation in 1918. (Aboriginal women did not similarly obtain this right until 1960.)
- The Persons Case of 1929 where women were finally acknowledged as persons within the *British North America Act*.
- The *Royal Commission on the Status of Women*, reporting in 1970, which led to a host of policies and programs to redress the status of women.
- The *Canadian Human Rights Act*, 1977, which prohibited sexual discrimination in employment and assured women equal pay for work of equal value.
- The inclusion of equality between the sexes as part of the *Canadian Charter of Rights and Freedoms*, 1982.
- Amendments to the *Indian Act* in 1985 returning status and the right to band membership to Aboriginal women who had lost these rights by marrying non-Aboriginal men.

All of these efforts involved the work of a large number of women identifying specific issues and then joining together on an ad hoc basis and in established groups within and outside government. They strategized, formed alliances, acted out, and pressured wherever they could. Key to the success of these efforts was the unwillingness to categorize those working for government as the 'enemy' of those working on the outside in action groups. Instead there were efforts to introduce feminist thinking and structures within government and to deploy feminists—sometimes called 'femocrats'—in a wide range of state positions where they could, through daily actions within government and connections with community feminist groups, seek to change the culture of policy-making (Rankin and Vickers, 2001). Indeed it was the partnership between those on the inside and those on the outside that produced results (Rebick, 2005; Cohen Griffin, and Pulkingham, 2009b).

Although the state has significantly reduced efforts to address the needs of women, this has not led to increased feminist activism. In fact, the strength of feminist action groups has also diminished over the past two decades as neo-liberal thinking has gained prominence. Those protesting the restructured state appear to be out of step with the times, hanging on to the old 'nanny state'[3] with no new visions to inform governments.

Not surprisingly, many feminist activists have turned away from opposing state actions to protest global economies and systems that are wreaking havoc with deeply held beliefs about citizenship, environment, and social responsibility.

Naomi Klein's *No Logo* (2001) is a good example of feminist analysis about the connections between social and economic well-being at an international level. Feminist groups have many international connections with women's organizations and use these to challenge basic tenets of globalization. Yet it is important to continue to confront inequalities even in a country as prosperous as Canada where conditions may not seem as bleak but where gains that have been fought for by courageous citizens could be quickly lost.

Making connections between local and global issues affecting women is one very promising area. The Canadian Feminist Alliance for International Action (FAFIA) is an example of a coalition of over 75 Canadian women's groups that aim 'to further women's equality in Canada through domestic implementation of its international human rights commitments' (Canadian FAFIA website, 2009). Their website includes a 'Who's Who' of women's groups throughout the country. Canada's 1980 commitment to the UN *Convention on the Elimination of all Forms of Discrimination against Women* (CEDAW) and the Bejing Platform for Action provide leverage to press for change. By holding the Canadian government accountable for its formal commitments made an international level, women's organizations such as FAFIA are challenging the notion that they are merely left-leaning 'special interest' groups who seek to advance exceptional privilege for its members without regard for the whole, a charge that is often used to diminish their efforts. To say that feminist thinking is passé in policy and practice is to ignore the very substantial efforts that have survived and prospered in spite of disappearing state funding. This approach is highlighted by Rankin and Vickers:

> Our research concludes that, particularly in an era marked by globalization and decentralization, 'bothering with government' is still pivotal to the achievement of equality and justice for all women. We encourage feminist organizations to engage in an ongoing evaluation of the political opportunity structures they face and call for renewed debate on how feminists can work most effectively with policy-makers. Finally, we argue that women's policy machinery can be an important partner with feminists in public policy debates, but new channels of communication between state feminism and women's movements are required. (2001: 36)

## Making Connections among Social Workers and between Social Workers and Service Users

Central to feminist analysis of policy and practice is the notion of making connections between individuals, groups, and their larger context; the personal is indeed political. Feminist thinking does not begin and end with an analysis of an individual case and the ways in which workers could practice differently. This central reality was brought home to me in a recent study on risk assessment in child welfare conducted by Karen Swift and myself and situated in two provinces, Ontario and British Columbia (Swift and Callahan, in press).

In the study we identified a common phenomenon in human service practice: how workers and their clients consciously *disconnect* policy from practice when policy seems harmful. We interviewed practitioners and mothers involved in risk assessment, a process whereby practitioners investigating a situation of possible child maltreatment are required to complete a checklist of possible risks and assign each one a score based on a common set of descriptors. These scores are then analyzed to determine whether further investigation is required, whether children should be removed from or returned to their parents, and/or whether the family is eligible for supportive services.

While some practitioners felt very positive about the risk assessment process, others chose to go along with it reluctantly, and still others found different ways to subvert it. For instance, these latter workers sometimes raised the risk scores on intake so that people who would not be eligible for service based on their scores could access them nonetheless. In some cases, social workers even ignored the risk assessment altogether by working with the clients as they always had and filling out the forms later to satisfy the demands of the procedures and files. This most often occurred in remote towns and villages where applying the risk assessment instrument dutifully may have resulted in the removal of most children in the local communities. When those social workers who managed to work around the risk assessment process talked to us about their actions, they referred to themselves directly or indirectly as the 'good' practitioners, and considered others who complied with risk assessment policy as less professional and more bureaucratic.

Even though these practitioners disagreed with risk assessment policy and practice, they did not appear to make public their concerns in any cohesive fashion. Instead, they reasoned that by subverting it in their practice yet appearing to follow it in their paper work, they were doing what they could to undermine the risk policy while keeping their jobs and reputations. They knew that should the case go badly wrong, it was important to have completed the procedures correctly to protect themselves.

We also noted some of the same behaviour occurring with mothers who were the subject of risk assessments in child welfare. Many of these mothers had been complained about many times and had repeatedly experienced risk assessments. They did not think much of the risk assessment process and disputed many of its claims, at least to us. They told us about the many times they had had been required to attend different programs designed to reduce their risks. Like the social workers, they indicated that they were different than other mothers who had complaints made against them. They did not leave their children alone, nor keep an untidy house, nor use alcohol and drugs, and so forth, all stereotypical behaviours of mothers who maltreat their children. These women kept themselves apart from other mothers under investigation lest they be 'tarred with the same brush'. They pretended to follow the rules set down by the worker, at least on the surface, in order to get the worker out of their lives. Even though they doubted the efficacy of repeating programs and other activities, they did not usually make their views known to the workers or others. They did not want to appear noncompliant lest they jeopardize further their position as mothers.

This phenomenon of subverting policy by appearing to comply with it in practice and of positioning oneself in the process as 'I'm not like the rest of them', in fact, 'I'm better than them' has been observed in other studies about workers and clients in the humans services (Munro and Rumgay, 2000; Callahan, Rutman, Strega, and Dominelli, 2005). Most of us have done some version of it ourselves. Rather than connect policy and practice, it is a conscious effort to disconnect it without actually challenging it.

Those with postmodern inclinations might argue that everyday rebellions such as this wear away at policy and eventually change it, much like walking diagonally on the grass may lead to the creation of a formal path in time. But is it the same? The results of walking on the grass can be seen. Individual challenges to policy through subversive practice may create benefits for a few and occasional satisfactions for workers, but do they necessarily lead to policy changes?

Traditional feminist thinking, based upon liberation theory, would argue somewhat differently (Memmi, 1967; Friere, 1970, Roberts, 1983). Public compliance and private rebellion are viewed as a necessary but insufficient component to change: that is, it is only a good starting place. These theorists contend that many people who have overcome oppressions have begun by first learning to rejoice in their own perspectives and debunk the myths about them, sharing their stories of individual rebellions and, from these stories, forging relationships amongst each other and a common agenda for change.

In the risk study, we did not see social workers and mothers joining together to challenge either the science of risk assessment (doubtful) or its negative effects on their practice, in effect taking the next steps. After a decade (1998–2008) the risk assessment was eventually modified somewhat, making it less prescriptive and more focused on strengths. One of the central reasons for the changes was the number of children removed from their parents and the costs of this care. The outcomes of risk assessment were expensive, unexpected, and a high price to pay for a largely failed experiment.

A contrasting example of trying to change policy by collectively challenging it in practice is provided by the school teachers in British Columbia (Coutts, 2009). Because they were alarmed by the government policy that focused on mandatory and standardized tests for school-aged children, a few teachers refused to administer such tests. Eventually their individual protests were made public in the media. At the same time, teachers organized within their professional association to put pressure on individual school boards; as a result, some boards withdrew from the testing process. Some school boards also introduced policies permitting individual parents to authorize (or not) the tests for their children. While the provincial government was successful in requiring school boards to administer the tests, the opt-out clause for individual parents remained. More parents are presently choosing to exercise this option as teachers educate the public about the resource costs of these tests and their dubious educational value.

Although there is substantial difference in the power of public school teachers, their professional association and parents compared to social workers and parents in child welfare, the lessons of making visible the effects of policy in practice remain.

## Making Connections between Policy and Program Purposes and their Outcomes

Feminist thinking is focused on results because it is tied to a movement with a cause. Therefore it is focused on how some policies may flounder and others are transformed remarkably from their original intent during implementation.

Pence and Shepard (1999), along with the Praxis International organization in Duluth, Minnesota, have developed an interesting approach that combines monitoring implementation and evaluation. The organization works on addressing violence against women, particularly in the home. The authors observed that although new and progressive policies against violence in the home had been implemented, they often took very different expressions in actual practice and sometimes made matters worse. So, they became interested in evaluating the work of police, the courts, and social workers. In particular, the authors noted that the work of one organization often contradicted the work of another.

An outcome of these observations was the development of the safety audit. Based on the research methods of Dorothy Smith (1987), the safety audit begins with an examination of what happens on the ground: How do police officers decide what should be done when they receive a call involving a domestic dispute? What are the tools that they use to make that decision? What forms do they fill out? Who do they call, and what happens then? By examining the decision-making processes and the attendant work that accompanies these decisions, the safety auditors trace what happens in the case and whether the outcomes actually led to improved safety. They can identify points in the process where other options could occur and they can raise questions about the data used to make decisions. The safety audit pays attention to interorganizational relationships (or their absence) and it is a useful tool for government organizations and community groups to evaluate how policies work in practice. The safety audit is similar (although perhaps a more systematic framework) to the process of tracking individual circumstances and outcomes for service users that should be a primary component of practice in the human services.

# Summary and Conclusion

Oscar Wilde once said that the trouble with socialism was 'that it took up too many Sundays'. Some feel that one of the troubles with feminism is similar: it takes too much time and demands too much effort. Throughout the chapter, I have tried to indicate the value of using feminist thinking in policy-making and practice as well as some of the successes associated with such efforts. When I began to participate in feminist groups in the 1960s, the world was a very different place for women. There were few women in any of the well-paid professions such as law and medicine; divorcing women had no claim to the matrimonial property; First Nations women lost their status if they married non-status men; sexual assault was often blamed on women; and most young women did not expect to have a career and children at the same time. Dramatic changes have occurred since then and feminist groups can take credit for many of these, working both outside and within policy-making structures.

What have changed less are these policy-making structures and processes. They still creak along, founded on beliefs about who the experts are and what the proper processes for making decisions are. Some have argued persuasively that the changes to policy-making that have occurred have been primarily negative ones. As managerial thinking about human services as commodities and professionals as suppliers has gained ground, decision-making has become even further removed from the realities of those on the front line and those who are the clients.

Feminist thinking presents a challenge to these processes. It argues for more time, broad consultation, and different expertise. It doesn't fit well with governments in a hurry and governments under attack: thus the title of this chapter—chalk and cheese—an expression that means 'worlds apart' (Schur, 1987). How to open up these processes while recognizing the realities of the hurly-burly of policy-making is the ongoing challenge.

If I were to identify the most important contributions of feminist thinking to policy-making, it would be the feminist practice of building relationships across differences—a process grounded in feminist challenges to dichotomous thinking. For instance, as Pence and Shepard (1999) illustrate, demanding government attention to the issue is only one part of addressing violence against women. Feminist action groups must build relationships with other social movements and with sympathetic professionals, and encourage them to put the issues on their agendas. They must also forge connections with those inside bureaucracies such as hospitals, police, and governments who may be able to do something specific about the problem. Relationship-building is essential so that large, sometimes recalcitrant, organizations can move in different directions. It requires the development of tolerance and respect amongst people with very different views of the world and the relinquishment of a self-righteous stance by groups within and outside the 'system'. These relationships must be genuine if they are to succeed. All this is well known by human service practitioners and others who have learned the importance and skills of relationship-building as the cornerstone of practice.

Helping to put a problem on the agenda of others is indeed important but having solutions to those problems is another essential contribution of feminist thinking: women are agents of change as well as victims of oppression. Transition houses are a clear example of the success of this strategy. Women simply opened up safe houses, initially squatting in abandoned buildings and gradually gaining community and government support for their efforts (Pizzey, 1977). By working out solutions, even those that are small and short-lived, groups with little contact can sit down face-to-face and dispel myths about one another. Relationship-building occurs. Other solutions may be sought. Again, social workers and other human service workers know the value of promoting small steps in the process of change, of celebrating them, and using them for more relationship-building.

Changing policy-making and practice processes to include the women who are affected by the issues is common sense. And without such changes, the process of addressing inequalities may simply reinforce them, an outcome of no small irony.

## Recommended Reading

S. Bear, with the Tobique Women's Group, 'You Can't Change the Indian Act', in J.D. Wine and J.L. Ristock, eds, *Women and Social Change: Feminist Activism in Canada* (Toronto: James Lorimer and Company, 1991), 185–209. This chapter provides an excellent example of Aboriginal women organizing to affect change in the Indian Act.

J. Brodie, *Politics on the Margins: Restructuring and the Canadian Women's Movement* (Halifax: Fernwood Publishing, 1995). This book provides a thorough examination of the challenges facing the Canadian women's movement in light of globalization.

L. Briskin and M. Eliasson, eds, *Women's Organizing and Public Policy in Canada and Sweden* (Kingston, ON: McGill-Queen's University Press, 1999). This book provides a rare opportunity to compare the efforts of Canadian and Swedish women and their organizational strategies.

M. Cohen Griffin and J. Pulkingham, eds, *Public Policy for Women: The State, Income Security and Labour Market Issues* (Toronto: University of Toronto Press, 2009). This book is a collection of chapters by prominent Canadian scholars who address how recent public policies have failed women on many fronts.

## Critical Thinking Questions

1.  What impact (if any) has feminist thinking and analysis had in your agency and in your practice? If you do not work in an agency, think of an organization where you may have acted as a volunteer or with which you are familiar.
2.  In the Introduction of this chapter it was noted that in some fields feminist thinking and analysis have been subsumed under broader theorizing about oppression (e.g., anti-oppressive practice). Do you agree with this view? If so, is this a positive development? Why or why not? If you do not agree with this view, explain why?
3.  Are we now in a post-feminist era? If so, what are the possible consequences for the human services? What is your perspective on any of these consequences?

# Notes

1. Professor Callahan and Professor Karen Swift (York University) have recently completed research into the concept of risk. Their book, *At Risk: Social Justice in Child Welfare and Other Human Services*, will be published by the University of Toronto Press later this year.
2. Section 15(1) of the Charter states: 'Every individual is equal before and under the law and has the right to the equal protection and equal benefit of the law without discrimination and, in particular, without discrimination based on race, national or ethnic origin, colour, religion, sex, age or mental or physical disability.'
3. The term 'nanny state' is a derogatory reference to the period when social welfare provisions were more generous than is the case today.

# Chapter Nine

# Policy Resistance: The Rise and Fall of Welfare Time Limits in BC

*by Bruce Wallace and Tim Richards*[1]

In Chapter Six a variety of strategies designed to lead to more inclusive policy-making were identified and in Chapter Seven a number of approaches that involve influencing policy development from outside the system were reviewed. In Chapter Seven, and earlier in the book, the dilemma that often confronts both human service workers, as well social activists outside the system, was identified: What do you do when faced with policies that have been designed to reduce benefits to service users, and impose punitive procedures or otherwise restrict access to benefits and services? Although individuals may, on occasion, subvert these policies, the benefits that result are at best restricted to a limited number of individuals. Group advocacy, as a form of resistance, is sometimes possible but such efforts often appear to make little difference to a government with a strong ideological investment in the policy. This chapter presents a detailed case study analysis of policy resistance that involved the BC Liberal government's failure to impose time limits on recipients of income assistance as a requirement for eligibility to receive welfare. 'Welfare time limits' were introduced as part of an overall policy of disentitlement, based on the belief that welfare is not a basic support that should be available to anyone in need; rather it is a temporary benefit accorded only to people who prove that they are worthy of assistance.

In 2002, the BC provincial government enacted legislation under which certain classes of recipients would have their monthly benefits reduced or eliminated if they remained on income assistance for more than 24 months in a 60-month period. This was one among a number of punitive welfare reforms, but was noteworthy for being the first such eligibility requirement in Canadian history. While the welfare reforms that disentitled and denied assistance to applicants would ultimately have more devastating consequences for larger numbers of individuals, the welfare time limits reform best symbolized the way in which the government intended to reshape the welfare system. This new eligibility requirement was also notable because of the unprecedented opposition which developed against it, opposition that extended into mainstream civil society and well beyond groups traditionally opposed to punitive changes to the welfare system. Ultimately, the government was unable to salvage the welfare time limits policy, and on 6 February 2004 it capitulated by effectively eliminating time limits through legislative amendment.

This result is significant. Historically, opposition to punitive welfare policies has not been successful. In BC since the mid-1990s, when the percentage of people on income assistance approached 10 per cent of the population, successive governments have legislated cuts to welfare benefits and restricted eligibility rules to reduce the numbers of people receiving welfare. Though the impacts have been harsh, none of these previous welfare reforms generated significant public opposition. Time-limited welfare was different, and it is important to understand why.

In analyzing the rise and fall of welfare time limits, this chapter addresses two interrelated questions. First, why was the government unable to impose time limits to income assistance? And second, what can be learned from the process that may have broader implications in resisting the adverse effects of what are essentially 'bad policies'?

By answering these questions, we document the first attempt in Canadian history by a government to impose welfare time limits. We have drawn extensively on over a thousand pages of internal government material acquired through a *Freedom of Information* (FOI) request, and have also examined public documents and media reports. These materials enable an analysis of the complexities underlying the failure of this policy by examining the opposition to the policy both within the Welfare Ministry and within civil society.

The reader is cautioned that the chronology and analysis in this paper has limitations. The dynamics of the process regarding time limits both within the Ministry and amongst the public were very complex. Further, we are working with partial information; the *Freedom of Information* materials we received were heavily censored by the provincial government. The FOI process in this research was an arduous two-year ordeal characterized by the government denying the existence of the records requested, needlessly requiring requests to be reworded in special language; withholding information; and using other tactics to avoid release of information.

## The Rise of Welfare Time Limits—2001–02

In 2001, the BC Liberals were elected, promising a 'New Era' for the province. Once elected, they promised to end what they described as the culture of welfare dependency: 'We will find them jobs, we will get them training and, for the rest of their lives, they will be self-sufficient', stated the Minister of Human Resources. As part of this program, on October 2001 the front-page headline of Victoria's daily newspaper announced 'Welfare Time Limits Expected in Spring', and quoted the

Minister as saying: 'we are in the early stages of redefining welfare' and that a time limit on welfare payments to people who are capable of being employed would be implemented in the near future (Lavoie, 2001: A1).

In early 2002, the government translated its election slogans into spending priorities with a budget that required significant cuts to social spending in BC. The Welfare Ministry was directed to achieve a reduction of $581 million—a full 30 per cent cut—over the course of three years. This was the greatest reduction to any ministry. In response, the Ministry established caseload reduction targets that corresponded to the drastic reduction in its projected budgets. In the Legislature in February 2002, Premier Gordon Campbell assigned the Ministry responsibility to 'reduce total income assistance caseload' as part of the Government's Strategic Plan (BC Ministry of Human Resources, 2004a: 3). The Premier also established performance measures for the Ministry's Deputy Minister (DM) along with bonus pay for (1) reducing the number of welfare recipients by two per cent and (2) reducing the growth rate in disability assistance by two per cent regardless of the need (Francis, 2003: A16).

The specifics of time-limited welfare were delineated in the Ministry's 'Service Plan Summary':

Eligible employable singles and couples will receive assistance for a maximum of two years out of every five years. Eligible employable parents with dependent children will receive full income assistance for a maximum of two years out of every five years, after which their rates will be reduced by an average of 11 per cent. (BC Ministry of Human Resources, 2002: 5)

There were eight different groups of recipients exempted from the rule, including those over 65, those receiving certain types of disability benefits, and single parents with a child under three years of age or caring for a disabled child.

In anticipation of public opposition to time limits, an internal briefing note[2] prepared before the new welfare legislation was introduced discussed the likely opposition and the potential grounds for legal challenges. The note advised that 'negative reaction may be expected from advocacy agencies, clients and not-for-profit social services agencies who provide emergency shelter, temporary accommodation and food for homeless individuals' and that 'new Acts establish a number of provisions that may attract legal challenges'— specifically mentioning the welfare time limits. Of greatest concern to Ministry staff was the outstanding Supreme Court of Canada decision on the Gosselin v. Quebec case, which argued the state had a legal obligation to provide adequate assistance under welfare legislation. The briefing note explained how the planned legislation had been purposefully written to impose sanctions such as time limits while avoiding legal challenge, but warned that if the pending Supreme Court of Canada's decision created an obligation on provinces to provide adequate assistance, the Ministry would be in a weaker position to defend its time limits sanction.

As anticipated by the provincial government, the proposed welfare time limits were immediately controversial. Policy analysts from across the political spectrum agreed that this initiative was drastically different than other aspects of welfare restructuring, that this was unprecedented in Canada, and that the introduction of time limits in BC could have national implications. The Fraser Institute called welfare time limits 'a watershed development in Canadian welfare reform' (Schafer and Clemens, 2002: 16). The Canadian Centre for Policy Alternatives wrote that the time limit rule represented 'a fundamental shift in Canadian social policy—the denial of welfare when in need as a basic human right' (Klein and Long, 2003: 4).

Advocates and community groups working with people in need of assistance quickly registered their opposition and their predictions of harm. The planned changes to welfare legislation, and especially the unprecedented time limits, prompted challenging legal and ethical questions from anti-poverty advocates. University of British Columbia professor Graham Riches stated 'Let there be no doubt that [the] welfare reform decisions violate international law and in certain respects the *Charter of Rights and Freedoms*. The Government actions require legal challenges' (Riches, 2002: 1). In February 2002, a coalition of community agencies and poverty law advocates sent their concerns about the new welfare laws to the *United Nations Committee on Economic and Social Cultural Rights*, which the media reported, noting that 'poverty-law experts have claimed that the Campbell government's proposed welfare reforms could violate Canada's Constitution' (Smith, 2002: 10).

The new legislation, identified as the *Employment and Income Assistance Act*, was debated in the Provincial Legislature in April and received Royal Assent on 30 May 2002. However, the welfare time limits were not to come into effect until they were implemented by regulation four months later, on 30 September 2002. This regulation backdated the beginning of time-limited income assistance by six months to 1 April 2002. For an unknown number of individuals in receipt of welfare, their welfare time limit clock had started ticking.

Dr Reitsma-Street from the University of Victoria summed up community concerns about the legislative review process in this way:

> In spite of the significant changes no witnesses were called, no hearings were held, and no research into the legislation's impact was examined. The government permitted only a few hours of debate on the bills before approving them, despite requests of hundreds of people and groups who volunteered to appear before them. (2002: 5)

The public responses varied from condemnation to acclaim. In June 2002, at the BC Association of Social Workers' Annual General Meeting, members voted to censure the Minister (who identified himself as a former social worker), asserting that the legislation violated the principles espoused in the provincial Social Work Code of Ethics, and suggesting the legislation would place social workers in the position of being asked to carry out unethical policies. In contrast, Vancouver's

Fraser Institute praised the government's introduction of time limits in their report card on welfare reform, stating that the 'Province leaps to the forefront of intelligent welfare reform and sets new standard for Canadian welfare' and that BC's welfare reforms 'catapulted it beyond any Canadian jurisdiction and into the realm of reform-minded US states' (Fraser Institute, 2002: 1).

On 20 December 2002, the Supreme Court of Canada announced its decision in Gosselin v. Quebec, ruling that the Canadian Charter of Rights and Freedoms guarantee to equal treatment did not encompass a distinct right to social welfare benefits.[3] In this landmark case—the first claim under the Canadian Charter of Rights and Freedoms to a right for welfare—the decision split the court 5–4, with the majority stating there was no breach of the Constitution. However, the justices also did not rule out the possibility for further challenges that Section 7 may be interpreted to obligate a government to provide social assistance.

# The Erosion of Time Limits from Within the Ministry—Spring 2003

## Time Limits and the Mandate of the Ministry

In the spring of 2003, senior staff within the Ministry of Human Resources (later renamed the Ministry of Employment and Income Assistance) struggled to implement the politically motivated legislation as Ministry practice. Concerns were repeatedly raised by policy analysts that the current wording of the regulations would see time limits imposed in questionable situations, situations which were 'contrary to the policy intent'. The FOI documents show that in March 2003 the Social Policy Branch of the Ministry provided a list of clients who would face time limits sanctions but who were in fact not 'employable' because they may be in job training programs, in hospitals, or caring for a Child In the Home of a Relative (CIHR).[4] A private briefing note[5] to the Deputy Minister warned of 'undue hardship' for some clients under the current welfare time limits legislation; individuals who reached the time limits and lost benefits would continue to be ineligible even if they experienced periods during which they were unemployable. In this briefing note, staff pointed out the potentially negative public reaction to the fact that the legislation had no provision to issue assistance to ineligible applicants who had no other resources. In particular:

> Clients who lose their eligibility for assistance due to time limits, and who subsequently become temporarily unemployable due to medical condition, pregnancy, separating from an abusive spouse, or entering a treatment or rehabilitation program will not be eligible for assistance. In families where all adults are unable to work and who have no other resources, the denial of income support would create undue hardship…

As stated in a 'Decision Note to the Deputy Minister', 'A reduction [to families] appears to imply a double penalty—one for reaching the time limit, and another for being unable to work or achieve independence through employment.'[6] In this document Ministry staff also noted that the imposition of time limits could contribute to an individual's inability to be employable and independent, and potentially precipitate health issues such as addictions or depression.

In response, the government began to backtrack on welfare time limits through legislating exemptions. The result was *BC Regulation 116/2003*, which took effect on 1 April 2003, which exempted certain classes of welfare recipients from the time limits policy. In addition, Ministry staff explored policy mechanisms such as hardship grants to ensure that assistance would remain available to welfare recipients who were unable to seek or maintain employment.

Although internal information and analysis had already indicated that welfare time limits were inconsistent with the Ministry's mission and mandate, the Minister maintained its public message supporting welfare time limits. In March 2003 the BC government published an 'Opinion Editorial' by the Minister stating that in the past 'government policies led to a culture of entitlement: there was widespread expectation that welfare could be a lifestyle for employable people...we placed time limits on income assistance for employable people to discourage them from returning to welfare as a way of life' (Coell, 2003: 1).

## Time Limits and the Number of Recipients Facing Sanctions

In January 2003, the Ministry of Human Resources established a Time Limits Project Group to advise senior management on issues related to implementation of welfare time limits. In their first internal report[7] in January 2003, the Time Limits Project Group noted that they did not yet know what the impacts of welfare time limits would be: 'we require preliminary analysis to determine the potential Time Limits impact to clients, number of clients and their demographics.' One week later staff provided the first estimate, stating that preliminary analysis indicated that '19,000 chronic cases may have 24 months accumulated by May 2004.'[8] None of this information was made public, and further internal analysis was subsequently scheduled.

In the summer of 2003, internal documents revealed that the Minister of Human Resources was provided with estimates of the number of people facing time limits sanctions. According to an 'Information Note' prepared for the Minister's Briefing, 'Time limits will begin to affect clients as of the March 26, 2004 cheque issue. Caseload projections indicate that 7,900 cases are likely to be impacted, either through ineligibility or reduction, in April 2004.'[9] In this 'Information Note', Ministry staff warned the Minister that of these 7,900 clients, as many as 60 per cent could be characterized as difficult to employ, and advised that, 'It will be important in applying time limits to try to ensure both that they apply to those who reasonably can be expected to work, and that they not unfairly impact children or others who are vulnerable.'

The disclosure and leaks of government information began in this time period, with a CBC Vancouver report (2003: 1) on 'heavily censored files' obtained under the

*Freedom of Information Act* showing that 'senior bureaucrats warned the Minister of Human Resources last year that BC's welfare reforms could create hardship for some people.'

By the end of the summer, in a confidential note to Cabinet the Minister appeared to request a significant change in the approach to welfare time limits. The Minister advised Cabinet that 'advocates are already beginning to focus on time limits' and that 'the decision on the Gosselin Charter challenge on welfare as an entitlement leaves room for further challenge and a challenge is pending in British Columbia in October.'[10] In this same note, the Minister also presented Cabinet with the estimated total number of cases that might be impacted by April 2004: 1,321 families would face reductions to their benefits and 1,882 people would be completely cut off welfare.

# A Groundswell of Public Opposition—Summer and Fall 2003

Throughout the fall of 2003, diverse sectors of civil society began questioning the acceptability of welfare time limits. This was prompted in part by the work of anti-poverty individuals and organizations that had opposed time limits on principle prior to their enactment into law. However, the opposition soon spread to 'mainstream' portions of society who traditionally had not voiced concerns about poverty or welfare rights. The government's failure to be forthcoming with information and its failure to justify the rationale for welfare time limits soon put the government on the defensive and set the stage for the demise of time limits in the spring of the following year.

By October 2003, concerns about the pending time limits were mounting and critics were becoming more vocal and more diverse. The month began with the Canadian Centre for Policy Alternatives releasing the editorial 'The Ticking Time Bomb of BC's Welfare Time Limits' (Klein, 2003), which questioned the assurances from the Minister not to worry and repeated the risks outlined by Ministry staff, as outlined in information obtained through a FOI request on CBC Radio earlier in the summer.

Numerous groups and individuals launched public campaigns against the welfare time limits, including poverty advocates releasing plans for a legal challenge to the welfare time limits legislation that would build on the Gosselin case. Lawyers from the BC Public Interest Advocacy Centre (BCPIAC) explained: 'Sections 7 and 15 of our *Charter of Rights and Freedoms* guarantee security of the person and equality…cutting people off welfare will leave people without the means to meet basic needs. This is a threat to their physical and psychological security, and a denial of their dignity and equal worth as human beings' (BCPIAC, 2003: 1).

At a major speech to the Union of BC Municipalities, the Minister of Human Resources assured the crowd that 'people are better off working than on welfare',[11] however, more and more people were wondering what their municipalities would look like with an unknown number of people neither working nor receiving welfare.

On 8 October 2003, in the provincial Legislature, the Opposition quoted an internal report acquired through a FOI request that provided the estimated number of people affected by the welfare time limits, although the numbers were blanked out. The Minister's refusal to provide an estimate of the number of recipients facing time limits undermined the government's position that time limits are in the best interests of the public, instead lending support to the perception that the government was withholding information to manage an increasingly sensitive and damaging political issue.

Two days later, a leaked government memo resulted in the front page newspaper headline '28,000 Could Be Caught in Two-Year Welfare Squeeze' (Lavoie, 2003: A1). The leaked document was dated 9 October, the day after the Minister stood in the Legislature refusing to provide an estimate of the number of clients affected. In the Legislature, the Minister of Human Resources retorted that the Opposition had completely misunderstood the report and that it was not a forecast of people who would be affected by the time limits but rather a simple picture of the entire caseload, including all of those who would be excused from the time limits by the different categories of exemptions. The Minister added: 'I believe that by the time we get to April [2004], those people who have been on income assistance for two years, who are employable, will have jobs, I am hoping that's the case.' In response to the Opposition's earlier press release warning 'Communities across BC should brace for an explosion in the number of homeless British Columbians... BC communities need to make preparations in advance of April 1, 2004, when over 27,000 British Columbians will be kicked off income assistance' (BC New Democratic Party [NDP], 2003: 1), the Minister shot back, 'This is another example of the NDP using numbers that they know are wrong yet persist in putting before the public to cause confusion, fear, anxiety and stress among BC's most vulnerable.'[12]

A 'Confidential Issues Note' of 17 October 2003, prepared in response to the increasing outcry against welfare time limits, provided the Minister with his 'key message': 'The number of people affected by time limits at any one time is a small percentage of the caseload.'[13] Despite the message, the public and a number of key institutions were not buying it.

By November 2003, the efforts of grassroots organizing against the time limits started to yield results in the form of statements of public institutions. On 4 November the Vancouver City Council passed a motion urging the provincial government to rescind the time limits law and resolving to write other municipalities encouraging them to pass similar motions. The meeting included four hours of speakers supporting the motion. Two weeks later the Vancouver School Board passed a resolution condemning the provincial welfare time limits policy, noting that 'the provincial government has failed to provide accurate numbers on Vancouver citizens who will be impacted, but it is estimated that it could be in the thousands.'[14] The passing of resolutions continued through the month, with the City of Victoria passing a motion on 22 November, Smithers the same week, and Saanich one week later. The BC Association of Social Workers passed a 'Resolution to Repeal the Two-year Time Limit on Welfare Assistance in British Columbia' at their Annual General Meeting, while the Deans and Directors of the Canadian Association of Schools of Social Work passed a similar motion.

In response to the pressure, the Ministry implemented a referral of all inquiries directly to the Premier's office. In the Legislature the Opposition read an internal Ministry memo, which it referred to as a 'gag order':

> Please do not provide any information to the public regarding the potential numbers of clients being cut off or the effect of time limits on caseloads...The reason for this, likely obvious, is this is a very hot news story, and we can't speculate on how the policy will affect people or the numbers.[15]

In a press release the BC Government Employees Union summarized the situation as gagging their own Ministry staff to keep secret the number of people who would be cut off welfare as a result of the time limits.

On 14 November 2003, in a *Vancouver Province* article, the Ministry tried to reinforce the message that its policies were working and resulting in far fewer people on welfare, enough to justify a smaller system. The 'good news' message was overshadowed by the story's headline, 'Welfare Jobs Axed, Offices to be Closed' (2003: A16). The closure of welfare offices and the laying off of Ministry staff again prompted media speculation that thousands of people may lose their benefits and raised concerns that the Minister had no idea of how many people will be affected by the welfare time limits.

A week later, the Vancouver Sun ran a column by Stephen Hume with the headline 'What Happens When More Poor Hit the Streets?':

> [C]ome April, the province intends to put a lot more impoverished British Columbians on to the streets. That's when people now receiving social assistance will have to rely on their own resources once time limits imposed by the province off-load them from the welfare rolls—a first for Canada. I say off loading because that is what the province is doing—transferring the social costs to municipalities while pretending it's balancing the books. (2003: C7)

Without specific information from the Ministry, the public was left to speculate how many people would be living with no incomes and how this would affect their municipalities. This speculation played into affluent people's fear of living with people in dire poverty, and public opposition to the time limits increasingly framed itself as a matter of self-interest. For example, the Vancouver School Board resolution listed impacts not just as 'children arriving to school hungry' but also 'homeless people sleeping on our school steps'; the Saanich City Council resolution raised the concern of business and their ability to 'do business as a result of the new law'. While the affluent public may be willing to support harsh welfare laws, there seems to be less willingness to accept policies and outcomes that could negatively affect their own lives.

Throughout December, public opposition to the time limits continued to mount and diversify. The Social Planning and Research Council of BC (SPARC-BC) released a factsheet on welfare time limits which became an integral resource for concerned citizens less familiar with welfare rights. The factsheet capitalized on the fact that the provincial government had 'not been forthcoming about the anticipated impact of the time limits policy'.

Meanwhile a vocal *Anti-Two Year Time Limit Coalition* was organized in Vancouver. Described in its pamphlet as a 'coalition of anti-poverty groups, women's groups, faith groups, unions and other concerned organizations and individuals', the group called on people to come together for 'leafleting, petitioning, advocating for people's rights, organizing days of action, etc.'. In Victoria, the Anglican Diocese of Vancouver Island, representing 70 parishes, passed a resolution to write to every parish in the Diocese encouraging people to lobby the Minister and Premier to stop the welfare time limits policy.

With no credible response from the provincial government, the Fraser Institute stepped forward to attempt to counter the opposition. In an article titled 'Staying the Course on Welfare Time Limits' they observed that 'social advocacy groups have singled out the time limits policy as their main point of criticism. But the concerns have no foundation' (Gabel, Clemens, LeRoy, and Veldhuis 2003: 22). The authors went on to implore the provincial government to disregard public opinion:

> Unfortunately, in BC there is an increasingly vocal objection to time limits, and the province's government has thus far shown weak resolve on a number of its initiatives including spending cuts, tax relief, and privatization. It is important that they not cave in on time limits. With enough political will to limit exemptions and enforce this policy effectively, time limits can save a new generation of British Columbians from welfare dependency. (2003: 24)

Within the Ministry, staff responded not by staying the course on welfare time limits but rather by urgently preparing mitigation strategies, including the possibility of providing 'time limit extensions to singles and couples without children, who have been and continue to be, compliant with employment plans'.[16] According to this internal document '[t]he first large stream of recipients will be impacted by time limits starting in April 2004. If no changes are made to Time Limits it is estimated that 1378 cases will be impacted (662 single recipients, 55 couples, 143 two-parent families with children, 518 single parent families with children).' In the same memo, Ministry staff repeated the warning that the current policy would result in people who are unable to work being ineligible for income assistance, and that, under the current policy, clients cut off welfare due to time limits while deemed 'employable' could later face barriers to employment yet still remain ineligible for assistance for three years. Ministry staff also raised the risk of 'constitutional challenges' and specifically noted that 'legal fees associated with *Charter* challenges on the Ministry's time limits legislation could be very costly. Numerous advocacy groups have stated their intention to launch a charter challenge on time limits.' Despite staff concerns about welfare time limits, the document noted that a possible negative consequence of mitigating the time limits would be that 'the Ministry may be perceived as reacting to interest groups and media pressure' and that 'cost-savings will be significantly reduced.'

The year would end with one more challenge as Aboriginal leaders raised unique concerns about the impending time limits. An internal document dated 31 December 2003 noted that 'Aboriginal leaders have expressed concern that the two-year time limit, which will impact recipients as of April 2004, may lead to an influx of band members returning to reserves. The Sto:lo First Nation in the Upper Fraser Valley estimate that 60 per cent of its members live off-reserve and up to half may receive income assistance. There is growing concern that an influx of natives returning to reservations will place tremendous pressures on resources including housing and existing programs'.[17]

The Minister's speaking notes—included in the document obtained through the FOI—sought to calm the fears of Aboriginal leaders by stating the 'the final number impacted by time limits in April 2004 is expected to be quite small' as a result of 'successful employment planning and employment programs'. The Minister offered assurances that the Ministry 'wants people to be employed, rather than lose eligibility due to time limits or return to reserves'. He attributed the fears of Aboriginal groups not to the welfare policy but rather 'reports by the media and others [who] have greatly over-estimated the number of recipients who may reach their time limit. This may have fuelled fears by native leaders that large numbers of band members may return to reserves.'

# Government Capitulation—Spring 2004

The period from the start of 2004 until the effective end of time limits on 6 February 2004 was a time of intense activity within both the Ministry and civil society. The FOI documents indicate that, by this time, the government had concluded it would have to amend welfare legislation to negate the effects of time limits. It faced the challenge of a very short timeline to achieve this, and the public relations problems of backtracking on a centerpiece of its welfare reform. Within civil society, the opposition to time limits intensified and unified, in part in response to the government's failure to clarify its plans.

## Developments within the Ministry

On the first work day of the New Year, the Minister of Human Resources made a significant shift in position. In a radio interview the Minister said he was 'willing to take another look at sweeping changes to welfare guidelines that are set to start in April',[18] and stated that if a government committee examining the potential changes reported tens of thousands of people would be suddenly cut he would re-think the changes. However, he added he did not think that would be the case because of the provisions already developed to exempt certain classes of welfare recipients.

The media continued to pressure the Minister of Human Resources to say how many recipients would face time limit sanctions. On 4 January 2004 the Ministry's spokesperson promised to release a statistical report that would provide 'full disclosure of accurate information that will help people see what the whole picture looks like at the end of the month' (Anderson, 2004: A9). In this interview, Minister Coell insisted that '60 to 70 per cent' of current welfare clients did not fall into the work category and so would be at no risk of being cut off welfare as of April 2004.

Less publicly, government staff scrambled to push back the time limits clock. An internal email emphasized the urgent need to amend the welfare legislation prior to 1 April 2004 when the cut offs would begin. Ministry staff were told: 'The new message is we may be mitigating time limits but our focus is still employment for clients and we will emphasize this by strengthening EP [Employment Plan] sanctions.'[19] A subsequent email from the Ministry to Attorney General staff explained: 'Currently the Ministry is developing an RFL [Request for Legislation] to amend the *Employment and Assistance Act* in order to provide the Ministry with regulation making power to suspend the consequences of time limits in specific circumstances, provided a welfare recipient was compliant with their employment plan'.[20]

Ministry staff now faced two looming deadlines: (1) to provide the public with the estimated number of people likely to be impacted by the end of January and (2) to make the necessary legislative changes to mitigate the number of clients affected before the April welfare cheques were released. At the same time, the Deputy Minister sought a legal opinion from the Attorney General's Legal Services Branch regarding the possible impact of the Charter in relation to the provision for time-limited income assistance.

On 15 January 2004 Ministry staff submitted their request for an amendment to the *Employment and Assistance Act* to the Ministry of Attorney General. This application, accessed through a FOI request, was heavily censored but it was noted that the request was a 'significant policy change' that has 'significant financial implications'.[21] The request appears to be more than an appeal to add an additional exemption; the Ministry had clearly noted they already had the authority to exempt categories of recipients from the welfare time limits. Instead, the request appeared to seek an amendment to the legislation to allow for the suspending of the consequences of reaching the time limit for some clients in order to allow for case-by-case decisions. At this point, it was the Ministry describing the ineffectiveness and inappropriateness of current time limits legislation in accomplishing its policy intent, citing examples such as a client receiving welfare could be non-compliant with their employment plan for 23 months, and then comply for one month to be exempt from the welfare time limits; conversely clients could become unable to work after reaching their time limit (e.g., due to pregnancy). The Ministry noted in this memorandum that it did not wish to penalize family units making good faith efforts to find employment but it also did want to entirely exempt them from the time limits requirement.

As the mitigation strategies were unfolding, Ministry staff also appeared to be continually seeking the much-promised statistic of how many people would actually be cut-off assistance on 1 April and in the subsequent months. Throughout the correspondence and reports accessed, there were various estimates. Based on our analysis it appeared that Ministry staff were continually seeking mitigation strategies and corresponding estimates until the number was brought down to a figure that was felt to be publicly acceptable. The focus was on two estimates: first, the number of clients/cases who could potentially be affected by time limits in the future (i.e., their current months are counting towards time limits); and second, the smaller number of clients/cases who were actually expected to face sanctions (i.e., reduction or total removal of welfare benefits). In January 2004, an internal document[22] calculated that 21,112 adults (45 per cent of all adults on welfare) were on time-limited income assistance in BC—in other words, nearly half of adults on welfare were considered employable and were not protected under any of the existing 24 exemptions. The estimated number of people that had actually reached the 24-month time limit, promised for public release by the end of the month, continued to be worked and reworked throughout January.

In the two weeks leading to the promised announcement on 31 January, staff drafted and redrafted a document titled 'Time Limits Management Strategy'.[23] According to this document, 1,200 clients would reach their time limit on April 2004 but it was expected that many of these would have significant barriers to employment.

By the end of January, documents[24] obtained indicated that the Ministry was more confident of its ability to assess clients affected by time limits, to provide opportunities for employable clients to find work, and to exempt those with barriers to employment. These documents also appeared to reflect a more realistic view that a significant number of recipients had barriers that would prevent employment.

Although the tone of the Ministry's internal documents had shifted, on 31 January 2004 the promised release of the number of people facing time limits did not happen. The media reported: 'just how many British Columbians will be forced off welfare rolls this spring remains unclear after the provincial government missed a self-imposed deadline Friday to release that information' (Rud, 2004: A4). Although internal records clearly show the Minister knew the numbers of people that would be affected, the Minister told reporters 'that a report from Ministry staff isn't complete', that he 'hasn't seen it yet', and that 'staff are taking their time coming up with a figure in order to ensure that the information is accurate' (Rud, 2004: A4).

## Community Opposition

In the face of Ministry silence, community opposition to the welfare time limits gained strength and media attention throughout January 2004. Labour activists predicted that 'the 'Two-year Time Limit' would be the next significant 'front' on which to base a unified 'Fight Back' against the BC Liberal Government'. On 19 January 2004 there was a rally in Vancouver to 'Fight the Two-Year Time Limit and the Closure of Welfare Offices'. Resolutions were passed by Cranbrook City Council and the Greater Victoria School Board urging the Provincial Government to rescind the time limits law as well as the laws that reduce welfare benefits. The Canadian Centre for Policy Alternatives initiated a long-term study to analyze the impact of the new welfare time limits.

In the last days of January, a news conference was held in a downtown church in Victoria, where school boards, churches, and city councils sat side by side demanding an end to the time limits rule. The event demonstrated the widespread disapproval from mainstream society—not just anti-poverty activists—and portrayed the Province as out of step with the shared values of church, school, and local government. The news conference attracted national news coverage, including the Canadian Press article 'Preacher to Protest BC Welfare Cuts' in which Reverend Harold Munn vowed to sleep in the streets to protest the welfare time limits. Robert Arnold of the National Anti-Poverty Group (NAPO) declared that the time limit policy would soon become the focus of a countrywide campaign, stating 'We're picking up the two-year time limit in BC as one of our major campaigns' (Meissner, 2004). A week later a letter was sent to the Prime Minister and BC Premier, signed by over 125 groups, requesting that the time limits be rescinded before 1 April 2004 and that no similar provision be implemented in BC or any other province in the future.

## The 25th Exemption: 6 February 2004

On 6 February 2004, the Ministry delivered the news release 'Time Limit Policy to Protect People in Need' (BC Ministry of Human Resources, 2004b: 1) which estimated 'the number of clients to be affected as the government follows through on its commitment to limit income assistance for employable clients as two out of every five'.

According to this news release, just 339 clients would be affected by the time limits over the coming year—'far lower than the tens of thousands that the opposition claimed'. Although a number of exemptions to the policy had been earlier included in the policy, the news release contained a less triumphant message, that the government would be implementing a new 25th exemption to the time limits policy to ensure that those clients who were employable and looking for work would be protected. Specifically, the 25th exemption was intended to ensure that time limits would not affect people 'who have an employment plan, are complying with their plan, are actively looking for work, but have not been successful in finding employment' (BC Ministry of Human Resources, 2004c: 2).

The media were quick to file stories based on the news release, focusing on the numbers. Many did not immediately notice the significant policy change, and instead repeated the Minister's message that the opposition was wrong to claim tens of thousands would be affected. But when reporters called on social policy critics for additional commentary, they were made aware of the significance of the policy shift and the fact that the landmark policy was now essentially made redundant by the government. The next day the front page story on the Vancouver Sun read 'Province Backs Off Plan for Dramatic Cuts to Welfare' (Kines, 2004: A1). This headline was more similar to the Canadian Centre for Policy Alternatives (CCPA)'s news release 'Government Backs Down on Welfare Time Limits, But Cutoff Should Be Scrapped all Together' than the Minister's own release 'Time Limit Policy to Protect People in Need' (BC Ministry of Human Resources, 2004b).

The CCPA was one of several groups to quickly counter the message of the Minister, stating,

> Until today thousands of people were at risk of hitting the two-year time limit. The new exemption makes the whole two-year time limit policy redundant... [R]egardless of whether the number is 15,000, 300 or one, this is a bad law. It remains an awful precedent and should be removed from the books. (CCPA, 2004: 1)

Although community groups, media, and social policy commentators were critical of the government's decision to keep welfare time limits legislation, there was also celebration that the numbers of people who would be affected had been significantly reduced. The BC Coalition of People with Disabilities called the 25th exemption 'a significant victory for the community' in a letter of congratulations to community groups for their hard work in speaking out against welfare time limits. The Leader of the Opposition said she believed the Liberals originally planned to cut off far more people, but bowed to public pressure; this message was echoed by several media outlets.

The following week the initial reactions shifted to deeper reflections. The *Vancouver Sun* editorial noted the following:

> Had the rule been in place at the time it was unveiled, there were, by the human resources minister's reckoning, 30,000 people on welfare who would have been kicked off. After almost two years of speculation, during which the government has refused to divulge its own estimates, we now learn that at most, 37 people will become ineligible on April 1. We say at most because between now and then any or all of those people could fall off the list by virtue of finding a job or meeting the requirements for any of the 25 exemptions that have been created to the rule. So what happened? How could a policy shift of such magnitude have resulted in so little impact? ('Victoria Should Dispense with Welfare Time Limits', 2004: C7)

The editorial answered its own question, stating 'This extraordinary outcome was achieved partly by the last-minute decision to exempt anyone who is genuinely looking for work', calling the released numbers 'a mockery of the two-in-five rule' and stating that the provincial government should 'scrap this useless rule'.

Three days later the *Vancouver Sun* ran two opposing editorials on the announced 25th exemption. Shelagh Day, a lawyer with the Poverty and Human Rights Project in Vancouver, claimed 'What happened last week is that the government retreated in the face of mounting pressure from community organizations, churches, unions, city councils, social policy experts and individuals who let Victoria know that the 24-month rule is both impractical and morally repugnant.' She identified the 25th exemption 'a backhanded admission by the Liberals that applying a time limit to welfare doesn't work', and concluded that 'A rule that requires 25 exemptions is a feeble rule. And a rule that, to save the government's face, requires an exemption that guts the rule itself—as the 25th exemption does—needs to be scrapped' (Day, 2004: A9). The Fraser Institute agreed that the government capitulated, characterizing the government action as 'backtracking' and calling the addition of the 25th exemption a 'policy change that effectively nullifies the time limit rule'. However, it described the 25th exemption as 'a disastrous U-turn on welfare reform' that 'delegitimized what was one of Canada's most important social welfare reforms to date' (Clemens, Veldhuis, and LeRoy, 2004: A9).

Within the Ministry, staff prepared damage-control speaking notes for the Minister. One Information Note[25] stated: 'the Ministry has been accused of "gutting" time limits policy.... The small number of clients impacted by time limits is primarily due to thousands of clients who have found employment and who no longer require assistance, and not the newest exemption.' While this public statement sounded positive, it was false and in fact a direct contradiction to the Ministry's own budget Fact Sheet publicly released at the same time that states: 'The Ministry believes the most recent exemption to time limits policy will increase the annual average caseload by about 1,200 cases' (BC Ministry of Human Resources, 2004a).

On 15 April 2004 the government implemented the change of policy through BC Regulation 160/2004. It exempted from time limits any individuals, couples, or families where one person has received welfare for more than 24 months, as long as 'each recipient in the family unit who is subject to an employment plan complies with the employment plan'. Thus, while still enacted as legislation, welfare time limits were limited to pre-existing provisions regarding ineligibility. Welfare time limits ended, not with a bang, but with a whimper.

# Resisting Regressive Welfare Policies: Lessons Learned

The data accessed through the FOI clearly show that thousands of clients were facing time limit sanctions in BC. As a result of events that unfolded to mitigate the policy, early estimates that 10,000 clients would be sanctioned were replaced with a number of less than 50 in the first two years, and even fewer in the third year. As many argued, following the introduction of the 25th exemption time limits for welfare is now a redundant policy, and the law and its regulations should be repealed. That said, approximately 50 people still fell through the cracks and faced severe hardship, driving home the need for action to repeal the time limits legislation in its entirety.

The downfall of welfare time limits is noteworthy because it is one of the few successes in defeating the regressive welfare reforms that have been implemented in Canada over the past decade. A key to this success was the pressure exerted by mainstream society through its representatives, such municipal councils, based largely on a perception of harm to their communities that might occur from a large increase in the number of homeless people. However, the success of this mainstream opposition depended in part on the organizing work of smaller groups involved in the anti-poverty field. And while the opposition from these groups was loosely organized, it was effective in providing accurate and timely information and analysis that resonated with the concerns of mainstream organizations. These smaller groups acted as catalysts to bring divergent groups, such as city councils, school boards and faith communities, together to voice their shared opposition to time limits to welfare.

The opposition to welfare time limits also demonstrates the potential effectiveness of public interest research. Some of the most vocal criticisms of time limits came from individuals and organizations that would not normally consider themselves activists, such as city councils, school boards, and church groups. They knew that this was an unjust law, but they also knew that the issue was complex and that they did not have enough information to speak to its complexities. Public interest research was available to fill this gap and it provided the necessary evidence for diverse groups to speak out in a convincing fashion. Although activists opposed time limits, they were often not the most visible face of dissent. Rather activists and advocates were often behind the scenes providing needed analysis and assisting with media releases and press conferences; this enabled mainstream groups and organizations to voice their opposition in an informed and effective fashion. These activists linked concerned citizens to public interest research and facilitated their involvement in the issue.

Public interest lawyers also played a leading role in the opposition to time limits in arguing that the rule violated rights protected in the *Canadian Charter of Rights and Freedoms*. The threat of legal challenges repeatedly emerged in internal Ministry discussions and documents as a significant concern. Legal action, if this option is feasible, may be an important tool for future campaigns regarding welfare eligibility.

As revealed by the FOI materials, within the staff of the Ministry there was also opposition to time limits based in part on the beliefs of the Ministry's staff regarding the purpose or mandate of the Ministry. Time limits were resisted by Ministry staff because they were contrary to this purpose and mandate. It appears that this originated from both front-line staff and policy analysts. Both groups expressed concern that the policy would be harmful to the beneficiaries of income assistance and also would defeat the employment-related objectives of the program. They also cautioned the Minister that imposing time limits on certain classes of recipients could lead to negative public reactions and become a difficult political issue. The result was an ongoing process of amendments to exempt classes of recipients from the time limits policy. This was an important indication that the policy was fundamentally flawed; in this case it also serves to remind us that simplistic, politically-motivated social policy can be ill-conceived, difficult to implement, and disastrous for those it may affect.

The logic of time limits contained the seeds of its own downfall. Its purpose was to cut recipients off welfare, and inherent in the policy was the reality that a potentially large number of recipients would be affected at the same time. This inevitably raised the numbers question. If the policy was to have any useful consequence relative to its purpose, then the number had to be significant. However, the greater the success of the government in cutting recipients off of welfare, the greater would be the harmful consequences for the public. As events unfolded, it became apparent that public acceptance of the policy depended on it having minimal impact. Public concerns over this found expression in the resolutions of city councils, school boards, and other institutions. These concerns were fueled by the government's secrecy and failure to respond to basic questions concerning the number of recipients who would reach time limits. This secrecy led to media itself becoming a force of pressure upon government, for regardless of whether the media supported time limits to welfare, their irritation at the government's refusal to answer their questions regarding numbers of recipients facing ineligibility contributed to the government's loss of credibility. In the face of widespread public opposition, the government was left defending its policy to save face while at the same time declaring that the number of recipients affected would be insignificant.

By late January 2004 the government decided that the political price to be paid for its deeply unpopular social policy outweighed its ideological commitments, and the time limits policy was essentially sacrificed. Regrettably, its decision was not based on recognition of human and ethical considerations.

## Summary and Conclusion

Research by the authors and colleagues in 2006 demonstrated that the decline in welfare caseloads between 2002 and 2006 was largely a result of restricting entry and not increasing 'exits' of people who were receiving welfare (Wallace, Klein, and Reitsma-Street, 2006). In hindsight, it is clear that the two-year independence requirement and the three-week wait period imposed in the new legislation led to far greater caseload reductions than time limits to welfare. In fact, before the time limits would have taken effect in BC in April 2004, the cost-cutting and caseload reduction targets would already be surpassed as 'far more people are denied assistance, than cut off' (Reitsma-Street and Wallace, 2004: 175). Welfare restructuring led to people in need of help being systematically denied, discouraged, and delayed in receiving income assistance (Wallace, et al., 2006). However, it is also true that the welfare time limits policy would have caused additional harm to the most vulnerable people in BC, and the risk remains that it could be adopted in other jurisdictions in the future.

The downfall of time-limited welfare in BC prevented thousands of recipients from having their benefits reduced or ended. Many of these individuals would have been those least able to provide for themselves and least able to challenge the government's policies and decisions. Many would have been left homeless and hungry if time limits taken effect as initially legislated.

In part the end of time-limited welfare was also the assertion of values basic to a humane society. The time limits provision was a policy that tied income assistance to arbitrary rules rather than the needs of individuals. After years of cuts to welfare, the public reacted in limiting the extent to which punitive government policies towards people in need of income assistance would be tolerated. At the same time, it is important to recognize that the opposition to time limits was diverse and included those who opposed time limits in principle and for purely humanitarian reasons, and those who felt that a dramatic increase in the number of homeless citizens would be harmful to their communities. While it was the work of groups with a social justice agenda that led to broader opposition, it was likely the political pressure from more self-interested community groups that led to the eventual defeat of the time limits policy.

The internal government documents related to time limits indicate that government decision-makers are very sensitive to the prospects of court challenges to legislation. However, it is also significant that the defeat of the time limits policy was achieved through public pressure and opinion rather than legal action. While legal action is a legitimate method of challenging ill-conceived and harmful policies, it is equally important not to leave this work to lawyers and judges alone. Politicians must be reminded that the public itself can and will act to curb efforts that will do harm to vulnerable citizens.

## Recommended Reading

B. Wallace, S. Klein, and M. Reitsma-Street, *Denied Assistance: Closing the Front Door on Welfare in BC* (Vancouver: Canadian Centre for Policy Alternatives and Victoria Island Public Interest Research Group, 2006). This report provides a review of the nature and scope of the cutbacks in welfare that followed the election of the Campbell Liberal government in BC in 2001.

## Critical Thinking Questions

1.   The Fraser Institute and the Canadian Centre for Policy Alternatives took opposing views on the 'Welfare Time Limits' policy. Based on an analysis of

their responses, as outlined in this chapter, what underlying values appear to shape their positions? How would you classify the ideologies of these two groups?

2.    The authors of this chapter identify a number of factors that appeared to influence policy outcomes in this example of 'policy resistance'. They also suggest a particular role for social activists in pursuing policy resistance strategies that involve the public. What is this role? Do you agree or disagree? Explain why.

3.    Assess how government handled its own policy-making process. What mistakes did the government make? Do you think this had any impact on the outcome? Identify any different actions the government may have taken in dealing with the media or the public in order to gain acceptance for its reforms. Do you think these actions might have made any difference in the way groups and organizations responded?

4.    The authors of this case study suggest that both altruism and self-interests played a role in shaping opposition to this policy. Although it is possible that some groups voiced a combination of these concerns, most are depicted as developing positions that reflected more emphasis on one or the other of these two motivations. What were the groups and organizations identified in the chapter that reflected more altruistic motivations? What were the groups and organizations that reflected more self-interested motivations? What conclusions do you draw about using both of these motivations in organizing public opposition to regressive social policies or public support for positive reforms?

5.    In this particular case neither front-line staff nor service users figure prominently in resisting this policy, although such involvement may have occurred behind the scenes. What are the possible reasons for this lack of involvement? Is it more difficult to obtain such engagement in policy resistance than it might be if one was developing a new policy designed to benefit service users through a more inclusive policy-making process? How important are other factors, such as the characteristics of these groups, their vulnerability, and the nature and scope of the policy reform? Can any of these factors be mitigated?

# Notes

1.    Bruce Wallace is a community based researcher in Victoria. He was the lead researcher and author of *Denied Assistance: Closing the Front Door on Welfare in B.C.* Tim Richards is a Senior Instructor in the Faculty of Law, University of Victoria. From 1994 to 2002 he worked as a front line legal advocate assisting people in poverty with their income assistance and employment insurance rights and is now involved in research to establish a living wage in British Columbia.

2.    Internal Briefing Note (undated) prepared for Legislative Review Committee regarding the 'Introduction of the Employment and Assistance Act and the *Employment and Assistance for Persons with Disabilities Act* for the Spring 2002 Legislative Session'.

3. [2002] 4 S.C.R. 29, 221 D.I.R. (4th) 257, online: CanLII at http:www.canlii.ca/c/sas/scc/ 2002/2002scc84.html [Gosselin cited to S.C.R.].
4. 'Time Limits Scenarios' document attached to emails sent 12 March 2003.
5. 'Ministry of Human Resources Decision Note' dated 3 April 2003. (Document heavily severed.)
6. 'Ministry of Human Resources Decision Note' dated 23 May 2003.
7. 'Time Limits Phase I Summary Report (Status Report)', dated 31 January 2003
8. 'Time Limits Phase I Summary Report (Status Report)', dated 7 February 2003.
9. 'Ministry of Human Resources Information Note 'Strategies to Refine Specific Elements of Time-limited Assistance', prepared for Minister's Briefing on 18 June 2003.
10. Confidential A & P Note: Advice to Cabinet 'Impact of the Two-Year Time Limit on Income Assistance', dated 27 August 2003.
11. Confidential Issues Note: 'Advice to Minister—Time Limits UBCM', dated 22 September 2003.
12. Confidential Issues Note: 'Advice to Minister—Time Limits—Opposition Numbers', dated 20 October 2003.
13. Confidential Issues Note: 'Advice to Minister—Time Limits (Oct Update)', dated 17 October 2003.
14. Vancouver Board of School Trustees SD No 39 Board Meeting Minutes of 17 November 2003.
15. Hansard Debates, 6 November 2003 (J. MacPhail).
16. Ministry of Human Resources Decision Note 'Time Limits Mitigation Strategies for Singles and Childless Couples'—dated 3 December 2003.
17. Ministry of Human Resources Information Note 'Background for Minister's Meeting with the Attorney General on the Impact of Time Limits on First Nations Reserves', dated 31 December 2003.
18. CKNW, 'Human Resources Minister Might Re-Think Upcoming Changes to Welfare Guidelines', 2 January 2004.
19. Email dated 7 January 2004, sent from Ministry of Human Resources Legislation and Legal Services Branch to Ministry of Attorney General lawyer.
20. Email dated 13 January 2004 from a Ministry of Attorney General lawyer.
21. Ministry of Human Resources Memorandum to Ministry of Attorney General RE: *Amendments to the Employment and Assistance Act*, dated 15 January 2004.
22. One page document titled 'BCEA Clients by Time Limit Status—December, 2003'.
23. 'Time Limits Management Strategy' which was an internal document attached to email dated 30 January 2003 which states the Strategy document 'was just finalized yesterday'.
24. The internal document titled 'Time Limits Management Strategy' attached to emails sent on 4 February 2004.
25. Ministry of Human Resources Information Note 'Differences between BC Employment and Assistance and BC Benefits', dated 12 February 2004.

# Chapter Ten

# Policy-Making in Aboriginal Child and Family Services

The primary objective of this chapter is to explore how three of the approaches to inclusive policy-making identified in Chapter Six—shared decision-making, a policy community, and community governance—have been applied in an Aboriginal service context. Our exploration of these three approaches in the child welfare field attempts to clarify both the processes that were followed and some of the results that have emerged to date. Limitations of these approaches are identified and, in the case of the shared decision-making example, we identify actions that occurred 'when inclusive approaches were not enough' to move the policy agreement forward to the execution stage. This case study approach could also be applied to other fields of practice such as health and education if specific attention to an inclusive model of policy-making has been selected as the approach to building a new policy or program in these areas. In addition, one could apply this case study approach using a 'backwards mapping' method where one begins with an existing policy and traces the steps that occurred to establish the policy by 'looking back' to locate the key actors, decision points, and processes that were involved. This approach would allow one to examine the extent to which inclusive approaches were used in the development of a particular policy or program.

An Aboriginal context has been selected as a focus for this chapter for three reasons. First, Aboriginal people, particularly in First Nations communities, are a particularly marginalized population in Canada. Second, differences in worldviews, cultural values, and aspirations between Aboriginal people and 'mainstream' approaches in Canada demand a respect for diversity that only comes with active engagement with these communities on a more equal footing than the approach that has characterized historical approaches to policy-making on Aboriginal issues. Finally, despite present disadvantages that characterize many Aboriginal communities there is evidence of resiliency and strengths that must be used in shaping the best possible policies for Aboriginal people. These reasons require a more inclusive approach to policy-making in Aboriginal communities; indeed to develop policies in any other way is to continue a legacy of oppression associated with colonialism, discrimination, and second class citizenship. At the same time we recognize that inclusive approaches should not simply be reserved for policy-making in Aboriginal communities. These are essential in other diversity contexts but they are also important to the human services in all communities. We begin with a review of the policy-making context in Aboriginal communities.

# The Policy-Making Context

Data from the *Aboriginal Peoples in Canada in 2006: Inuit, Métis and First Nations, 2006 Census* (Statistics Canada, 2008), reported that the Aboriginal population was about 1.17 million in a nation of approximately 33 million. However, Statistics Canada (2008) notes that the actual Aboriginal population is likely much higher due to gaps in enumeration on reserves and lack of participation. However, these data represent the best information available. In this survey, approximately 59 per cent of the total population identified as First Nations, 33 per cent identified as Métis, and slightly more than four per cent identified as Inuit. The remaining total identified more than one Aboriginal identity. Although Aboriginal peoples represent a relatively small proportion of Canada's population, in the 10-year period up to 2006 the Aboriginal population increased by 45 per cent, or almost six times faster than the growth rate for the non-Aboriginal population in Canada. Given this pattern, it is not surprising that the Aboriginal population is much younger than their non-Aboriginal counterparts. For example, approximately 17 per cent of the non-Aboriginal population is 14 years of age or younger whereas 30 per cent of the Aboriginal population falls within this age cohort (Statistics Canada, 2008). These data also suggest that approximately 53 per cent of all Aboriginal people live in urban areas.

The oppression of Aboriginal people has been well documented (e.g., Report of the Royal Commission on Aboriginal Peoples [RCAP], 1996) and this oppression cannot be separated from the colonial history that has characterized relationships between mainstream society and Canada's indigenous peoples. Notwithstanding some improvements Aboriginal peoples continue to experience extreme levels of poverty, high rates of unemployment, low levels of educational attainment, and inadequate housing conditions. First Nations communities are particularly vulnerable. For example, one in four First Nations children live in poverty, more than half of First Nations people are unemployed, the rate of disabilities among First Nations children is almost double the rate for all Canadian children, diabetes among First Nations people is at least three times the national average, and one-third of First Nations households with children are overcrowded (Assembly of First Nations website, 2008).

These structural factors are closely connected to the overrepresentation of Aboriginal children in care in that the primary form of maltreatment in these communities involves parental neglect exacerbated by poverty, substandard housing, and substance abuse (Trocmé and Blackstock, 2004; Blackstock, Prakish, Loxley, and Wien, 2005). The intrusive approaches of the mainstream child welfare system began with the '60s scoop', a term coined by Johnston (1983) in reference to the pattern of providing child welfare services 'on reserves' whereby these services were limited to the apprehension and placement of large numbers of children in non-Aboriginal communities, often on a permanent basis. This pattern of child removal has continued, even with the transfer of jurisdictional authority to Aboriginal child and family service agencies. For example, in 2000–02 it was estimated that 30–40 per cent of the 76,000 children in care in Canada were Aboriginal (Farris-Manning and Zandstra, 2007). In First Nations communities alone the number of children in out of home care increased by 71.5 per cent between 1995 and 2001 (McKenzie, 2002a) and, in 2007, Indian and Northern Affairs Canada reported that 5.5 per cent of on-reserve status Indian children were in care.

There are also other effects. For example, suicide accounts for 38 per cent of all deaths for First Nations youth aged 10–19 (Assembly of First Nations website, 2008). As well, the incarceration rates of Aboriginal people are five to six times the national average, and Aboriginal women are among the most disadvantaged in Canada (RCAP, 1996).

These circumstances are important to recognize; however, they do not tell the whole story. First, these data vary a great deal among groups and communities. Second, descriptive information on social conditions is inadequate without a discussion of causality. Finally, such information neglects the strengths and resiliency of Aboriginal people, and these are essential to any discussion of policy-making in the Aboriginal context.

The prevalence of health and social problems in many Aboriginal communities is closely related to the history of Aboriginal–white relations in North America. The legacy of colonization is reflected in government policies that deliberately undermined the viability of Aboriginal communities, divesting them of their land, culture, and tribal authority (RCAP, 1996; Frideres, 1998). The treaties, which created reserves to deal with the 'Indian problem' and the Indian Act were instrumental in this process. But the residential school system and, after the 1960s, the mainstream child welfare system also played key roles, not only in the assimilation of Aboriginal people but also in undermining Aboriginal communities and culture. In residential schools, which were operated primarily by Catholic and Protestant churches with government support, Aboriginal traditions including one's language were banned (Miller, 1996).

In a Manitoba study conducted in 1994, 43 former residents of residential schools were interviewed (Manitoba Joint Committee on Residential Schools, 1994). Respondents related stories of excessive discipline and abuse, ridicule, and demeaning punishment. Almost half the respondents related experiences of sexual abuse. Three additional traumas were identified as having lasting effects on adult adjustment and parenting. One was the lack of love in most relationships with caregivers and teachers. Second was the denial of cultural expression, such as language, and the ridicule heaped on Aboriginal traditions, including spiritual beliefs. Third was the loss of a family experience, including the opportunity for positive bonding with parents; this was identified as having a continuing impact on adjustment and intergenerational parenting practices. As described by one respondent: '[I]t robbed me of my family life because I don't think I learned how to love—my whole childhood was stolen from me.' For many, the loss of a family experience was the most traumatic experience of the schools.

While the residential school system was an obvious instrument of colonialism, others (see Johnston, 1983; McKenzie and Hudson, 1985; Fournier and Crey, 1997) have demonstrated how the child welfare system, beginning with the earlier noted '60s scoop' acted in similar ways by separating Aboriginal children from the families, communities, and culture.

Although the impact of the residential school system and conventional child welfare practices, prominent during the 1960s and 1970s, are essential aspects of understanding Aboriginal reality, not all problems can be fully explained by these developments. Other structural causes such as systematic racism, poverty, and inadequate opportunities are also important.

Problem analysis and needs assessment, as documented in Chapter Four, is an essential step in the policy-making process yet it needs to be matched with an understanding of strengths and resilience. Many individuals who attended residential schools not only survived but also emerged to play leadership roles within the Aboriginal community. At the collective level, cultural traditions and practices, including the role of the extended family, have become key elements in the renewal of Aboriginal communities and their way of life.

Much has changed in Aboriginal services, in relation to both practice and policy in the past three decades. New agencies have been established to provide a variety of child and family-focused interventions, often using traditional frameworks such as the medicine wheel or circle as methods of organizing interventions (Graveline, 1998; Hart, 2002). Healing in an Aboriginal context is closely linked to spirituality, beginning with the individual and building outward to include family, community, and society (Assembly of First Nations, 2000; Connors and Maidman, 2001). For example, a successful community model of healing from child sexual abuse using the circle and concepts based on the medicine wheel has been established in Manitoba on the Hollow Water First Nation (Aboriginal Corrections Policy Unit, 1997). Within an Aboriginal worldview, healing and wellness are based on a commitment to holism, which can be defined as achieving harmony and balance among the physical, mental, spiritual, and emotional components of one's being. Holism is also connected to the development of a positive Aboriginal identity, and the focus on identity and its relationship to cultural expression has recently received increased attention in the literature on social work practice (McKenzie and Morrissette, 2003).

Despite relative differences between Aboriginal and non-Aboriginal people on a number of social well-being measures, improvements in education and employment, particularly in the urban context, are apparent. For example, between 1996 and 2006, the number of Aboriginal adults with high school diplomas living in the urban areas increased by nine per cent to 59.9 per cent and the number with university degrees increased from 4.2 per cent to 6.8 per cent. During this same period of time the median income for urban Aboriginal people increased by 52 per cent and the unemployment rate dropped from 24.2 per cent to 14 per cent (Rabson, 2009a: A9).

Local governance in the human services has also transformed policy-making in many Aboriginal communities. In First Nations, local control of many health and education services are common, and the majority of these communities now have locally controlled child and family service agencies providing child welfare services under agreements that require federal funding and compliance with provincial legislation and standards. For example, between 1990 and 2008, the number of First Nations child and family service agencies grew from 34 to 108, and these agencies provide at least partial child welfare services to 442 of the 606 reserve communities in Canada served by INAC in 2008 (Auditor General of Canada, 2008). Aboriginal agencies have been developed in the urban context to provide early childhood education, interventions related to family violence, and a variety of youth and family related services. As well, child and family service agencies have been developed in major urban centres such as Toronto, Vancouver, and Winnipeg to provide services to Aboriginal people in these cities.

Some of the services that have developed have been quite innovative. On the Kahnawake First Nation near Montreal, a highly successful model of community social services based on the principles of integration and wrap-around services has been developed. An effective model of community-controlled child welfare services has been established by the Cowichan tribes in BC (Brown, Haddock, and Kovach, 2002). A wide range of community-based prevention services have been developed by West Region Child and Family Services in Manitoba and on the Blood First Nation in southern Alberta. Another example is the development of a custom adoption program by the Yellowhead Tribal Family Services Agency in Alberta.

There have also been some important developments at the national and provincial levels. Aboriginal control of service delivery has been extended to Aboriginal people living off reserve in many provinces, and in Saskatchewan the Federation of Saskatchewan Indian Nations has developed its own child welfare legislation. Although this legislation does not have legal authority, it is frequently referenced as guidance in agreements that are established with First Nations in that province. Aboriginal political organizations at both the national and provincial levels now exert considerable influence on social policy, both through a social advocacy stance and direct involvement in policy and program development. As well, specialized social policy organizations have been established. For example, in child and family services the First Nations Child and Family Caring Society

(FNCFCS) of Canada has emerged as a key research and advocacy organization on behalf of Aboriginal families and children. These organizations, which perform roles often identified with both policy communities and advocacy groups, have the potential of influencing ongoing policy development in child and family services. Unfortunately, the First Nations Child and Family Caring Society has very limited resources, and of course, this restricts its overall capacity to influence policy developments.

There are many descriptive accounts of the evolution of social policy affecting Aboriginal people over the past decades; however, there is a noticeable absence of material to describe either the policy-making processes or preferred models of policy-making within the Aboriginal context. What follows is a synopsis of three different case studies on policy-making in the field of Aboriginal child and family services. One example is drawn from the federal policy-making arena, a second comes from the provincial level, and the third reflects an organizational approach.

Two of the critical issues in Aboriginal policy-making are funding and jurisdictional control and these issues are central to the field of child and family services. Funding for First Nations child welfare agencies on reserves in all provinces, except Ontario, is received directly from the federal government; this funding is based on a formula outlined in Directive 20-1. Although the current funding approach to First Nations child and family services is in transition, this formula has not been fully reviewed and revised since its introduction in 1991, and this has been a significant factor in the underfunding of First Nations child and family services agencies on reserves. First Nations families living on reserves are not eligible for certain provincial services, such as the range of services provided to children and adults with disabilities, and even when eligible, they have limited access to such services due to geographic or financial disadvantages. In addition, reserve communities and other more remote Aboriginal communities lack the range of voluntary services and programs that exist in most urban centres. Finally, differences in funding policies between the federal and provincial levels of governments over services to First Nations people deemed to be living 'on reserve' lead to frequent clashes between these levels of government over who must pay for services. In some cases, these disputes have delayed or prevented the provision of needed services. Although the adequacy of funding and the management of these funds are critical to all policy-making processes, this issue is particularly important to the federal policy-making example described next and the third example on community governance.

Jurisdictional control over human services affecting Aboriginal people reflects the aspirations of Aboriginal people to gain some measure of self-governance over the services affecting their people. However, this is not simply a question of political control and how this might be operationalized within a nation state like Canada with a well entrenched governance model that includes federal, provincial, and city or municipal levels of responsibility. It is also about the rights and responsibilities to develop policies and programs that will include culturally appropriate principles and practices. Jurisdictional control, then, can be examined from two perspectives: the political perspective, which asserts the inherent right to self-government; and the service perspective, which focuses on decolonization through an emphasis on Aboriginal focused practices as a counterpoint to historical patterns of colonization that were largely based on strategies of subjugation and assimilation

# Shared Decision-Making at the Federal Level

In Chapter Six, shared decision-making was discussed as a model of inclusive policy-making. Such a model is important in policy-making where interactions are required between communities and government or where groups with power and authority are required to establish mutually acceptable policies and programs. However, the authenticity of shared decision-making processes is often difficult to establish, except through experience. Indeed, these processes are often described as collaborative or as partnerships even though many fail to live up to this potential. Partnership and collaboration, like shared decision-making, requires a commitment to shared power in shaping policy solutions; in addition, it requires policy actions that emerge from shared understanding of the joint decisions that have been made.

The Joint National Policy Review process is examined as an example of shared decision making. This process—a collaborative effort between the Assembly of First Nations, represented by First Nations child and family services agency directors, and the Department of Indian Affairs and Northern Development (DIAND OR INAC)—was initiated to address problems in funding and related service development in First Nations child and family services.

As earlier noted, funding formulas and the level of funding are central to policy-making in child welfare because they play a key role in defining both the nature and scope of services that can be provided. The level of funding is closely tied to service quality, and the funding formula is an important determinant of the nature of services that will be provided. For example, if funding is provided primarily for protection services related to investigation, risk assessment, and out of home placement costs, this restricts the ability of an agency to provide early intervention and family support services.

Most First Nations child and family services agencies located on reserves operate on the basis of a 'delegated model' where the province or territories grant First Nations agencies the authority to provide child welfare services subject to provincial or territorial legislation and standards and funding is provided by the federal government.

Federal funding for First Nations child and family services was rationalized in a new funding formula established by INAC that became effective in 1991. This formula, known simply as Directive 20-1, has been the model for funding all First Nations child and family services agencies on reserves, except those in the province of Ontario. In Ontario, the federal government provides a general grant to the province based on a 1965 agreement, and the province allocates funding to First Nations agencies based on the provincial funding formula. Directive 20-1 provides for operational grants to First Nations agencies on reserves based on the child population served by the agency and several other factors, including an allowance for remoteness. It also indicates that funding for child maintenance (i.e., the cost of maintaining children placed in alternative care) is to be reimbursed based on actual costs allowed by the relevant provincial authority. This formula, established as a top-down directive with little input from First Nations service providers, has been criticized for some time. Among other inadequacies, the formula used to establish the basic allocation for an agency has not been adjusted for changes in the cost of living since 1995, there is no identified allocation for family support services, and there is only a limited adjustment factor for higher costs due to remoteness (e.g., higher travel costs, limited access to specialized services, etc.).

In the mid-1990s new First Nations child and family service agencies were beginning to develop in Saskatchewan. These First Nations controlled agencies, funded by INAC, provided child and family services on reserves subject to provincial child welfare legislation. Concerns were raised in the province about funding issues with a request that INAC address these; however, First Nations child and family service agencies in other provinces objected to a regional approach to issues that were, in fact, national in scope. Following meetings with INAC officials in Ottawa, an agreement was struck to conduct a national policy review into First Nations child and family services in 1998. It took approximately one year to negotiate terms of reference for a process that would include equal representation from INAC and First Nations child and family service agencies operating under the umbrella of the Assembly of First Nations. Each INAC region (New Brunswick and Nova Scotia make up one region and other regions are equivalent to provincial boundaries) appointed one INAC representative and one First Nations child and family service director to a Joint Steering Committee. A Project Management Team and a Policy Review Group, each adhering to the equal representation principle between INAC and First Nations, were established (McDonald, Ladd, et al., 2000).

The first task was to hire research consultants to complete policy reviews on four thematic areas: agency governance, legislation and standards, communication issues, and funding issues. Funding issues, including the approach to funding service delivery and child maintenance, were central issues. The research projects were initiated in December 1999 and completed in May 2000. Project reports were then combined in a final report (McDonald, Ladd, et al., 2000) with a series of recommendations. Recommendations included the need to revise funding formulas to provide for a wider range of early intervention services, address inadequate elements in the current formula for supporting agency operations, and develop culturally appropriate service standards. An action plan for ratifying the report of the Joint National Policy Review and implementing recommendations through an ongoing partnership model was outlined.

The implementation phase included the development of a joint national committee to coordinate implementation activities at the national level and the establishment of regional tables, again based on the principle of partnership. Regional tables were established because of the recognition that it was also important to engage with representatives of provincial governments and that regional variations created issues that needed to be resolved at that level.

After the completion of the Joint National Policy Review, a separate study on the use of block funding in child maintenance was commissioned (McKenzie, 2002a). This review was designed to lead to a Cabinet submission for authority to establish flexible funding agreements for the child maintenance component (i.e., costs for foster, group, and institutional care) of an agency's child welfare budget. Agencies that entered into these agreements would receive a block grant that could be used for early intervention and family support programming if savings in the money spent on out-of-home care were realized.

Results from this experience in shared decision-making at the federal level have been mixed. The process initially generated goodwill and a shared understanding of issues that has helped senior policy-makers in INAC in their efforts to promote policies on behalf of First Nations agencies. As well, special submissions for the 2003–4 budget were made for increased funding for family support services in First Nations communities and for authority to establish flexible funding arrangements for First Nations' agencies. While the flexible funding proposal was approved, new funding for family support services was not included, and this resulted in considerable frustration on the part of those who were invested in the process. First Nations participants at the policy tables were not involved in meetings beyond the divisional level in INAC. Thus, the development of final proposals and the presentation of these proposals to central bodies such as Cabinet and Treasury Board were handled by senior departmental staff. Delays were also a factor. For example, ratification of the report of the Joint National Policy Review by the Minister of Indian Affairs was delayed by several months and meant that implementation of the shared decision process was delayed. And while there was support for both the process and many of the recommendations within the Social Policy Division of INAC, resistance was encountered at other levels, including Cabinet and Treasury Board. Some of this resistance reflected concerns about cost implications, but there was also little appreciation for the partnership approach to policy-making and the need to expedite the process in light of the excessive bureaucratic procedures that too often impede rather than enable new policy initiatives at the governmental level.

After the initial failure to obtain a special allocation for family support services or make changes to the funding formula included in Directive 20-1, one last effort was made to address funding issues. In 2004 INAC secured federal funding that permitted the National Advisory Committee of the Joint Policy Review to fund a research project to identify more clearly three optional funding models for First Nations child and family services agencies: (1) revisions to the current formula as outlined in Directive 20-1; (2) linking First Nations child and family services funding to provincial models; and (3) a new First Nations based funding formula. A contract was established with First Nations Child and Family Caring Society (FNCFCS), and a multidisciplinary research team was recruited. The *Wen:De (We are Coming to the Light of Day)* report was released in 2005 by the First Nations Child and Family Caring Society of Canada. This report documented a number of issues pertaining to jurisdictional disputes (see Box 10.1) and the gaps in funding between First Nations and provincial child welfare agencies. Although a number of gaps were identified, the failure to incorporate an inflationary factor in the Directive 20-1 funding formula alone accounted for a shortfall of $112 million between 1999 and 2005 or a loss of approximately 14 per cent of operational funding allocated to these agencies over this seven-year period of time.

Additional funding for inflationary adjustment, infrastructure development, and new family support programs (identified as support for 'least disruptive measures') was recommended, and the report demonstrated through cost–benefit

## Box 10.1  Jordan's Principle

One of the critical issues documented in the *Wen:De Report* (First Nations Child and Family Caring Society, 2005) pertains to jurisdictional disputes between departments within one level of government and between the federal and provincial or territorial levels of government over funding responsibility for services to individuals. The report noted that jurisdictional disputes were not unique, and a survey of 12 First Nations agencies indicated that 393 incidents of such disputes had occurred over a one-year period of time. Most disputes involved children with complex medical needs. Jordan, a young child with a limited life expectancy who had been hospitalized in Winnipeg for a lengthy period of time, illustrates the effects of these disputes.

The family, living in a northern reserve, requested that the child be returned to his home community because there were no treatment advantages to remaining in hospital. However, there were costs involved in transportation and the provision of maintenance supports at home. Jurisdictional wrangling between federal government departments over the payment of these costs dragged on for a prolonged period of time. Before the child had an opportunity to live in a family environment he died in the only home he ever knew—a hospital. This has led to the development of Jordan's Principle, which requests that a 'child first' policy be adopted whereby the government or department that first receives a request for the payment of services for a First Nations child will pay without disruption or delay when these services are otherwise available to non-Aboriginal children in similar circumstances. The government then has the option of resolving the final responsibility for funding the service or referring the matter to a jurisdictional dispute resolution process. The federal government has endorsed Jordan's Principle but not all provincial governments have adopted this principle or implemented measures to ensure compliance with it.

calculations how investment in prevention and early intervention would not only improve child and family outcomes but also reduce social expenditures over time. Although the research indicated that additional work was required to establish a clear template for a new funding model, it rejected the provincial option and recommended a blend of the Directive 20-1 model and a new First Nations based funding formula that would address some of the special issues facing First Nations communities, including the overrepresentation of First Nations children in care and the need to better support a community-based model of service delivery.

Shortly after the release of the *Wen:De Report*, the Martin Liberal Government was replaced by the Harper Conservative government in Ottawa. The new federal government refused to accept the recommendations made in the *Wen: De Report* and indicated it would do its own review. A private firm in Winnipeg was contracted to complete a review; however, the federal government has never released the results.

Frustrated with the lack of government response to the funding needs documented in the *Wen:De Report*, in February 2007 the FNCFCS and the Assembly of First Nations filed a complaint under the *Canadian Human Rights Act,* alleging that chronic under-funding of First Nations child and family services agencies amounts to discriminatory treatment of First Nations children. In October 2008 the Canadian Human Rights Commission agreed to conduct an inquiry into these allegations. Although the results of the inquiry are not yet known, the Auditor General of Canada reported in 2008 that the funding formula used by INAC was inadequate to meet provincial standards and the needs of First Nations children and families. It is not yet clear whether the results of the human rights inquiry will produce a remedy that might lead to implementation of at least some of the recommendations of the *Wen:De Report* or whether more recent actions by INAC to increase funding will overshadow any outcomes that might occur from the Human Rights complaint.

Although there is little evidence that shared decision-making is now central to the process, the federal government has taken some steps to increase First Nations funding to First Nations agencies on reserves. One is left to speculate about whether evidence from the Joint National Policy Review process, the *Wen:De Report*, or the still secret policy review conducted by the government influenced these actions, or whether the Human Rights complaint and the Auditor General's report were more influential. In any event, INAC has been setting up framework agreements with each region (roughly similar to provincial boundaries) to increase funding to agencies on reserves on a region-by-region basis. Eventually these agreements will replace the outdated funding formula in Directive 20-1. Although this departs from the *Wen:De Report* in adopting a model that fits with the provincial funding system, new funding is being provided for family support and enhancement services with an expectation that this will lead to a reduction of children in care and future cost savings to government. Notwithstanding these developments, the piecemeal approach taken by INAC was strongly criticized in March 2009 by the House of Commons Public Accounts Committee, which noted an immediate need to adjust the funding formula for all regions in the country (Rabson, 2009b: A6).

# Creating a Policy Community at the Provincial Level

The second example described in this chapter is a provincial initiative launched in Manitoba to restructure child welfare services in the province, whereby new Aboriginal authorities would assume responsibility for the provision of child and family services to most, if not all, Aboriginal service users throughout the province. This initiative is known as the *Aboriginal Justice Inquiry Child Welfare Initiative* because the recommendation on which the policy was based first appeared in the *Report of the Aboriginal Justice Inquiry* released in 1991 (Hamilton and Sinclair, 1991).

This model reflects aspects of shared decision-making in that policy-makers from Aboriginal organizations and government became involved in negotiations that led to new proposals on how child welfare services would be transferred to new Aboriginal authorities. However, because both Aboriginal and government partners shared a strong commitment to a common policy outcome at the outset, that is, the transfer of jurisdiction to Aboriginal authorities, this example is more reflective of a policy community. Participants worked together in developing ways to make this policy goal a reality, and although differences emerged, these have been largely related to operational and implementation issues rather than the essential purposes and intent of the new policy.

In 1999, the NDP government initiated a process that was designed to transfer responsibility for the provision of child welfare services for all Aboriginal people in Manitoba to new Aboriginal Child and Family Service Authorities. This initiative was not designed as a cost-saving venture but as a method to support Aboriginal jurisdiction over child welfare services. As noted, the policy change reflected a recommendation originally made in an inquiry into Aboriginal justice in the province, and it was consistent with requests from both the Manitoba Métis Federation and First Nations groups in the province for greater control, particularly over services provided to Aboriginal people living off-reserve.

In Manitoba, First Nations-controlled child and family service agencies have been providing a full range of child welfare services on reserves since the mid-1980s under a delegated arrangement that includes provincial legislation and standards and federal funding. However, approximately one-half of First Nations people in the province live off-reserve, and these families and children had generally received services from non-Aboriginal agencies. In addition, Métis people had no separate child welfare agency designed to respond to their particular needs and aspirations. Aboriginal children make up the majority of children-in-care population in the province; for example, in 2001 it was estimated that Aboriginal children made up about 21 per cent of Manitoba's population under the age of

15, yet they accounted for 78 per cent of the children in care (Manitoba Family Services and Housing as cited in Joint Management Committee, 2001). The policy change contemplated, then, was designed to provide Aboriginal people with greater control over the provision of child welfare services to Aboriginal families and children and to enable more community-based, culturally appropriate models of service delivery.

An inclusive policy-making process that involved the provincial government and Aboriginal political organizations in the province was established, based partly on the new NDP government's commitment to a more collaborative approach and Aboriginal demands for greater control over both the process and outcomes of policy-making in child welfare. Three Aboriginal partners were identified: the Manitoba Métis Federation (MMF), the Assembly of Manitoba Chiefs (AMC) representing Southern First Nations, and Manitoba Keewatinowi Okimakanak (MKO) representing Northern First Nations.

The first step involved negotiations between the province and Aboriginal organizations. This led to the signing of three separate Memorandums of Understanding (MOUs) between the province and each Aboriginal group. Subsequently, all four parties signed a Service Protocol Agreement that identified a framework and principles for the planning process. Each stakeholder group (the two First Nations groups were defined as one stakeholder group in determining committee memberships) had an equal number of representatives on the various policy-making structures, a decision that put government members in the minority. The structure included an Executive Committee, a Joint Management Committee, an Implementation Committee, and working groups.

The Joint Management Committee was generally responsible for the initiative and it reported to the Executive Committee, which included two provincial ministers and representatives from the three Aboriginal partners. The more detailed policy-making activities occurred at the Implementation Committee level that was responsible for coordinating the planning process, developing the initial conceptual plan, and establishing detailed implementation guidelines. This committee also received reports from seven working groups that had been set up to review and make recommendations on topics such as legislative change, financing, and service delivery models.

Policy-making discussions at the committee level produced some interesting policy debates. For example, the Minister of Family Services and Housing had outlined three key principles for the new initiative. The reforms were to be cost-neutral, new services would be provided under a delegated authority model (i.e., services must adhere to provincial legislation and standards, as amended), and service users would have a choice about which authority to access for services: the General Authority (non-Aboriginal), Métis, First Nations North, or First Nations South. Although the principle of delegated authority was accepted, modifications were made to the other two principles because of Aboriginal objections. For example, the province provided significant transitional funding and new funding since implementation; as well, the choice of which authority provides services has been somewhat restricted. The right to choose a service provider was a particularly contentious issue. Given the dominant society's historical pattern of assimilating Aboriginal people, it was argued that the new Aboriginal authorities should not be denied the right to reclaim their members by becoming the service providers of first resort. Those opposing this viewpoint asserted the rights of service users to self-determination as a guiding principle. Under the present arrangement, the service user still has some level of personal choice; however, the first priority is to refer users to the service provider that best matches their cultural background.

Four different child and family service authorities have been established under new legislation that entrenches the right of Aboriginal people to receive services from agencies established under a governance structure composed of persons ratified by the political body that represents their people. Each authority has a province-wide mandate and can provide services to families and children from its cultural group anywhere in the province. However, each authority does not have service delivery units in all parts of the province, and contractual arrangements with the primary service provider in a community occurs in circumstances where the designated authority does not have an office in the area. For example, in most cases a Métis family living on reserve will receive service from the First Nations agency providing service on that reserve. Joint intake procedures have been developed to provide emergency and short-term services in each region and to identify the Authority of Record for the child and family (i.e., the authority from which they would normally receive service based on their cultural affiliation). If an agency representing their Authority of Record exists in the area, they would normally be referred to this agency for continuing services. There was an assumption at the beginning that members of First Nations, persons identifying as Métis, and non-Aboriginal persons would want to be served by service providers mandated by their respective authorities. For the most part this has been the case although the General Authority still provides services to a significant number of Aboriginal children and families.

The implementation planning process proceeded reasonably well although initial time lines were extended in recognition of the many complexities involved in developing a service model that is based on concurrent jurisdictional responsibility (i.e., more than one agency with responsibility for service provision within regional areas). There was a significant level of collaboration between government and Aboriginal participants, including a determination to circumvent bureaucratic imperatives that interfered with the general policy intent. For example, the drafting of the *Child and Family Services Authorities Act* was done in close consultation with the Implementation Committee. This Committee developed detailed specifications of what should be in new legislation and then government personnel drafted the legislation. Draft legislation was then returned to the Committee for comments and suggestions for revision prior to debate in the legislature and government was responsive to most of these suggestions. A problem-solving approach based on respect and goodwill characterized the process, and this has enabled the development of a model that, over time, promises to facilitate the provision of more culturally appropriate child welfare services in the province. Government was also responsive on other issues, including funding for training and the transitional costs pertaining to the development of new authorities and Aboriginal agencies.

Despite the collaborative approach taken by government with representatives from Aboriginal groups in the province, this was not replicated with other important constituencies, particularly in the formative stages of the policy process. For example, there was a general public consultation process in the fall of 2001 after the development of the conceptual plan but this process was quite limited in that only 12 town hall meetings and 15 focus groups were held throughout the province. In addition, the province made little effort to involve non-Aboriginal agencies or staff in the process. This failure contributed to feelings of low morale that had implications for the policy implementation stage. Although some of these reactions are normal in any major policy change, much of this could have been avoided. Indeed, most child welfare staff were supportive of the general policy goal even if they were concerned about implementation issues and processes. And as noted in Chapter Five, the involvement of existing staff is essential in ensuring service quality and continuity in the implementation phase.

There were also some shortcomings to the policy-making process itself. The initial goal was focused primarily on a change in jurisdiction where service users in child welfare would receive services from authorities based on their cultural affiliation. Of secondary importance was a shift in the service paradigm to a more family enhancement model of child welfare. Although this issue was not neglected entirely, it was initially anticipated that new agencies, established as a result of a change in jurisdiction, would create their own model of service. For example, it was assumed that agencies might reduce expenditures on high cost methods of out-of-home care and re-invest these savings in more community-based services. How this shift would occur without new resources in a model that focuses almost exclusively on 'search and rescue' to one that includes a major emphasis on early intervention and family support was not clearly outlined in the initial planning process. In some respects this issue has presented some of the most significant challenges during the program implementation stage.

Legislation was passed in 2002 to enable this policy change and implementation of the new service model, including the transfer of cases to new agencies, occurred between 2003 and 2005. The field implementation stage has involved a number of challenges. In the early stages there were significant problems in coordinating service responsibilities between authorities and agencies, and the requirement to coordinate planning among the four authorities has caused delays in addressing important issues. There were also a number of highly publicized deaths in the first couple of years which promoted a series of special reviews that identified a wide range of recommendations for change. Service-related issues are being addressed with new government support for training and the expansion of early intervention programs, which are loosely labelled as 'family enhancement services'. As well, the provincial government remains strongly committed to the new service model. Nevertheless, some uncertainties remain.

One of these pertains to governance, and the relationship of authorities to government, and in the case of Aboriginal authorities, to their respective political constituencies. Each Aboriginal authority, which has responsibility to fund and oversee policy development and service delivery for its defined constituency, reports to a Board which is at arm's length from the politicians (i.e., Chief or President and Board of the Métis Society). The General Authority, which has responsibilities that are similar to Aboriginal authorities, reports to an administrative unit within government. However, some First Nations agencies, which may be governed by boards composed of Chiefs, see the role of these authorities as interfering with the direct control that local politicians would like to have over child welfare programs. In some cases, the concerns reflect management problems and a lack of communication between the respective authority and politicians. However, this response is also apparent when authorities make decisions that limit the control of Chiefs, even when those decisions reflect efforts to address problems in agency management or services that are not in the best interests of children and families. Some of these conflicts at the community and tribal council level led the Assembly of Manitoba Chiefs to approve a motion in January 2009 to hand over direct leadership and responsibility of the Southern Child and Family Services Authority to the Southern Chiefs Organization. If this occurs, the Authority will become more directly accountable to the 36 chiefs that make up the Southern Chiefs Organization. This action by the Southern Chiefs is quite interesting because the Southern Authority has been particularly successful in the developing new and forward looking reforms. Although this change has not occurred, and it is questionable whether major changes in structure can occur without a change in legislation, some have expressed the fear that the move by the Southern Chiefs could lead to unwarranted political interference in the management of the Authority or in day to day decision-making (Welch, 2009: A4).

## Community Governance and Child Welfare

In this case study, we explore both the outcomes and processes associated with an inclusive approach to policy development undertaken by a First Nations child and family services agency operating under a community governance structure.

West Region Child and Family Services has provided a full range of child welfare services to nine First Nations communities in Manitoba since 1985. It is recognized as an agency that exhibits best practices in child and family services, and in 1998 it received the Peter T. Drucker Award for Canadian Non-Profit Innovation for its work in early intervention and family support and the use of the medicine wheel as an organizing framework for these services.

The agency has made innovative use of flexible funding for child maintenance since 1992 when it negotiated the first block funding agreement in First Nations child welfare with INAC. This agreement capped the amount of money received for child maintenance (i.e., foster, group, and institutional care costs) based on the previous year's expenditures and a projected cost increase for the upcoming operating year. However, the agency was permitted to use any money not required for out-of-home care costs to develop alternative programs focusing on early intervention and family support. By developing lower-cost alternative care options for children, such as a therapeutic foster care program, the agency was able to provide good-quality, culturally appropriate care for children requiring placement while reducing some of its costs on expensive residential care in places like Winnipeg. In turn, these savings have helped to establish a wide range of early intervention and family support programs. Based on 2004 data, about 40 per cent of the agency's funding for child maintenance was being spent on alternative programs while the agency continued to provide high service to those children requiring out-of-home placement (McKenzie and Shangreaux, 2006).

Service outcomes have been evaluated on three separate occasions (McKenzie, 1994, 1999; Shangreaux and McKenzie, 2005). As well, a cost–benefit analysis of agency programs was completed for the *Wen:De Report* (Blackstock et al., 2005). Results indicate a decline in the rate of 'on reserve' children in care from 10 per cent in 1992–93 to 5.2 per cent in 2003–04, a change in the placement pattern of children in care with more children in placements involving Aboriginal caregivers and closer to their home communities, a significant increase in early intervention and cultural healing approaches, and a decline in the incidence of reported cases of child abuse and neglect despite an increase in the on-reserve child population. The results of the cost–benefit analysis indicates that the agency's investment in a continuum of primary, secondary, and tertiary prevention saved $1.5 million each year as more children were able to stay at home rather than being placed in high cost substitute care (Loxley and Deriviere, 2005: 120). As previously indicated, doing the best thing for children and their families can, over the longer term, lead to economic benefits.

Two factors have been particularly important to the agency's success. One is that agency services and the engagement with front line staff and community stakeholders have been guided by the medicine wheel approach and traditional Ojibway teachings. Values derived from these traditions have emphasized a holistic approach to community-based practice that integrates First Nations' values, world views, family and community structures, and national helping systems in a coordinated approach to working with families whose children are at risk of maltreatment. This philosophy is reflected in a program structure which emphasizes four 'circles of care'. The 'Staying at Home Circle of Care' focuses on supporting children at home through a continuum of family support and family preservation services. The 'Alternate Care Circle' supports foster and group care programs with a special emphasis on strengthening kinship care and improving outcomes for children in care. The 'Family Restoration and Treatment Support Circle' directs services to families where children have been placed in care or are at risk. These treatment support services are designed to support children with special needs and their families and to facilitate family reunification where appropriate. There is also a special focus on caring for children with Fetal Alcohol Syndrome Disorder (FASD). The final program is identified as 'Supporting Community Circles of Care' with includes community-based prevention programs and supportive services to local child and family service communities.

A second and related factor is its adoption of an inclusive approach to policy-making that includes staff, community members, and service users (McKenzie, 2002b). There is a strong leadership team and an agency commitment to professional development that has provided incentives to staff to obtain post-secondary education degrees and other professional training. The agency uses a community-based planning approach at both a regional and local level to receive feedback on existing services and to develop new initiatives. For example, regional operational workshops, involving all staff and a wide range of representatives from each community, are held every two years. A similar exercise occurs at the local level; each community-based service team organizes a community-planning workshop on child and family services annually or every two years. Not only are these helpful in realizing the goal of community accountability, but they also serve as a means for setting priorities, community education, and recruiting community volunteers.

The organizational structure of the agency also facilitates community involvement. Each local community has a community-based service team, and these staff work in collaboration with a Child and Family Services Committee. This committee of local volunteers plays an active role in providing advice and assistance on both child protection and prevention matters. This collaborative process to community building also characterizes work with service user groups. One illustrative example was the Vision Seekers Program, a partnership program designed with other service providers to provide work and life-skills training to young adults with children who are or are likely to become at risk.

A collaborative working style is characteristic of the agency's internal operations as well, and staffs play an important ongoing role through their participation in service team meetings and the management team. In addition, they are engaged in special initiatives such as the planning and management of community prevention initiatives (see Box 10.2).

## Summary and Conclusion

Aboriginal people, more than any other group in Canadian society, have had policies 'done to them'. In the past three decades this has begun to change; however, uncertainties persist because of problems in funding and the inconsistent approach of governments in establishing a policy framework that will promote both local autonomy and service quality. In addition, there are contradictions within some Aboriginal organizations and communities where top-down hierarchical models of policy-making prevail.

## Box 10.2  Community Governance in Action

Faced with a dilemma of how to plan and deliver community-based prevention programs to nine First Nations communities, West Region Child and Family Services developed a collaborative approach to planning, implementing, and evaluating the variety of community-based initiatives that could be financially supported through a fund set up for this purpose. Although the amount of funding is significant, there is never enough to fund all programs that can be sponsored to support at-risk children and families. Thus there was a need to establish priorities among a variety of proposed new initiatives, and to institute a process for doing this that could be used for each annual budget cycle. The first step was to design a method that would enable good decisions, involve key people in the process, and be regarded as fair by participating staff and communities. This involved the participation of community-based prevention staff, along with senior staff, in setting criteria for the selection of projects, and a protocol for proposal development and accountability. On an annual basis in each community, local staff now undertake a planning process to design and prioritize program initiatives, in collaboration with their local child and family service committee. These are then formally submitted to the agency's selection committee, which is comprised of selected senior staff and one prevention worker from each community. Following an agency decision on the amount of money to be allocated to community prevention programs, the selection committee then meets to make decisions on which programs will receive funding and the amount of funding to be allocated. As the budget is significant, each community receives approval for several initiatives. Responsibility is then transferred to the local prevention workers and child and family services committees to complete the detailed planning and implementation stages for each approved project. Local staff and committees are also responsible for submitting a report to account for expenditures and provide evaluative feedback after each community project has been completed.

We first consider the contradictions that exist within some Aboriginal communities and organizations. It is often argued that the more hierarchical models of power and control that exist in some Aboriginal organizations reflect patterns learned through the legacy of colonization. This may be true, yet many involved in the human services (both service providers and service users) are left with unmet needs and feelings of disempowerment. Under these circumstances, local control is an imperfect solution. Although we recognize this problem, it is equally clear that substituting government authority for local control is unlikely to resolve these difficulties. First, the state has a poor record of protecting the rights and aspirations of Aboriginal people; and second, changes that are likely to be both responsive to community and long-lasting must come from within. This is not to suggest the government has no role. It has a responsibility to ensure the essential rights of citizens no matter where they live and facilitate processes consistent with the basic tenets of democracy and community capacity-building. Standards and accountability mechanisms for services delegated to community-based organizations are necessary, and these can enhance the provision of high-quality services.

We turn now to an examination of the role of government and Aboriginal organizations in the making of Aboriginal social policies.

Some of the seeds of change were sown in the 1970s but the more dramatic changes in the development of Aboriginal social policy have occurred since the 1980s. The impetus for many of these changes resulted from two parallel processes. On the one hand, Aboriginal organizations became an effective social movement in making the case for a number of changes consistent with the goal of self-government. Although some disruptive tactics, including various kinds of blockades, were expressions of discontent, strategies also included advocacy and negotiation. As well, there were a growing number of reports and studies that documented both high levels of need and the failures of past government policies.

Three examples of inclusive models of policy-making were summarized in this chapter, and some tentative conclusions can be drawn from these experiences. The shared decision-making approach at the federal level which focused on funding in First Nations child and family services was a very time-consuming process. The absence of a clearly defined outcome from this experiment in shared decision-making may reflect, in part, the complexity of policy-making processes at the federal government level. Without a genuine commitment on the part of government to modify the bureaucratic procedures that often get in the way of collaborative approaches to policy-making, shared decision-making can raise expectations that may not be realized. However, the information generated from the process coupled with more direct actions including a human rights complaint appear to have influenced a neo-liberal federal government to respond in some fashion to the funding crisis in child welfare services on reserves.

The policy community approach in the Aboriginal Justice Inquiry Child Welfare Initiative appears to have been successful in establishing a framework for policy change that has already influenced the provision of child welfare services to Aboriginal people in Manitoba in some profound ways. Control over all child welfare services in the province has been transferred to Aboriginal authorities, and new legislation provides a framework for the development of culturally appropriate services. The realization of intended policy outcomes has been hampered somewhat by problems in implementation but there is still a strong commitment among the key stakeholders to adjust the model in an effort to improve the outcomes for all children and families in the province. The future benefits of this policy change will depend on an ongoing commitment to an adaptive approach to implementation, and the development of processes which facilitate collaboration without politicizing the policy environment in ways that lose sight of the needs and rights of children and families.

The community governance approach to policy development established by West Region Child and Family Services provides an exemplar of what can be accomplished when an inclusive model is embraced as a comprehensive approach to policy-making at the local level. However, the success of this model is also dependent on other factors, and two of the most important of these are effective leadership and skilled and committed staff.

# Recommended Reading

B. McKenzie and V. Morrissette, 'Social Work Practice with Canadians of Aboriginal Background: Guidelines for Respectful Social Work', in A. Al-Krenawi and J.R. Graham, eds, *Multicultural Social Work in Canada* (Don Mills, ON: Oxford University Press, 2003), 251–82. This chapter considers factors, including the important role of cultural identity, that affect social work practice with Aboriginal peoples.

Aboriginal Corrections Policy Unit, *The Four Circles of Hollow Water* (Ottawa: Supply and Services Canada, 1997). This report outlines a model for dealing with sexual abuse that was developed in a small First Nations community in Manitoba.

E. Connors and F. Maidman, 'A Circle of Healing: Family Wellness in Aboriginal Communities', in I. Prilleltensky, G. Nelson, and L. Pierson, eds, *Promoting Family Wellness and Preventing Child Maltreatment* (Toronto: University of Toronto Press, 2001), 349–416. This chapter identifies a variety of programs and practices to promote healing in Aboriginal communities.

M. Saulis, 'Program and Policy Development from a Holistic Aboriginal Perspective', in A. Westhues, ed., *Canadian Social Policy: Issues and Perspectives*, 4th edn (Waterloo, ON: Wilfrid Laurier University Press, 2006), 115–30. This chapter provides additional information on the circle framework for policy and program development and compares Aboriginal and mainstream planning processes.

United Nations Committee on the Rights of the Child website, available at http://www2.ohchr.org/English/bodies/crc/index.htm. This UN Committee monitors the implementation of the *Convention on the Rights of the Child*, but also provides other reports on issues such as circumstances affecting indigenous children across the world.

# Critical Thinking Questions

1.  It is argued in this chapter that inclusive approaches are particularly appropriate to policy-making in Aboriginal communities. What are the arguments to support this position? Identify at least three challenges or potential risks.

2.  In June 2008, Primer Minister Stephen Harper made a speech in the House of Commons in which he apologized to Aboriginal people for the Indian Residential School system and the harms that the schools had caused to Aboriginal people. Locate this speech and critique this apology. In your

opinion how significant is this step to healing from the effects of residential schools?

3. Select one of the inclusive policy-making approaches described in this chapter. Identify some of the factors required to make this approach work.

4. Select an Aboriginal or non-Aboriginal organization with which you are familiar. Critically examine the power structure and approach to decision-making. How inclusive is the organization in developing its policies?

# Conclusion

In our concluding chapter we briefly summarize our case for more attention to connecting policy to practice. Simply put, we argue the case for inclusive approaches to policy-making but recognize these efforts alone will not be enough. We then examine the relationship between the policy-practice model this requires and the approaches outlined in critical approaches to human service practice, including arguments in the literature for a focus on structural social work and anti-oppressive practice.

## Policy-Practice for Progressive Policy-Making

A major obstacle to the development of more inclusive policy-making is the influence of neo-liberal governments and the related social policies that they champion. Policy-makers associated with this ideology prefer secrecy over transparency, centralized control over participatory democracy, and the preferences of the elite over the needs of citizens. This is evident in approaches to establish global free trade agreements, but it is also evident in the managerialist approach to program development and the centralized bureaucratic structures that support this style of policy-making. This model of policy-making was evident in the approach to risk assessment described in Chapter Eight as well as the approach to welfare cut-backs in BC described in Chapter Nine. The reason is not hard to understand. Those with power recognize that increased public involvement would lead to more progressive policies than they are willing to tolerate. This is reflected in market surveys that consistently show the public ahead of the curve on issues such as medicare and welfare state provision despite the best efforts of more conservative think tanks, the media, neo-liberal governments, and the corporate elite to shape public opinion in their own interests.

We introduced the notion of *grand and ordinary* policy issues in the Introduction. We do acknowledge that introducing more inclusive policy-making approaches on grand issues, such as globalization and monetary and fiscal policy, would be exceedingly difficult to develop. Advocacy through engagement with social movements, and in the case of globalization, international alliances with other groups and organizations, are much more likely to make a difference. However, with respect to the ordinary issues of health, education, and social service programs, more inclusive approaches can make a difference. To be fair, there are significant barriers, such as the managerialist models in many large organizations, and practical issues, such as the available time and energy of practitioners and service users. However, there are experiences which support other ways of working. In the kinship care project described in Chapter Six, not only was a manager supportive of more engagement with front-line practitioners but also a significant number of practitioners responded by engaging in a process that led to important policy recommendations. This experience demonstrates the important roles that must be played by those formally responsible for policy-making as well as front-line practitioners in building an inclusive policy-making approach. Similar experiences were documented in Chapter Ten on the use of policy communities and community governance in Aboriginal child and family services.

In general, it is more difficult to engage service users than staff in some fields of practice, such as child welfare. However, even here it is not impossible, and their participation in the areas of education, health care, and feminist policy-making is well-known.

We argue strongly for a renewed commitment to inclusive policy-making. First, we note that the models of policy-making described in Chapter One and the approach to policy analysis described in Chapter Four can be adapted to facilitate increased participation from service users, other citizens, and front-line staff. This is particularly true in the policy analysis stage. The use of special lenses, including the steps outlined in the gender inclusive model of policy analysis, as well as the steps in the integrated model of policy analysis we outlined, encourage an inclusive approach. In our discussion of implementation, we noted the importance of an adaptive approach to implementation in many types of social programs. This model supports the active engagement of front-line practitioners and service users; simply put, we suggest that the success of the implementation stage of policy-making depends on their engagement and the commitment of policy-makers to incorporate their input.

A second and related approach to incorporating inclusivity in policy-making emerges from some of the approaches highlighted in Chapter Six. The adoption of one of the particular approaches outlined in this chapter may be used to ensure an inclusive approach to policy-making, a more participatory approach to activities associated with policy analysis, or the active involvement of front-line staff and service users in implementation. In some ways the approaches that are selected have something in common with the ladder of citizen participation introduced in Chapter Four. The engagement of staff and others in a backwards-mapping approach or a model of decision-making based on the *vertical slice approach* reflect relatively low levels of inclusivity. We see a *shared decision making approach* and a commitment to a policy community model as involving a higher level of commitment to engagement. And *community governance*, where decision-making authority rests with the community, involves a higher level of commitment to inclusive planning. It will also be apparent that one must distinguish between the rhetoric and the reality in any of these approaches in that these models can either be established as ways of co-opting participants or ensuring more meaningful participation.

Three final observations on incorporating inclusive approaches are noted. First, we emphasize that a commitment to inclusive policy-making requires the active involvement of policy analysts and policy-makers within central agencies and structures. These individuals have an important role in developing policy relevant options to be considered through engagement with stakeholders. Second, it is recognized that it is not practical that all policy-making decisions will be made with the full participation of relevant stakeholders. Some decisions must be made quickly and a longer term participatory process is simply not feasible. However, even in these cases a more inclusive approach to implementation may be advisable. Third, while we have argued for the inclusion of practitioners and service users in the policy-making process, we have been remiss in failing to apply the concept of inclusivity to practice. We note here our conviction that practitioners must involve service users in determining action plans. For example, in implementing risk assessment instruments, practitioners usually take on the sole responsibility for gathering information and determining the severity of risk factors. In many instances these tasks could be performed in a joint fashion with service users providing information and participating in discussions around risk factors and how to deal with these.

We have also argued in this edition of the book that inclusive approaches are not enough when decision-makers deliberately adopt more centralized, authoritarian models of policy-making. Policy resistance; engagement in advocacy, often through unions, interest groups, or professional organizations; the use of legal challenges; using think tanks to influence policy-makers or shape public opinion; participation in social movements, and whistle-blowing are some of the methods that can be used in trying to influence policy-making from outside the system. The case study on opposing welfare time limits in BC provides a useful example of strategies that can be employed, and both this example and the shared-decision-making example around funding for First Nations child and family services demonstrate how working both inside and outside the system can increase the odds of achieving promising policy outcomes.

## Policy-Practice and Critical Social Work

There is a great deal of attention paid these days to rebranding progressive or radical human service work based on principles associated with social justice as *structural* or *anti-oppressive* practice, and it is important to consider how our arguments for progressive policy-making connect with these models. Mullaly, in *The New Structural Social Work* (2007: 288), associates anti-oppressive practice with structural social work and identifies the transformation of society along socialist lines as the goal of structural social work. While he is careful to recognize that structural social work includes practical responses to personal needs the emphasis in the structural model he proposes is that both personal change and social change (system change) is needed to transform society.

Hick and Pozzuto (2005) recognize that critical social work involves a number of different perspectives, that some perspectives may be complimentary, and that others may be in conflict. They also talk about 'transformative practice' but resist attempts to establish a hierarchy of approaches and argue that a theory is needed that begins with people's experiences and struggles but goes on to explore how these are connected to larger social structures and issues (2005: xvi).

Baines (2007) contrasts anti-oppressive practice (AOP) with more conventional mainstream approaches steeped in professionalism, the authority of the workplace, and the role of the social worker as the expert. She identifies 10 core insights or themes associated with social justice-oriented practice models. These include the recognition of multiple oppressions as causes of social problems for individuals and society in general, that social justice oriented practice assists individuals while simultaneously seeking to transform the forces that generate inequality and oppression, that participatory approaches between practitioners and clients are necessary, and that self-reflexive practice is essential. Although a blended approach to social justice is advocated Baines claims that 'AOP represents the current "state-of-the art" thinking and practice by social justice oriented social workers concerned with how best to "push the envelope" within the context of neo-liberalism, globalization and restructuring' (2007: 19).

These models have much in common with the arguments we have advanced. For example, they identify prevailing causes related to neo-liberalism, globalization, and managerialism as issues which have adversely affected social benefits for those in need, and made it more difficult to introduce progressive policies and services. The central tenet of structural social work includes work both within and outside the system to respond both to the needs of individuals and to promote changes that counter the way current structures promote injustices. This is not inconsistent with the changes to policy-making approaches that we advocate. As well, many of the central themes of practice within a social justice framework that Baines (2007) associates with AOP, such as participatory approaches, the need for self-reflexive practice and the ongoing need for analysis of the ever-changing impacts of structural factors, such as neo-liberalism, on inequality and other forms of oppression resonate with the type of policy-practice we advocate.

At the same time there are important criticisms of these approaches to be considered. First, there is a tendency to label these approaches as preferred approaches to practice in ways that discount the efforts of those who make significant contributions to social change but are not considered to be practising within the particular confines of these models. Conversely, those who adopt these so-called progressive approaches may fail to 'practise what they preach'. These tendencies can lead to a new form of elitism that is counter-productive to the underlying principles of these models. A second criticism pertains to the recognition in anti-oppressive practice of the intersecting and overlapping nature of oppressions. While this can be a strength, Tester (2003) notes problems associated with 'who determines who is oppressed' and 'which oppressions take precedence' in circumstances where almost everyone can identify as a victim of some type of oppression. In a similar fashion the approach to 'overlapping oppressions' may tend to dilute or minimize the central concerns of those who advance more specific claims regarding injustices based on race, class, or gender in society. Finally, and notwithstanding their general commitment to structural reform, there is a tendency in both anti-oppressive and structural approaches to focus more attention on the individual manifestations of oppression and the changes required at this level. For example, despite recognizing that the 'personal is political', strategies for making policy changes that affect significant groups of service users are not yet well developed.

This discussion of anti-oppressive practice and structural approaches within the human services has been included to establish a basis for our position on these important but often contested perspectives within the field and their more particular application to policy-practice. As earlier noted, we agree with many of the underlying principles, including the goals and practices associated with these approaches; however, we prefer to base our approach to policy-making more directly on core social justice principles, including the need to address inequality and other forms of oppression, the rights of those affected by policies to play a key role in the design and evaluation of policies and programs designed to respond to these purposes, and the need to assess the results against criteria related to social justice imperatives. We also argue that specialized attention to policy-making goals and processes is required in the human services if we are to improve the connections between policy and practice in ways that will have a positive impact on groups of service users, the staff that provide these important services, and the ongoing development of more progressive social policies.

# Appendix: Annotated Websites and Selected Canadian Journals

## Social Policy Sites

*Assembly of First Nations Website*
www.afn.ca
This site provides information on current issues affecting First Nations in Canada, including information on poverty in First Nations communities.

*C.D. Howe Institute/Institut C.D. Howe*
www.cdhowe.org
The C.D. Howe Institute provides policy analysis based on 'objectivity, professionalism, and relevance', but is widely known as the conservative research institute recommended by the Canadian Taxpayers Federation.

*Caledon Institute*
www.caledoninst.org
The Caledon Institute 'does rigorous, high-quality research and analysis and promotes practical proposals for the reform of social policy at the government and non-government sector'. The Institute is a private, non-profit organization focusing on social and economic inequalities in a broad range of social policy areas.

*Canadian Centre for Policy Alternatives*
www.policyalternatives.ca
The Canadian Centre for Policy Alternatives undertakes and promotes research on a wide range of issues pertaining to social and economic justice. In addition to

reports and books on particular issues, the centre publishes a monthly newsletter, *The Monitor,* which is available free to members.

*Canadian Health Coalition*
www.healthcoalition.ca
The Canadian Health Coalition is dedicated to preserving and enhancing Canada's public health coalition. The coalition includes groups representing unions, seniors, women, students, consumers, and health care professionals.

*Canadian Policy Research Networks*
www.cprn.ca
Established in 1995 the Canadian Policy Research Networks is a non-profit think tank that coordinates research networks focusing on work, family, and health. These networks involve collaboration by researchers in universities and government agencies across the country. The research is funded by a number of federal, provincial, and private-sector agencies.

*Canadian Research Institute for the Advancement of Women*
www.criaw-icref.ca
The institute is a non-governmental organization devoted to advancing gender equality through research and action. Online resources include fact sheets about violence against women in Canada, and women and poverty.

*Canadian Council on Social Development*
www.ccsd.ca
The Canadian Council on Social Development (CCSD) is a voluntary, non-profit organization that 'aims to develop and promote progressive social policies inspired by social justice, equality and the empowerment of individuals and communities through research, consultation, public education and advocacy'. CCSD is supported by membership fees and contracts with government. It publishes a quarterly magazine Perception that is free to members.

*Canadian Feminist Alliance for International Action*
www.fafia-afai.org
The Alliance is a coalition of over 75 Canadian women's groups 'that aim to further women's equality in Canada through domestic implementation of its international rights commitments'.

*Centre for Social Justice*
www.socialjustice.org
The Centre for Social Justice conducts research, education, and advocacy on issues of equality and democracy in Canada and globally.

*Council of Canadians with Disabilities*
www.ccdonline.ca
The Council of Canadians with Disabilities focuses on disability rights including access to job, housing, and democracy.

*First Nations Child and Family Caring Society of Canada*
www.fncfcs.com
This website provides reports and information on First Nations children and families in Canada with a particular focus on child and family services issues.

*Fraser Institute*
www.fraserinstitute.ca
The Fraser Institute is a think tank dedicated to 'competitive market solutions to public policy problems'. It is funded mainly through corporate contributions.

*Human Rights Education Associates*
www.hrea.org
Human Rights Education is an Ottawa-based organization dedicated to the empowerment of human rights activists and organizations and to the education of people on human rights issues and the role of civil society. It includes databases, publications, and news items.

*Innocenti Research Centre (UNICEF)*
www.unicef-irc.org
The Centre, formally known as the International Child Development Centre, has as its prime objectives to improve international understanding of the issues relating to children's rights, to promote economic policies that advance the cause of children, and to help facilitate the full implementation of the United Nations Convention on the Rights of the Child in industrialized and developing countries. The Centre produces a wide range of publications which contribute to the global debate on children's issues and include a wide range of opinions.

*Institute on Governance*
www.iog.ca
The Institute is an independent, non-profit think tank founded in 1990 to promote better governance for public benefit. It undertakes research and provides consultation services.

*Metropolis Canada Website*
canada.metropolis.net
Metropolis is an international network for comparative research and public policy development on migration, diversity, and immigrant integration in cities in Canada and around the world.

*Prairie Women's Health Centre of Excellence*
www.pwhce.ca
The Prairie Women's Health Centre of Excellence is dedicated to improving the health status of Canadian women in Manitoba and Saskatchewan by supporting policy-oriented and community-based research and analysis on the social and other determinants of women's health.

*Rights and Democracy*
www.dd-pd.ca/site
The International Centre for Human Rights and Democratic Development, now known as *Rights and Democracy* is a non-partisan Montreal-based organization created by the Parliament of Canada to work with citizens' groups and governments in Canada and abroad to promote human and democratic rights. It focuses on four themes: democratic development and justice, women's rights, indigenous people's rights, and globalization and human rights.

*Social Administration and Planning Links*
www.geocities.com/john_g_mcnutt/administ.htm
The links listed on this website are provided courtesy of John G. McNutt, Graduate School of Social Work, Boston College, Chestnut Hill, MA 02467.

*Status of Women Canada*
www.swc-cfc.gc.ca
This website contains resources for gender-based analysis of public policy.

*The Council of Canadians*
www.canadians.org
The Council of Canadians 'is an independent, non-partisan public interest organization established in 1985. The Council provides a critical voice on key national issues: safeguarding our social programs, promoting economic justice, renewing our democracy, asserting Canadian sovereignty, promoting alternatives to corporate-style free trade and preserving our environment'. The council is supported solely by membership dues.

*Women and the Economy – UN Platform for Action Committee*
www.unpac.ca/economy
UNPAC was founded in Manitoba after United Nations Fourth World Conference that took place in Beijing in 1995. The site contains information on projects related to women's economic inequality, women, and globalization. It indicates that its main goal is to demystify the economy and women's place in it.

# Poverty Related Sites

*Campaign 2000*
www.campaign2000.ca

Campaign 2000 was established in 1991 to bring pressure on the federal government to implement the all-party resolution of 1989 to eliminate child poverty by the year 2000. Campaign 2000 is now supported by national, provincial, and local partners. The principle strategy used by Campaign 2000 is the annual report card released on the anniversary of the all-party resolution. The national report card documents the extent of child poverty in Canada but the site includes some provincial information as well.

*Canada Without Poverty*
www.cwp-csp.ca
Canada Without Poverty  is a voluntary organization committed to advocacy on behalf of low-income Canadians. It was formerly known as the National Anti-Poverty Organization (NAPO).

*HIV/AIDS and Poverty*
www.cdnaids.ca/web/is.nsf/pages/is.0017
This site provides information outlining the relationship between HIV and poverty in Canada, based on the resources available through Canadian AIDS Society

*Introspect Poverty Website*
intraspec.ca/povertyCanada_news-and-reports.php
This is a non-profit website that presents statistics, news, and research on issues of poverty, child poverty, and social policy in Canada. It provides information on national and provincial projects, research and policy organizations, gives a list of food banks by province, and other additional resources.

*Luxembourg Income Study*
www.lisproject.org
The Luxembourg Income Study (LIS) is a cross-national Data Archive and a Research Institute located in Luxembourg. It provides information on public policy, income issues, and its indicators, both in Canada and other countries.

*National Council of Welfare*
www.ncwcnbes.net
The National Council of Welfare (NCW) was established in 1969 as a citizen's advisory body. It advises the Minister of Human Resources Development on matters of concern to low-income Canadians. The council consists of representatives from across Canada and appointed by the Governor-in-Council. Reports by the NCW deal with a range of issues on poverty and social policy in Canada, including income security programs, welfare reform, medicare, and taxation. These reports are free of charge to individuals who are on the mailing list. The address is: National Council of Welfare, 9th floor, 112 Kent Street, Place de Ville, Tower B, Ottawa, ON K1A OJ9.

*Ontario Coalition Against Poverty*
www.oacp.ca
OACP is a direct-action anti-poverty organization based in Toronto. OACP mounts campaigns against regressive government policies as they affect poor and working people. They also provide direct-action advocacy for individuals against eviction, termination of welfare benefits, and deportation.

*Organisation for Economic Co-operation and Development*
www.oecd.org.home
OECD's website provides information on sources of comparable statistics, economic and social data. Most of the information collected by OECD, its reports, and its publications are available electronically.

*PovNet*
www.povnet.org
PovNet is an Internet site for advocates, people on welfare, and community groups and individuals involved in antipoverty work. Up-to-date information on welfare and related matters in British Columbia is provided, but there are links to current antipoverty issues elsewhere.

*Townsend Centre for International Poverty Research*
www.bris.ac.uk/poverty
This International Centre for Poverty Research was established at the University of Bristol in 1999 and has a goal to eradicate poverty in the world. The University supports this goal by providing high quality interdisciplinary research to anti-poverty policies in both the industrial and developing countries.

# Government Research Sites

*Canadian Social Research Links*
www.canadiansocialresearch.net
This website is a social-research clearinghouse with links to national and international research focused on employment and evaluation.

*Government of Canada Main Site*
www.gc.ca/main_e.html
This site provides access to all federal departments and agencies and official information about Canada. Links to provincial governments are also provided.

*Public Health Agency of Canada*
www.phac-aspc.gc.ca
This site contains information as well as links to organizations, including Aboriginal health, minority groups, HIV/AIDS in Canada, environmental health, gender and health, people with disabilities, and violence prevention.

*Statistics Canada*
www.statcan.gc.ca
This is a general website with links to databases collected by Statistics Canada.

# Child Welfare and Family Support Sites

*Centre of Excellence for Child Welfare*
www.cecw-cepb.ca
This website provides information on research and activities undertaken by the Centre of Excellence for Child Welfare with links to the First Nations Research site at www.fncfcs.ca

*The Canadian Association of Family Resource Programs*
www.frp.ca
Family Resource Programs Canada is a national, not-for-profit organization representing more than 20,000 family resource programs, centres, and related services across Canada. Its mission is to promote the well-being of families by providing national leadership, consultation, and resources to those who care for children and support families.

*The Canadian Child Care Federation*
www.cccf-fcsge.ca
The mission of the Canadian Child Care Federation is to improve the quality of child care services for Canadian families. Research results and advocacy positions are provided.

*The Child Welfare League of Canada*
www.cwlc.ca
The Child Welfare League (CWL) is a national, voluntary organization dedicated to promoting the well-being of 'at risk' children, youth, and their families. It is governed by a board of directors from child welfare and family-serving agencies across the country.

*The Vanier Institute of the Family*
www.vifamily.ca
Established in 1965, the Vanier Institute of the Family provides important information on Canada's 8.4 million families. The Institute is an advocate for policies that can support the well-being of families.

# Useful Tools for Community-Based Practice

*Canadian Centre for Community Enterprise*
www.cedworks.com
This website includes a resource booklet for Community Economic Development

(CED) called *The Community Resilience Manual*. A separate publication called *Tools and Techniques for Community Recovery and Renewal* is also available at this site to provide further assistance to citizens wanting to strengthen or revitalize their local economies. The site lists important CED links and publications.

*Community Tool Box*
ctb.ku.edu
This site provides resources for all types of community work including how-to sections on many topics such as community assessment, advocacy, planning, grant applications, and much more.

*Human Resources and Skills Development Canada*
www.hrsdc.gc.ca
This website contains some useful tools including the *Community Development Handbook* and *The Partnership Handbook*.

# Selected Journals

*Canada's Children*
*Canada's Children* is published by the Child Welfare League of Canada three times a year. Articles are focused on policy and practices in child welfare and family services. Copies are provided to members and individual copies may be purchased by contacting info@cwlc.ca.

*Canadian Journal of Community Mental Health*
www.socialsciences.uottawa.ca/crecs/cjcmh
This interdisciplinary journal is published twice a year. Areas of priority interest include program evaluation in the human services, community needs assessment, and community development with a broad focus on community mental health. The subscription in 2009 was $25 for individuals.  The journal is only available electronically.

*Canadian Public Policy*
www.economics.ca
The aim of this interdisciplinary journal is to stimulate research and discussion of public policy problems in Canada. The journal publishes four issues each year. Articles are available electronically with a one-year delay.

*Canadian Review of Social Policy*
www.crsp.info
The *Canadian Review of Social Policy* is published twice yearly under the direction of an editorial working group. The articles cover a wide range of social policy issues. The annual cost in 2009 was $45 for individuals and $30 for students. Subscription inquires can be sent to crsp@yorku.ca.

*Canadian Social Work*
www.casw-acts.ca
*Canadian Social Work* is the journal of the Canadian Association of Social Workers (CASW). It is an annual publication available to members. The CASW Bulletin is published twice a year. The journal is available online.

*Canadian Social Work Review*
www.wlu.ca/press/Journals/cswr/index.shtml
The *Canadian Social Work Review* is published twice yearly by the Canadian Association of Schools of Social Work. The subscription rate for individuals was $35, and the student rate was $22 in 2009. Subscriptions are available online. The journal is also available electronically.

# References

Aboriginal Corrections Policy Unit. (1997). *The Four Circles of Hollow Water*. Ottawa: Supply and Services Canada.

Abelson, D.E. (2002). *Do Think Tanks Matter? Assessing the Impact of Public Policy Institutes*. Kingston, ON: McGill Queen's University Press.

Alexander, E.R. (1985). 'From Idea to Action: Notes for a Contingency Theory of the Policy Implementation Process', *Administration and Society* 16 (4): 403–26.

———. (2002). E-mail to L. Peirson, forwarded to B. Wharf.

'An Attack on Academic Freedom: Apotex vs. Oliveri'. (2009). *CAUT Bulletin 56* (1), January: A1.

Anderson, C. (2004). 'BC Promises Answers on Impact of Welfare Rule', *The Province*, 4 January: A9.

Arnstein, S.R. (1969). 'A Ladder of Citizen Participation', *Journal of the American Institute of Planners* 4: 216–24.

Asselin, R.B. (2001). 'The Canadian Social Union: Questions about the Division of Powers and Fiscal Federation', available at http://dsp-psd.tpsgc.gc.ca/Collection-R/LoPBdP/BP/prb0031-e.htm.

Assembly of First Nations. (2000). *First Nations and Inuit Regional Health Survey*. Ottawa: Author.

Assembly of First Nations website. (2008). 'Make Poverty History: The First Nations Plan for Creating Opportunity', 1 October, available at http://www.afn.ca/article.asp?id=2903.

Auditor General of Canada. (1988). 'Attributes of Well-Performing Organizations', in *Annual Report*. Ottawa: Author.

———. (2008). 'First Nations Child and Family Services Program—Indian and Northern Affairs Canada', in *Report of the Auditor General of Canada to the House of Commons*, available at http://www.oag-bvg.gc.ca.

Baines, D. (2007). 'Anti-Oppressive Social Work Practice: Fighting for Space, Fighting for Change', in D. Baines, ed., *Doing Anti-Oppressive Practice: Building Transformative Politicized Social Work*, pp.1–30. Halifax: Fernwood Publishing.

Bardach, E. (1977). *The Implementation Game*. Cambridge, MA: MIT Press.

Bashevkin, S. (2002). *Welfare Hot Buttons: Women, Work and Social Policy Reform*. Toronto: University of Toronto Press.

BC Ministry of Human Resources (2002). 'Service Plan Summary 2002/03–2004/05'. Victoria, BC: Government of British Columbia.

———. (2004a). 'Fact Sheet: $80 Million Budget Lift'. Victoria, BC: Government of British Columbia, 17 February.

———. (2004b), 'News Release: Time Limit Policy to Protect People in Need'. Victoria, BC: Government of British Columbia, 6 February.

———. (2004c), 'Factsheet: Time Limits Update'. Victoria, BC: Government of British Columbia, 6 February.

BC Ministry of Women's Equality. (1997). *Gender Lens: A Guide to Gender-Inclusive Policy and Program Development*. Victoria, BC: Government of British Columbia.

BC New Democratic Party (NDP). (2003). 'BC NDP Newswire: Homeless Explosion Coming with Welfare Changes', 8 October.

BC Public Interest Advocacy Centre (BCPIAC). (2003). 'News Release: Community Groups Prepare for Constitutional Challenge to Welfare Cut-Off', 20 October. Vancouver: Author.

Bear, S., with the Topique Women's Group (1991). 'You Can't Change the Indian Act', in J.D. Wine and J. L. Ristock, eds, *Women and Social Change: Feminist Activism in Canada*, pp. 185–209. Toronto: James Lorimer and Company.

Berman, P. (1980). 'Thinking about Programmed and Adaptive Implementation', in H. Ingram and D. Mann, eds, *Why Policies Succeed or Fail*, pp. 205–27. Beverly Hills, CA: Sage.

Blackstock, C., T. Prakash, J. Loxley, and F. Wien. (2005). 'Summary of Findings', in First Nations Child and Family Caring Society of Canada, ed., *Wen:De (We are Coming to the Light of Day)*, pp. 7–59. Ottawa: First Nations Child and Family Caring Society of Canada.

Bok, S. (1984). *Secrets*. New York: Vintage Books.

Boulding, K. (1964). 'Book Review, *A Strategy of Decision* by D. Braybrooke and C. Lindblom', *American Sociological Review* 25 (5): 29.

Bregha, F. (n.d.). *Public Participation in Planning, Policy and Program*. Toronto: Ministry of Community and Social Services.

Briskin, L., and M. Eliasson, eds. (1999). *Women's Organizing and Public Policy in Canada and Sweden*. Kingston, ON: McGill-Queen's University Press.

British Columbia Ministry of Community, Aboriginal and Women's Services. (2003). *Guide to Best Practices in Gender Analysis*, available at http://www.mcaws.gov.bc.ca/womens_services.

British Columbia Ministry of Women's Equality. (1994). *Gender Lens: A Guide to*

*Gender-Inclusive Policy and Program Development*. Victoria, BC: Author.

Brodie, J. (1995). *Politics on the Margins*. Halifax: Fernwood Publishing.

Brodtrick, D. (1991). 'A Second Look at the Well-Performing Organization', in J. McDavid and B. Marson, eds, *The Well-Performing Organization*, pp. 16–22. Toronto: Institute of Public Administration of Canada.

Brooks, S. (1998). *Public Policy in Canada: An Introduction*, 3rd edn. Don Mills, ON: Oxford University Press.

Brown, L., L. Haddock, and M. Kovach. (2002). 'Watching over Our Families: Lalum'utul'Smun'een Child and Family Services', in B. Wharf, ed., *Community Work Approaches to Child Welfare*, pp. 131–51. Peterborough, ON: Broadview Press.

Brownlee, J. (2005). *Ruling Canada: Corporate Cohesion and Democracy*. Halifax, NS: Fernwood.

Buchanan, J., and G. Tullock. (1965). *The Calculus of Consent*. Ann Arbor, MI: University of Michigan Press.

Callahan, M., and K. Callahan. (1997). 'Victims and Villains: Scandals, the Press and Policy-Making in Child Welfare', in J. Pulkingham and G. Ternowetsky, eds, *Child and Family Policies: Struggles, Strategies and Options*, pp. 40–58, Halifax: Fernwood Press.

———, L. Hooper, and B. Wharf. (1998). *Protecting Children by Empowering Women*. Victoria, BC: School of Social Work, University of Victoria.

———, and C. Lumb. (1995). 'My Cheque or My Children', *Child Welfare* 74 (3): 795–819.

———, D. Rutman, S. Strega, and L. Dominelli. (2005). 'Looking Promising: Contradictions and Challenges for Young Mothers in Care', in M. Gustafson, ed., *Unbecoming Mothers: The Social Production of Maternal Absence*, pp. 185–209. New York: The Haworth Clinical Practice Press.

Cameron, D., and E. Finn (1996). *10 Deficit Myths: The Truth about Government Debts and Why They Don't Justify Cutbacks*. Ottawa: Canadian Centre for Policy Alternatives.

Cameron, G., J. Karabanow, M-C Laurendeau, and C. Chamberlain. (2001). 'Program Implementation and Diffusion', in G. Prilleltensky, G. Nelson, and L. Peirson, eds, *Promoting Family Wellness and Preventing Child Maltreatment*, pp. 318–48. Toronto: University of Toronto Press.

Campaign 2000. (2008a). '2007 Report Card on Child and Family Poverty in Canada', 29 September, available at http://www.campaign2000.ca.

———. (2008b). 'Family Security in Insecure Times: The Case for a Poverty Reduction Strategy for Canada', 10 December, available at http://www.campaign2000.ca.

Campaign 2000 website. (2009). 'Introduction to Campaign 2000', 7 March, available at http://www.campaign2000.ca.

Campbell, M. (1999). 'Harris Slams Child Poverty Report Card', *Globe and Mail*, 25 November: A3.

'Can the Gun Registry Be Saved?'. (2003). *The Globe and Mail*, 4 January: A14.

Canadian Association of Social Workers website. (2009). 'Canadian Association of Social Workers (CASW) Social Policy Principles', 7 March, available at http://www.casw-acts.ca.

Canadian Centre for Policy Alternatives. (2000). 'Income Disparities', *The CCPA Monitor* 7 (6): 3.

————. (2004). 'Government Backs Down on Welfare Time Limits, but Cutoff Rule should be Scrapped Altogether' (News Release). Vancouver: Canadian Centre for Policy Alternatives—BC Office.

Canadian Centre for Policy alternatives website (2009). 7 March, available at http://www.policyalternatives.ca.

Canadian Council of Chief Executives website. (2009). 'About CCCE', 4 March, available at http://www.ceocouncil.ca/en/about/about.php.

Canadian Council on Social Development. (2008). 'Economic Security Fact Sheet #2: Poverty', 13 November, available at http://www.ccsd.ca/factsheets/economic_security/poverty/index.htm.

Canadian Feminist Alliance for International Action (FAFIA). (2009). 'About FIFIA', 4 January, available at http://www.fafia-afai.org/en/about.

Canadian Labour Congress. (2007). 'Towards a Better Employment Insurance (EI) System for Workers in Today's Job Market', available at http://www.canadianlabour.ca.

————. (2008). 'The Growing Gap: Inequality and the Fight for Women's Economic Equality (Document No. 8)'. Paper presented to 25th CLC Constitutional Convention, 26–30 May.

Carley, M. (1980). *Rational Techniques in Policy Analysis*. London: Heinemann.

Carmichael, K. (2008). 'U.S. Politicians Begin the Big Cleanup', *The Globe and Mail*, 20 September: A19–21.

Carroll, B., and D. Siegel (1999). *Service in the Field*. Kingston, ON: McGill-Queen's University Press.

Cassidy, F. (1991). 'Organizing for Community Control', *The Northern Review* 11: 17–34.

CBC Vancouver. (2003). 'Welfare Reforms Triggered Internal Warnings', 7 July, available at http://www.vancouver.cbc.ca.

Chambers, D.E., and K.R. Wedel. (2005). *Social Policy and Social Programs: A Method for the Practical Public Policy Analyst*, 4th edn. Boston: Pearson Education.

Clague, M., R. Dill, R. Seebaran, and B. Wharf. (1984). *Reforming Human Services: The Experience of Community Resource Boards in B.C.* Vancouver: University of British Columbia Press.

Clark, C. (2002). 'Martin's Plan Gives Back-Benchers More Clout', *The Globe and Mail*, 22 October: 1.

Clemens, J., N. Veldhuis, and S. LeRoy. (2004). 'Propping Up the Most Vulnerable: BC's U-Turn on Welfare Reform Spells Disaster', *Vancouver Sun*, 16 February, available at http://www.fraseramerica.org/commerce.web/article_details.aspx?pubID=3445.

Clement, W. (1975). *The Canadian Corporate Elite: An Analysis of Economic Power*. Toronto: McClelland and Stewart.

Clement, W. (1983). *Class, Power and Property*. Toronto: Methuen.

Coell, M. (2003). 'Opinion Editorial: Income Assistance Changes Support People in Need', Government of British Columbia, Victoria, BC, 5 March, available at http://www.2news.gov.bc.ca/nrm_news_releases/2003MHR0003-000229.htm.

Cohen, M., J. March, and J. Olsen. (1972). 'A Garbage Can Model of Institutional Choice', *Administrative Science Quarterly* 17 (1): 1–25.

Cohen Griffen, M., and J. Pulkingham, eds. (2009a). *Public Policy for Women: The State, Income Security and Labour Market Issues*. Toronto: University of Toronto Press.

————, and J. Pulkingham. (2009b). 'Introduction: Going Too Far? Feminist Public Policy in Canada', in M. Cohen and J. Pulkingham, eds, *Public Policy for Women: The State, Income Security and Labour Market Issues*. Toronto: University of Toronto Press.

Coleman, W.D., and G. Skogstad (1990). *Policy Communities and Public Policy in Canada: A Structural Approach*. Toronto: Copp Clark Pitman.

'College Vindicates Oliveri, Rejects HSC's Allegations'. (2002). *CAUT Bulletin 49* (1) January: 1.

Connors, E., and F. Maidman (2001). 'A Circle of Healing: Family Wellness in Aboriginal Communities', in I. Prilleltensky, G. Nelson, and L. Pierson, eds, *Promoting Family Wellness and Preventing Child Maltreatment*, pp. 349–416. Toronto: University of Toronto Press.

Coutts, M. (2009). 'B.C. Teachers Mutiny over Provincial Exam: Union, School Board tell Parents to Dodge Mandatory Test', *National Post*, 17 January, available at http://www.nationalpost.com/related/links/story.html?id=1187139.

Cruise, D., and A. Griffiths (1997). *On South Mountain: The Dark Secrets of the Goler Clan*. Toronto: Penguin.

Dahl, R. (1970). *After the Revolution*. New Haven: Yale University Press.

Davies, C. (2003). 'Policy Development: Making Research Count', in K. Kufeldt and B. McKenzie, eds, *Child Welfare: Connecting Research, Policy and Practice*, pp. 377–86. Waterloo, ON: Wilfrid Laurier University Press.

Day, S. (2004), 'Time Limits for Welfare Disregard the Humanity of Poor People', *Vancouver Sun*, 16 February: A9.

Dobbin, M. (2007). 'Elite's Deep Integration Plot Coming Out of the Shadows', *The CCPA Monitor 14* (3): 1, 6.

Doblestein, A.W. (1990). *Social Welfare: Policy and Analysis*. Chicago: Nelson Hall.

Dobson, W. (2002). *Shaping the Future of the North American Economic Space: A Framework for Action*. Toronto: C.D. Howe Institute.

Durie, H., and A. Armitage. (1996). *Planning for Implementation of B.C.'s Child, Family and Community Services Act*. Victoria, BC: School of Social Work, University of Victoria.

Dyck, R. (2004). *Canadian Politics: Critical Approaches*, 4th edn. Scarborough, ON: Nelson.

Ellsberg, D. (2002). *Secrets: A Memoir of Vietnam and the Pentagon Papers*. New York: Viking.

Elmore, R. (1982). 'Backward Mapping: Implementation Research and Policy Decisions', in W. Williams, ed., *Studying Implementation: Methodological and Administrative Issues*, pp. 18–35. Chatham, NJ: Chatham House.

Etzioni, A. (1967). 'Mixed Scanning: A 'Third' Approach to Decision-Making', *Public Administration Review* 27: 385–92.

———. (1976). *Social Problems*. Englewood Cliffs, NJ: Prentice Hall.

Fagan, T., and P. Lee. (1997). 'New Social Movements and Social Policy: A Case Study of the Disability Movement', in M. Lavalette and A. Pitt, eds, *Social Policy: A Conceptual and Theoretical Introduction*, pp. 140–62. London, UK: Sage.

Farris-Manning, C., and M. Zandstra (2007). 'Children in Care in Canada: A Summary of Current Issues and Trends with Recommendations for Future Research', in *Child Welfare League of Canada, The Welfare of Canadian Children: It's Our Business* pp. 54–72. Ottawa: Child Welfare League of Canada.

Fayant, J., and D. Kerr. (2007). *Living Without Food*. Edmonton: Bissell Centre.

Fetterman, D., and A. Wandersman. (2007). 'Empowerment Evaluation: Yesterday, Today, and Tomorrow', *American Journal of Evaluation* 28: 179–98.

Finkel, A. (2006). *Social Policy and Practice in Canada: A History*. Waterloo, ON: Wilfrid Laurier University Press.

Finn, E. (2008). 'Ending Child Poverty Has Economic as Well as Moral Benefits', *The CCPA Monitor* 14 (2): 4.

First Nations Centre (2007). *OCAP: Ownership, Control, Access and Possession.* Sanctioned by the First Nations Information Governance Committee, Assembly of First Nations. Ottawa: National Aboriginal Health Organization.

First Nations Child and Family Caring Society of Canada (FNCFCS). (2005). *Wen De (We Are Coming to the Light of Day)*. Ottawa: Author.

Flynn, J.P. (1992). *Social Agency Policy*, 2nd edn. Chicago: Nelson Hall.

Forsey, E.A. (2005). *How Canadians Govern Themselves*, 6th edn. Ottawa: Her Majesty the Queen in Right of Canada.

Fournier, S., and E. Crey. (1997). *Stolen From Our Embrace: The Abduction of First Nations Children and the Restoration of Aboriginal Communities*. Vancouver: Douglas and McIntyre.

Francis, R. (2003), 'Bonus Points for Welfare Cuts', *The Province*, 24 February: A16.

Fraser Institute. (2002). 'BC Welfare Reform Receives a "B"', (News Release), 21 October. Vancouver: Author.

Frideres, J. (1998). *Aboriginal Peoples in Canada: Contemporary Conflicts*, 5th edn. Scarborough, ON: Prentice Hall.

Friere, P. (1970). *The Pedogogy of the Oppressed*. Harmondsworth: Penguin.

Gabel, T., J. Clemens, S. LeRoy, and N. Veldhuis. (2003). 'Staying the Course on Welfare Time Limits', *Fraser Forum* (December), pp. 22–4. Vancouver: Fraser Institute.

Gallagher, J., and R. Haskins. (1984). *Policy Analysis*. New York: Ablex.

Gil, D. (1990). *Unraveling Social Policy*, 4th edn. Rochester, VT: Schenkman.

Government of British Columbia. (n.d.). 'Information for Persons with Disabilities'. Victoria, BC: Ministry of Employment and Income Assistance.

Graham, J., B. Amos, and T. Plumptre. (2003). *Principles for Good Governance in the 21st Century*, Policy Brief No. 15. Ottawa: Institute on Governance, available at http://www.iog.ca/publications/policy_briefs.

Graham, J., K. Swift, and R. Delaney. (2003). *Social Policy: An Introduction*, 2nd edn. Scarborough, ON: Prentice Hall.

Graveline, F. J. (1998). *Circle Works: Transforming Eurocentric Consciousness*. Halifax, NS: Fernwood.

Greider, W. (1992). *Who Will Tell the People? The Betrayal of American Democracy*. New York: Simon and Schuster.

Haddow, R. (1990). 'The Poverty Policy Community in Canada's Liberal Welfare State', in W. Coleman and G. Skogstad, eds, *Policy Communities and Public Policy in Canada: A Structural Approach*, pp. 213–27. Toronto: Copp Clark Pitman.

Hamilton, A.C., and C.M. Sinclair. (1991). *Report of the Aboriginal Justice Inquiry of Manitoba, Vol. 1: The Justice System and Aboriginal People*. Winnipeg: Queen's Printer.

Hart, M.A. (2002). *Seeking Meno-Pimatisiwin: An Aboriginal Approach to Helping*. Halifax: Fernwood Publishing.

Hart, R. (2001). 'The National Report', *Perspectives* 23 (1): 17.

Hausmann, R., L. Tyson, and S. Zahidid. (2007). *The Global Gender Gap Report*. Geneva: World Economic Forum, available at http://www.weforum.org/pdg/gendergap/report2007.pdf.

Hawken, P. (2007). 'Social Justice, Environmental Groups May Number a Million', *The CCPA Monitor* 14 (3): 48–9.

Health Canada. (2009). 'Health Canada's Gender-based Analysis Policy', 11 March, available at http://www.hc-sc.gc.ca/hl-vs/women-femmes/gender-sexe/policy-politique-eng.php#2.

Herman, J., L. Morris, and C. Fitz-Gibbon. (1987). *Evaluator's Handbook*. Newbury Park, CA: Sage.

Hick, S., and R. Pozzuto. (2005). 'Towards "Becoming" a Critical Social Worker', in S. Hick, J. Fook, and R. Pozzuto, eds, *Social Work: A Critical Turn*, pp. ix–xviii. Toronto: Thompson Educational Publishing.

Hirshfeld-Davis, J. (2008). 'Millions for Lehman Chiefs', *Winnipeg Free Press*, 7 October: B5.

Holzer, H. (2007). 'It Would Be Less Costly to Eliminate than to Tolerate Poverty', *The CCPA Monitor* 14 (2): 5.

Howlett, M., and M. Ramesh. (2003). *Studying Public Policy: Policy Cycles and Policy Subsystems*. Don Mills, ON: Oxford University Press.

Hume, S. (2003). 'What Happens When More Poor Hit the Streets?', *Vancouver Sun*, 22 November: C7.

Institute on Governance. (2007). *Citizen Deliberative Decision-Making: Evaluation of the Ontario Citizen's Assembly on Electoral Reform*. Ottawa: Author.

Johnston, P. (1983). *Native Children and the Child Welfare System*. Toronto: James Lorimer.

Joint Management Committee. (2001). *Aboriginal Justice Inquiry Child Welfare Initiative: Promise of Hope, Commitment to Change*. Winnipeg: Author.

Kernaghan, K., and D. Siegel. (1995). *Public Administration in Canada: A Text*, 3rd edn. Scarborough, ON: Nelson Canada.

Kerstetter, S. (2002). *Rags and Riches: Wealth Inequality in Canada*. Ottawa: Canadian Centre for Policy Alternatives.

Kettner, P.M., R.M. Moroney, and L.L. Martin. (2008). *Designing and Managing Programs: An Effectiveness-Based Approach*, 3rd edn. Thousand Oaks, CA: Sage.

Kines, L. (2004). 'Province Backs Off Plan for Dramatic Cuts to Welfare', *Vancouver Sun*, 7 February: A1.

Kingdon, J.K. (1995). *Agendas, Alternatives, and Public Policies*, 2nd edn. New York: Harper Collins.

Klein, N. (2001). *No Logo*. London: HarperCollins.

––––––––. (2007). *The Shock Doctrine: The Rise of Disaster Capitalism*. Toronto: Random House.

Klein, S. (2003). 'Editorial: The Ticking Time Bomb of BC's Welfare Time Limits'. Vancouver: Canadian Centre for Policy Alternatives, available at http://www.policyalternatives.ca/index.cfm?act=news&call=619&do=articles&pA=BB736455.

––––––––, and A. Long (2003). *A Bad Time to be Poor: An Analysis of British Columbia's New Welfare Policies*. Vancouver: Canadian Centre for Policy Alternatives and Social Planning and Research Council of BC, available at http://www.policyalternatives.ca/documents/BC_Office_Pubs/welfare.pdf.

Kouzes, J.M., and P.R. Mico (1979). 'Domain Theory: An Introduction to Organizational Behaviour in Human Service Organizations', *The Journal of Applied Behavioural Sciences* 15 (4): 449–69.

Lancaster House. (2002). 'Government Muzzled of Social Worker's Criticism Unjustified, Appeal Court Finds', 24 September, available at http://www.lancasterhouse.com/about/headlines_1,asp.

Lauzière, M. (2008). 'Quebec's Law Against Poverty and Social Exclusion', *Perception* 29 (3 & 4): 16–17, 22.

Lavoie, J. (2001). 'Welfare Time Limits Expected in Spring', *Victoria Times-Colonist*, 10 October: A1.

––––––––. (2003). '28,000 Could Be Caught in Two-Year Welfare Squeeze', *Victoria Times-Colonist*, 21 October: A1.

Lemann, N. (2002). 'Paper Tiger: Daniel Ellsberg's War', *The New Yorker*, 4 November: 96–9.

Lett, D. (2008). 'Taking Back the Territory', *Winnipeg Free Press*, 4 May: B1–2.

Lightman, E. (2003). *Social Policy in Canada*. Don Mills, ON: Oxford University Press.

Lindblom, C.E. (1959). 'The Science of Muddling Through', *Public Administration Review* 19: 79–88.

––––––––. (1968). *The Policy-Making Process*. Englewood Cliffs, NJ: Prentice Hall.

––––––––. (1979). 'Still Muddling, Not Yet Through', *Public Administration Review* 39 (6): 517–26.

––––––––. (1982). 'The Market as Prison', *The Journal of Politics* 44 (2): 324–36.

Lipsky, M. (1980). *Street-Level Bureaucracy*. New York: Russell Sage.

Love, A. (1992). 'The Evaluation of Implementation: Case Studies', in J. Hudson, J. Mayne, and R. Thomlison, eds, *Action-Oriented Evaluation in Organizations*, pp. 135–59. Toronto: Wall & Emerson.

Lowi, T. (1979). *The End of Liberalism*. New York: W.W. Norton.

Loxley, J., and L. Deriviere. (2005). 'Promoting Community and Family Wellness: Least Disruptive Measures and Prevention', in First Nations Child and Family Caring Society of Canada, *Wen:De (We Are Coming to the Light of Day)*, pp. 113–45. Ottawa: First Nations Child and Family Caring Society of Canada.

Lysack, C., and J. Kaufert. (1994). 'Comparing the Origins and Ideologies of the Independent Living Movement and Community Based Rehabilitation'. Presentation to Progress through Partnerships, National Independent Living Conference, Winnipeg, Manitoba, 24 August.

MacBeath, A. (1957). 'Can Social Policies be Rationally Tested?' (The L.T. Hobhouse Memorial Lecture). London, UK: Oxford University Press.

McDonald, R.J., P. Ladd, et al. (2000). *First Nations Child and Family Services Joint National Policy Review* (Final Report). Ottawa: Assembly of First Nations and Department of Indian Affairs and Northern Development.

McGrath, S. (1997). 'Child Poverty Advocacy and the Politics of Influence', in J. Pulkingham and G. Ternowetsky, eds, *Child and Family Policies: Struggles, Strategies and Options*, pp. 248–72, Halifax: Fernwood Publishing.

McKenna, B. (2008). 'A Desperate Disease, A Desperate Remedy', *The Globe and Mail*, 20 September: B5.

McKenzie, B. (1989). *Decentralizing Child Welfare Services: Effects on Service Demand and the Job Morale of Street-Level Bureaucrats*. PhD diss., Arizona State University, Tempe, AZ.

———. (1991). 'Decentralization in Winnipeg: Assessing the Effects of Community-Based Child Welfare Services', *Canadian Review of Social Policy*, 27: 57–66.

———. (1994). *Evaluation of the Pilot Project in Block Funding for Child Maintenance* (Final Report). Winnipeg: West Region Child and Family Services.

———. (1997). 'Developing First Nations Child Welfare Standards: Using Evaluation Research Within a Participatory Framework', *The Canadian Journal of Program Evaluation 12* (1): 133–48.

———. (1999). *Evaluation of the Pilot Project on Block Funding in West Region Child and Family Services: A Second Look* (Final Report). Winnipeg: Faculty of Social Work, University of Manitoba.

———. (2002a). *Block Funding Child Maintenance in First Nations Child and Family Services: A Policy Review* (Final Report). Winnipeg: Faculty of Social Work, University of Manitoba.

———. (2002b). 'Building Community in West Region Child and Family Services', in B. Wharf, ed., *Community Work Approaches to Child Welfare*, pp. 152–62: Peterborough, ON: Broadview Press.

———, and P. Hudson. (1985). 'Native Children, Child Welfare, and the Colonization of Native People', in K. Levitt and B. Wharf, eds, *The Challenge of*

*Child Welfare*, pp. 125–41. Vancouver: University of British Columbia Press.

———, and V. Morrissette. (2003). 'Social Work Practice with Canadians of Aboriginal Background: Guidelines for Respectful Social Work', in A. Al-Krenawi and J.R. Graham, *Multicultural Social Work in Canada*, pp. 251–82. Don Mills, ON: Oxford University Press.

———, and C. Shangreaux. (2006). 'From Child Protection to Community Caring in First Nations Child and Family Services'. Presentation at World Forum on Child Welfare, Vancouver, BC, 22 November.

McKnight, J., and J. Kretzmann. (1992). 'Capacity Mapping', *New Design* (Winter): 9–15.

McQuaig, L. (1987). *Behind Closed Doors*. Toronto: Viking.

McQuaig, L. (1991). *The Quick and the Dead*. Toronto: Viking.

McQuaig, L. (1993). *The Wealthy Banker's Wife*. Toronto: Viking.

McQuaig, L. (1995). *Shooting the Hippo*. Toronto: Viking.

Majchrzak, A. (1984). *Methods for Policy Research*. Newbury Park, CA: Sage.

Manitoba Joint Committee on Residential Schools. (1994). *Proposal for a Manitoba Healing and Resource Centre for First Nations Affected by Residential Schools*. Winnipeg: Assembly of Manitoba Chiefs.

Marchak, M.P. (1991). *The Integrated Circus: The New Right and the Restructuring of the Global Economy*. Kingston, ON: McGill-Queen's University Press.

Marris, P. (1986). *Loss and Change*, rev. edn. London: Routledge and Kegan Paul.

———, and M. Rein. (1967). *The Dilemmas of Social Reform*. New York: Russell Sage.

Maslow, A. (1954). *Motivation and Personality*. New York: Harper & Row.

May, K. (2002). 'Recipe for Disaster', *Times Colonist*, 25 August: 1–2.

Meissner, D. (2004). 'Preachers Will Sleep in Streets to Protest BC Government's Welfare Cuts', 28 January, distributed by *Canadian Press* at www.canada.com.

Memmi, A. (1967). *The Colonizer and the Colonized*. Boston: Beacon Press.

Miljan, L. (2008). *Public Policy in Canada: An Introduction*, 5th edn. Don Mills, ON: Oxford University Press.

Miller, J.R. (1996). *Shingwauks' Vision: A History of Native Residential Schools*. Toronto: University of Toronto Press.

Ministry of Children and Family Development (MCFD). (2008). *Kinship Care Review*. Victoria, BC: Government of British Columbia.

Montgomery, J. (1979). 'The Populist Front in Rural Development. Or Shall We Eliminate Bureaucracies and Get On With the Job', *Public Administration Review* (January/February): 58–65.

Moran, B. (2001). *A Little Rebellion*. Vancouver: Arsenal Pulp Press.

Moroney, R.M. (1991). Social Policy and Social Work. New York: Aldine de Gruyter.

Morse, J., and A. Bower. (2002). 'The Party Crasher', *Time*, 30 December/6 January 2003: 43–6.

Mullaly, B. (2007). *The New Structural Social Work*, 3rd edn. Don Mills, ON: Oxford University Press.

Munro, E., and J. Rumgay. (2000). 'Role of Risk Assessment in Reducing Homicides by People with Mental Illness', *British Journal of Psychiatry 176*: 116–20.

Murray, R. (1993). 'Transforming the "Fordist" State', in G. Albo, D. Langille, and L. Panitch, eds, *A Different Kind of State? Popular Power and Democratic Administration*, pp. 51–65. Don Mills, ON: Oxford University Press.

National Council of Welfare. (2008). *Welfare Incomes 2006 and 2007*. Ottawa: Author.

Newman, P. (1975). *The Canadian Establishment*. Toronto: McClelland and Stewart.

———. (1981). *The Canadian Establishment. Vol. 2: The Acquisitors*. Toronto: McClelland and Stewart.

———. (1998). *The Titans: How the New Canadian Establishment Seized Power*. Toronto: Penguin.

Nicolson, L. (1990). *Feminism/Postmodernism*. New York: Routledge.

Nutley, S.M., I. Walter, and H.T.O. Davies (2007). *Using Evidence: How Research Can Inform Public Services*. Bristol, UK: The Policy Press.

Nyp, G. (2002). *Reaching for More: The Evolution of the Independent Living Centre of Waterloo Region*. Waterloo, ON: Independent Living Centre of Waterloo Region.

Olsen, G. (2008). 'Lesson from Sweden', 29 September, available at http://www.policyalternatives.ca.

Olson, M. (1965). *The Logic of Collective Action: Public Goods and the Theory of Groups*. Cambridge, MA: Harvard University Press.

Organization for Economic Cooperation and Development (OECD). (2008). *Growing Unequal? Income Distribution and Poverty in OECD Countries*, 10 December, available at http://www.oecd.org/dataoecd/44/48/41525292.pdf.

Osberg, L. (2008). *A Quarter Century of Economic Inequality in Canada: 1981–2006*. Toronto: Canadian Centre for Policy Alternatives.

Owen, S. (1998). 'Shared Decision-Making: A Case Study', in B. Wharf and B. McKenzie, *Connecting Policy to Practice in the Human Services*, pp. 81–96. Don Mills, ON: Oxford University Press.

Pal, L.A. (1992). *Public Policy in Canada: An Introduction*. Toronto: McClelland and Stewart.

Palumbo, D.R. (1987). 'Introduction', *Policy Studies Review 7* (1): 97–101.

Panitch, L., ed. (1977). *The Canadian State*. Toronto: University of Toronto Press.

Pateman, C. (1970). *Participation and Democratic Theory*. Cambridge, UK: Cambridge University Press.

Peirson, L. (2002). E-mail to B. Wharf, 23 November.

Pence, E., and W. Shephard (1999). *Coordinating Community Response to Domestic Violence*. Newbury Park, CA: Sage.

Peters, T.J., and R.H. Waterman. (1982). *In Search of Excellence*. New York: Basic Books.

Phillips, S. D., and M. Orsini. (2002). *Mapping the Links: Citizen Involvement in Policy Processes*. Ottawa: Canadian Policy Research Networks.

Piven, F.F. (1993). 'Reforming the Welfare State: The American Experience', in G. Albo, D. Langille, and L. Panitch, eds, *A Different Kind of State? Popular Power and Democratic Administration*, pp. 66–74. Don Mills, ON: Oxford University Press.

———, and R.A. Cloward (1977). *Poor People's Movements: Why They Succeed, How They Fail*. New York: Pantheon.

Pizzey, E. (1977). *Scream Quietly or the Neighbors Will Hear*. Short Hills, CT: Ridley Enslow.

Popham, R., D. Hay, and C. Hughes. (1997). 'Campaign 2000 to End Child Poverty: Building and Sustaining a Movement', in B. Wharf and M. Clague, eds, *Community Organizing: Canadian Experiences*, pp. 248–72. Don Mills, ON: Oxford University Press.

Pressman, J., and A. Wildavsky (1973). *Implementation*. Berkeley, CA: University of California Press.

Prigoff, A. (2000). *Economics for Social Workers: Social Outcomes of Economic Globalization with Strategies for Community Action*. Belmont, CA: Wadsworth/ Thomson Learning.

Rabson, M. (2009a). 'Aboriginals Making Strides: Report', *Winnipeg Free Press*, 11 March: A7.

———. (2009b). 'Ottawa Blasted Over Child Welfare', *Winnipeg Free Press*, 25 March: A6.

Rainer, R. (2008). 'Towards a National Ideal: Canada without Poverty by 2020', *Perception 29* (3 & 4): 6–9.

Rankin, P., and J. Vickers, with the research assistance of A-M Field, (2001). *Women's Movements and State Feminism: Integrating Diversity into Public Policy*. Ottawa: Status of Women Canada.

Raphael, D. (2007). *Poverty and Policy in Canada: Implications for Health and Quality of Life*. Toronto: Canadian Scholars' Press.

Rawls, J. (1971). *A Theory of Justice*. Cambridge, MA: Harvard University Press.

Rebick, J. (2005). *Ten Thousand Roses: The Making of a Feminist Revolution*. Toronto: Penguin Canada.

Rein, M. (1970). *Social Policy: Issues of Choice and Change*. New York: Random House.

———. (1972). 'Decentralization and Citizen Participation in the Social Services', *Public Administration Review 32*: 687–701.

———. (1983). *From Policy to Practice*. New York: M.E. Sharpe.

Regehr, S. (2008). 'Solving Poverty: Four Cornerstones of a Workable National Strategy for Canada', *Perception 29* (3 & 4): 10–1

Reitsma-Street, M. (2002), 'The New Era of Welfare', *Perspectives 7*: 5.

———, and B. Wallace. (2004). 'Resisting Two Year Limits on Welfare in British Columbia', *Canadian Review of Social Policy, 53*: 169–77.

Report of the Aboriginal Committee. (1992). *Liberating Our Children: Liberating Our Nation*. Victoria, BC: Ministry of Social Services.

Report of the Committee on Local Authority and Allied Social Services. (1968). London, UK: Her Majesty's Stationery Office.

Report of the Community Panel, Family and Children's Services Legislative Review. (1992). *Making Changes: A Place to Start*. Victoria, BC: Ministry of Social Services.

Report of the Gove Inquiry into Child Protection. (1995). *Matthew's Story*. Victoria, BC: Queen's Printer.

Rice, J., and M. Prince. (2000). *Changing Politics of Canadian Social Policy*. Toronto: University of Toronto Press.

Riches, G. (2002). 'Statement by Graham Riches, Director, University of British Columbia School of Social Work at BC Association of Social Workers Press Conference', 2 February, available at http://toby.library.ubc.ca/webpage/webpage.cfm?id=105.

Rittel, H.W., and M.W. Webber. (1973). 'Dilemmas in a General Theory of Planning', *Policy Sciences* 4: 155–68.

Roberts, S.J. (1983). 'Oppressed Group Behaviour: Implications for Nursing', *Advances in Nursing Science* July: 21–30.

Romanow, R. (2002). *Building on Values: The Future of Health Care in Canada* (Final Report). Ottawa: Commission on the Future of Health Care in Canada, available at http://www.healthcarecommission.ca.

Royal Commission on Aboriginal Peoples (RCAP). (1996). 'Report Summary', *Report of the Royal Commission on Aboriginal Peoples*, available at http://www.ainc-inac.gc.ca.

Rud, J. (2004), 'Numbers Remain Vague on April Welfare Cutoff', *Victoria Times-Colonist*, 31 January: A4.

Russell, F. (2008a). 'NAFTA Costs Jobs, Create Pollution', *Winnipeg Free Press*, 18 June: A11.

———. (2008b). 'Suit Seeks to Open Canadian Health Care to Privatizers', *Winnipeg Free Press*, 24 September: A13.

———. (2009). 'Canadian Police Want to Keep Gun Registry Going', *Winnipeg Free Press*, 1 April: A10.

Rutman, D. (1998). 'A Policy Community: Developing Guardianship Legislation', in B. Wharf and B. McKenzie, *Connecting Policy to Practice in the Human Services*, pp. 97–113. Don Mills, ON: Oxford University Press.

———, M. Callahan, A. Lundquist, S. Jackson, and B. Field. (1999). *Substance Use and Pregnancy: Conceiving Women in the Policy Process*. Ottawa: Status of Women Canada.

Sabatier, P.A. (1986). 'Top-down and Bottom-up Approaches to Implementation Research: A Critical Analysis and Suggested Synthesis', *Journal of Public Policy* 1 (1): 21–48.

Saleebey, D. (1990). 'Philosophical Disputes in Social Work: Social Justice Denied', *Journal of Sociology and Social Welfare* 17 (2): 29–40.

Sancton, A. (1997). 'Reducing Costs by Consolidating Municipalities: New Brunswick, Nova Scotia and Ontario', *Canadian Public Administration* 39 (3): 267–90.

Sarlo, C. (2008). 'What is Poverty? Providing Clarity for Canada', 10 December, available at http://www.fraserinstitute.org/researchandpublications/publications/5547.aspx.

Saulis, M. (2006). 'Program and Policy Development from a Holistic Aboriginal Perspective', in A. Westhues, ed., *Canadian Social Policy: Issues and Perspectives*, 4th edn, pp. 115–30. Waterloo, ON: Wilfrid Laurier University Press.

Saunders, D. (2008). 'Trickledown Meltdown', *The Globe and Mail*, 27 December: B4–5.

Schafer, C., and J. Clemens. (2002). 'Welfare Reform in British Columbia: A Report Card'. Vancouver: Fraser Institute, available at http://www.fraserinstitute.org/researchandpublications/2748.aspx.

Schram, B. (1997). *Creating Small Scale Social Programs*. Thousand Oaks, CA: Sage.

Schroedel, J., and P. Peretz. (1994). 'A Gender Analysis of Policy Formation: The Case of Fetal Abuse', *Journal of Health Politics, Policy and Law 19* (2): 335–60.

Schur, N. (1987). *A to Zed*. New York: Harper Perennial.

Shangreaux, C., and B. McKenzie. (2005). *Strengthening and Protecting the Future of Our Children: Evaluation of West Region Child and Family Services Alternative Services Continuum*. Winnipeg: West Region Child and Family Services.

Shragge, E. (1990). 'Community-Based Practice: Political Alternatives or New State Forms?' in L. Davies and E. Shragge, eds, *Bureaucracy and Community*, pp. 137–73. Montreal: Black Rose Books.

Silver, R. (2002). 'Drive to Globalization Creating a Crisis for Nation States', *The CCPA Monitor 9* (2): 30–2.

Smale, G. (1995). 'Integrating Community and Individual Practice: A New Paradigm for Practice', in P. Adams and K. Nelson, eds, *Reinventing Human Services*, pp. 59–86. Hawthorne, NY: Aldine de Gruyter.

Smith, C. (2002), 'Are Welfare Changes Illegal?' *Georgia Straight*, 14–21 February: 10.

Smith, D. (1987). *The Everyday World as Problematic*. Toronto: University of Toronto Press.

Smith, K. (2005). 'Book Review of *Connecting Policy to Practice in the Human Services* by B. Wharf and B. McKenzie, 2nd edn', *Canadian Review of Social Policy* 55: 136–40.

Social Planning Council of Metropolitan Toronto. (1976). *In Search of a Framework*. Toronto: Author.

Sower, C., J. Holland, K. Tiedke, and W. Freeman. (1957). *Community Involvement: The Webs of Formal and Informal Ties That Make for Action*. Glencoe, IL: Free Press.

Spakes, V. (1984). 'Family Impact Analysis as a Framework for Teaching Social Policy', *Journal of Education for Social Work 20* (1): 59–73.

Stanford, J. (2008). *Economics for Everyone: A Short Guide to the Economics of Capitalism*. Halifax, NS: Fernwood and Canadian Centre for Policy Alternatives.

Statistics Canada. (2008). *Aboriginal Peoples in Canada in 2006: Inuit, Métis and First*

*Nations, 2006 Census*, available at http://www12.statscan.ca/english/census06/aboriginal/pdf/997-558-XIE2006001.pdf.

Status of Women Canada (1996). *Gender-Based Analysis: A Guide for Policy-Making*. Ottawa: Author.

————. (1998). *Gender-based Analysis: A Guide for Policy Making*. Ottawa: Author.

Surowiecki, J. (2008). 'The Open Secret of Success', *The New Yorker*, 12 May: 48.

Swanson, J. (2006). 'Why Poverty is Worse than It Was 30 Years Ago', *Vancouver Sun*, 21 February: A11.

Swift, K., and M. Callahan. (In press). *At Risk: Professional Practice in Child Welfare and Other Human Services*. Toronto: University of Toronto Press.

Taylor, P.S. (2008). 'Ontario's Big Poverty Plan: Bill Ottawa', *Maclean's 121* (5 & 12): 16.

Tester, F. (2003). 'Anti-Oppressive Theory and Practice as the Organizing Theme for Social Work Education: The Case Against', *Canadian Social Work Review 20* (1): 127–32.

Titmuss, R. (1968). *Commitment to Welfare*. London: George Allen and Unwin.

————. (1974). *Social Policy*. London: George Allen and Unwin.

Townson, M., and K. Hayes. (2007). *Women and the Employment Insurance Program*. Ottawa, ON: Canadian Centre for Policy Alternatives.

Trebilcock, M.J. (2005). 'The Choice of Governing Instrument: A Restrospective' in P. Eliadis, M.M. Hill, and M. Howlett, eds, *Designing Government: From Instruments to Governance*, pp. 51–73. Montreal and Kingston: McGill-Queen's University Press.

————, D.G. Hartle, J.R.S. Prichard, and D.N. Dewees. (1982). *The Choice of Governing Instrument*. Ottawa: Ministry of Supply and Services.

Trocmé, N., B. Fallon, and B. MacLaurin. (In press). 'Canadian Incidence Study of Reported Child Abuse and Neglect: Changing Patterns of Reported Maltreatment: 1998 and 2003', in K. Kufeldt and B. McKenzie, eds, *Child Welfare: Connecting Research, Policy and Practice*, 2nd edn. Waterloo, ON: Wilfrid Laurier University Press.

————, D. Knoke, and C. Blackstock. (2004). 'Pathways to the Overrepresentation of Aboriginal children in Canada's Child Welfare System'. *Social Service Review* 78 (4): 577–601.

————, B. MacLaurin, B. Fallon, J. Daciuk, D. Billingsley, M. Tourigny, et al. (2001). *Canadian Incidence Study of Reported Child Abuse and Neglect: Final Report*. Ottawa, ON: Minister of Public Works and Government Services Canada.

United Nations Committee on the Rights of the Child website. (2009). Available at http://www2.ohchr.org/English/bodies/crc/index.htm.

Valentine, F. (1994). *The Canadian Independent Living Movement: An Historical Overview*. Ottawa: The Canadian Association of Independent Living Centres.

'Victoria Should Dispense with Welfare Time Limits', *Vancouver Sun*, 13 February: C7.

Wallace, B., S. Klein, and M. Reitsma-Street. (2006). *Denied Assistance: Closing the*

*Front Door on Welfare in BC*. Vancouver: Canadian Centre for Policy Alternatives and Victoria Island Public Interest Research Group, available at http://www.policyalternatives.ca/documents/BC_Office_Pubs/bc_2006/deniedassistance.pdf.

Welch, M.A. (2009). 'Chiefs Demand More Say in Child Welfare', *Winnipeg Free Press*, 23 February: A4.

'Welfare Jobs Axed, Offices to be Closed'. (2003). *Vancouver Province*, 14 November: A16.

Westhues, A. (2006). 'Becoming Acquainted with Social Policy', in A. Westhues, ed., *Canadian Social Policy: Issues and Perspectives*, 4th edn, pp. 5–24. Waterloo, ON: Wilfred Laurier University Press.

Wharf, B. (1984). *From Initiation to Implementation: The Role of Line Staff in the Policy-Making Process*. Victoria, BC: School of Social Work, University of Victoria.

———, ed. (2002). *Community Work Approaches to Child Welfare*. Peterborough, ON: Broadview Press.

Wharf-Higgins, J.S. (1997). 'Who Participates: Citizen Participation in Health Reform in B.C.', in B. Wharf and M. Clague, eds, *Community Organizing: Canadian Experiences*, pp. 273–302. Don Mills, ON: Oxford University Press.

———, J. Cossom, and B. Wharf. (2006). 'Citizen Participation in Social Policy', in A. Westhues, ed, *Canadian Social Policy: Issues and Perspectives*, 4th edn, pp. 131–49. Waterloo, ON: Wilfrid Laurier University Press.

Williams, W. (1976). 'Implementation Analysis and Assessment', in W. Williams and R. Elmore, eds, *Social Program Implementation*, pp. 280–93. New York: Academic Press.

Williams, W. (1980). *The Implementation Perspective*. Berkeley, CA: University of California Press.

Witkin, S.L., and S. Gottschalk. (1988). 'Alternative Criteria for Theory Evaluation', *Social Service Review*: 211–24.

Yalnizyan, A. (2007). *The Rich and the Rest of Us: The Changing Face of Canada's Growing Gap*. Ottawa: Canadian Centre for Policy Alternatives.

———. (2008). 'Budget 2008: What's In It for Women?' Ottawa: Canadian Centre for Policy Alternatives, available at http:///www.growinggap.ca/files/Budget_2008_Whats_in_it_for-women.pdf.

Yeatman, A., and S. Gunew (1993). *Feminism and the Politics of Difference*. Sydney: Allen & Unwin.

# Index